*The Woman in
Latin American and
Spanish Literature*

The Woman in Latin American and Spanish Literature

Essays on Iconic Characters

Edited by
EVA PAULINO BUENO *and*
MARÍA CLAUDIA ANDRÉ

FOREWORD BY MARJORIE AGOSÍN

McFarland & Company, Inc., Publishers
Jefferson, North Carolina, and London

 # 770876288

LIBRARY OF CONGRESS CATALOGUING-IN-PUBLICATION DATA

The woman in Latin American and Spanish literature : essays on
   iconic characters / edited by Eva Paulino Bueno and María Claudia
   André ; foreword by Marjorie Agosín.
         p.   cm.
   Includes bibliographical references and index.

   ISBN 978-0-7864-6599-6
   softcover : acid free paper ∞

   1. Latin American literature — History and criticism.
2. Women in literature.   3. Gender identity in literature.
4. Women and literature — Latin America.   5. Spanish
literature — History and criticism.   I. Bueno, Eva Paulino.
II. André, María Claudia.
   PQ7081.43.W66 2012
   860.9'98 — dc23   2012007553

BRITISH LIBRARY CATALOGUING DATA ARE AVAILABLE

Front cover image © 2012 Shutterstock

Manufactured in the United States of America

*McFarland & Company, Inc., Publishers
   Box 611, Jefferson, North Carolina 28640
   www.mcfarlandpub.com*

Dedicamos este livro às mulheres
da América Latina e da Espanha,
todas personagens fundamentais da história e
da cultura de seus respectivos países.

Dedicamos este libro a las mujeres de América Latina y
de España quienes inspiraron a todos
los personajes femeninos fundamentales
de la historia y de la cultura de sus respectivos países.

Acknowledgments

If it is true that it takes a village to raise a child, it is no less true that it takes a small battalion of brave souls to write a book, especially in our times of tweets and half baked sentences. We owe a lot to many people who have helped us along the way, in different forms. First, we want to acknowledge the contributors to this book for their patience, good humor, and comradeship during the revision process. It has been a pleasure to work with each of you, and to learn about your expertise.

At St. Mary's University, Eva Paulino Bueno wants to thank Dean Janet Dizinno, who approved a timely sabbatical. In the Department of Languages, she wants to thank two people: her colleague Mark Lokensgard, who graciously took over the duty of chairing the department for the period of the sabbatical, and the always kind and competent Rosalinda Helbig, administrative assistant, for her dedication, friendship, and impeccable organization of everything. She also thanks her co-editor María Claudia André, who once again proved to be the best co-editor and colleague anyone can wish for. At home, Eva wants to thank her husband Terry Caesar, always an inspiration in scholarly and other ways. Finally, she wants to thank two creatures who cannot read this book, her dogs Nora Inu and Buddy-san, who provided countless walks and hours of joy, as well as the opportunity to talk silly without concern for propriety. María Claudia André extends her gratitude to her husband Scott and her son Axel, her constant sources of love, understanding, and support. She also thanks Eva P. Bueno for being the driving force of this project.

Table of Contents

Foreword

MARJORIE AGOSÍN

Any student of contemporary Latin American literature will be delighted to discover this collection of essays carefully edited by Eva Paulino Bueno and María Claudia André. Both the editors and the participants have succeeded in combining critical thought and originality. This important body of work explores the literary history of Latin America through the representation of iconic female characters; it is intended to help the reader understand how the female characters have changed and developed in their search for new identities and new ways of being and acting in accordance to the society and the customs of their times. Each essay is carefully crafted and supported by the most recent theories in literary criticism, gender, and Latin American studies.

The unifying thread of this collection consists in its innovative reading of some canonical texts and its deep appreciation and understanding of the role of women as symbols of struggle, perseverance, and creativity. Here, together for the first time, these women characters enable us to understand how Latin American women are portrayed by both male and female writers, and thus help us re-think and re-interpret the dynamics between genders across boundaries, and across the different historical periods. This collection of essays reveals a complex, vast literary corpus and demonstrates through a variety of interpretive techniques that iconic feminine characters not only identify with the cultural and national history of the countries to which they belong, but also provide a counter-discourse or a nonofficial version of their historical accounts. The essays also show us that the feminine character is never static, but changes according to the surrounding social and historical pressures in the lives of their authors.

Each of the essays presents an iconic woman as a central character, one

1

that discloses the complexity of the themes surrounding the historical and political period in which she lived, from the cultural complexities and the stereotypes throughout the years, to the complexities of the postmodern world. Making connections between and among the essays, readers may perceive, for instance, that the plight of the black woman in an earlier period reappears in the twentieth century, and that the passivity that a characters uses as a way to survive the rigors of a patriarchal society becomes the conduit to a rich interior life for another. Through these essays we distinguish the inner conflicts and passions of the female character, the development of her personality, and the constant dichotomy between the public and the domestic spaces, with the prevalence of the interior world as a shelter as well as a source of creativity and strength.

I celebrate this collection of essays; each illuminates different elements that are unique to the understanding of the feminine character in Latin American literature. Even though these characters were created in different chronological times, by writers from different backgrounds, and written in different languages, the critical reading and interpretation presented in this book enable us to understand the complex ways in which women characters explore their sense of belonging in the times and countries in which they live, using their own personal strength and wit, as women. The careful study of their physical, psychological, and emotional conflicts gives us, collectively, admiration and a sense of respect for the situation of women in Latin America, the source of inspiration for many of the characters in these novels.

To write the foreword for this book is a privilege and a great literary adventure because, finally, what makes these essays so fascinating is the fact that they do not simply present answers, but, rather, they inspire new questions and perspectives about the literature of Latin America.

Marjorie Agosín (Ph.D. Indiana) is a professor of Spanish at Wellesley College and has published books and essays on the plight of women in Third World countries.

Introduction

EVA PAULINO BUENO *and* MARÍA CLAUDIA ANDRÉ

This book is the result of decades of research and countless hours of dialogue among the contributors, as well as between the contributors and their students in different institutions. The impetus to transform our research into a book grew out of the editors' previous collaborative work leading to the publication of an encyclopedia of Latin American women writers in 2008. The work required for the encyclopedia enabled us to form a strong relationship with colleagues from different universities and to continue the discussion of aspects of the representation of women in Latin American literature and in Spanish literature written by both male and female writers. However, this collection of essays does not intend to be comprehensive; in fact, our first realization in the process of making this book is that it is hopelessly incomplete, as any project of this magnitude would be.

Hence, we must establish from the outset that the intention behind the selection of the essays included in this book is not encyclopedic; rather, the essays aim to foster discussion of *some* of the important issues that have been part of the representation of women in different times, and in different national literatures, without necessarily implying that these are the *only* novels treating the subjects, or that there are no other subjects that could perhaps also be included in the discussion. Each reader of Latin American and Spanish literature, as well as any colleague who teaches these literatures, may have other novels and short stories which constitute striking examples of how female protagonists have been used to represent different issues in different times. Our hope is that the reading of this book excites our readers to continue thinking about the subject and finding new connections and new inspirations in Latin American and Spanish literature.

We must also acknowledge the groundbreaking work of critics such as Roberto Schwarz, Doris Sommer, Octavio Paz, John Beverley, Jean Franco, Beatriz Sarlo, and Nadia Battella Gotlib, among others, who have made important contributions to a better and deeper understanding of other aspects of Latin American and Spanish literature, and whose discussions have been part of our teaching and writing careers. Given the great number of possible theoretical tools to be used in the essays, we must clarify that the contributors to this volume were left free to utilize a variety of theoretical orientations in their discussions. What interests us is to inquire how women characters have become the vehicle both of the interrogation of the "feminine"—and, by extension, of the "masculine" as well—and how the representation of women can be seen as a way to understand how relations of power have been present in the formation of the woman subject in the literatures of Latin America and Spain.

Our intention is not to make a chronological study of canonical texts. We do, however, recognize that for most of Latin America, literature came to its first meaningful expressivity during the crucial time of national formation and ideological consolidation, and that is why our first section deals with some early ways in which women characters were portrayed in Latin American literature, as representatives of nature. Without necessarily agreeing with Fredric Jameson's statement that "all" Third World literature—and Latin American literature included—"necessarily project[s] a political dimension in the form of a national allegory" (65), we concede that the writers of the young Latin American nations needed literature to accomplish many things, among them to praise the nature of the country, to instill in readers a sense of civic purpose, and to impart a certainty of the correctness, necessity, and urgency of the national enterprise.[1]

In other words, at that moment, in the presence of the enormous physical realities of the vast, unknown territories, the ruling elites—from where the writers came—needed to believe that they were in the process of creating a country that was at once different from the mother country, but also "civilized," as opposed to the indigenous, non-white, inhabitants. In Benedict Anderson's words, the elites needed to create "an imagined community."[2] That explains why we can find an abundant description of the nature of the country and of indigenous types in literature produced from the middle to the end of the nineteenth century.

The young nations matured, and their societies changed; the changes brought other problems, other anxieties to the forefront, and each of these aspects made their way into the fiction, the poetry, and the drama of the country. The arrival of new aesthetic influences from abroad, new political alignments, and the birth of the feminist movement all contributed to a different way of portraying women in Latin American literature. In addition, the recognition and increased acceptance of theoretical tools originating in Psychology and Philosophy have made the field of literary criticism even more vibrant, as the essays in this book demonstrate.

In order to stress the importance of these separate aspects, we have organized this book into five sections, each of them illustrating one issue that women characters have been particularly useful to carry the burden of representing. The contributors created each essay freely, working with ideas that the primary novels themselves suggested, using the theoretical approaches that each contributor found most appropriate for the essay. It was in the task of assembling the manuscript that we felt that, although none of the contributors knew at first which other essays were part of the final product, some texts "dialogued" with one another in very productive ways. This is obviously not to say that each of the essays discusses only the subject suggested by the title of the section; rather, each section serves as an indicator of major lines of thought that they share.

I. Woman as Nature

Literature, of course, is not history. Novels have no obligation to follow a chronological order, and they can, therefore, look back on past events and represent them as a way to look towards the future. To understand how women characters have been used to represent nature, the novel *María* (1867), by the Colombian Jorge Isaacs (1837–1895), is particularly instructive, especially considering that the eponymous character does not appear much in the novel as herself, but rather as the bountiful nature that surrounds the male character. Héctor Fernández-L'Hoeste argues that, precisely because he was a man who felt the sting of discrimination because of his Jewish origin, Isaacs tried to make his novel at the same time a glorification of the land of his country, and an affirmation of his Christian beliefs. But nature has not always been seen as a beneficial agent, and such is the case with *Doña Bárbara* (1929), a novel by Rómulo Gallegos (1884–1969) that can also be read almost as a political platform.

It is necessary to remember that in Latin America especially — but not exclusively — in the end of the nineteenth and beginning of the twentieth century, many writers were also politicians. As members of the privileged reading class, they were in the position to enact changes in the form of political and social influence. It is no coincidence that in Latin America so many writers became politicians or occupied political offices: Bartolomé Mitre in Argentina, José Martí in Cuba, José de Alencar and Aluísio Azevedo in Brazil, Andrés Bello and Rómulo Gallegos in Venezuela, Andrés Bello in Chile.[3] For each of these, and many others who occupied regional political positions, literature came hand in hand with politics: first the imagination, then action (or at least the will to action through political office). As Julio Ramos correctly points out, by the end of the nineteenth century, there was a profound connection between literature and politics; actually, they can be said to have been one and the same thing (62–63). In this light, it is possible to say that *Doña Bárbara* can be seen as the best possible political platform advocating the taming of nature and the introduction of "civilizing" processes such as those illustrated in the novel. Gallegos could have used *Doña Bárbara* as his campaign to the presidential office of Venezuela: the male force takes over and dominates the recalcitrant land, preparing it to be husbanded, controlled, and civilized. Patricia L. Swier reminds us, however, that reconceptualizations of gender and sexuality have given the character a new, iconic resonance.

But advancement to the higher office of the land was not always the most desired situation a writer could aspire to. The last essay of this group concerns *Balún Canán* (1957) by the Mexican Rosario Castellanos (1925–1974). We believe that this novel is a provocative bridge between the subject of nature and politics. Here we have a female child narrator who tries to represent the uncertainties, the class and race struggles happening around her. The natural and political world breaking down is the world of the Mexico where the first Mayan inhabitants — once the guardians of nature and of tradition — are being systematically destroyed or rendered as meaningless and undistinguishable as her beloved nanny becomes in the end of the novel. Jeanie Murphy argues that the figure of the father represents the phallocentric, white political culture that understands the land as something possessed by *men*. And here lies the female child's tragedy: she is the only one who can recognize the indigenous other, but because she is a female, she will not inherit the land, and therefore she will never be able to act upon her knowledge. The land — nature — is still under the power of the white man, no matter (or regardless of) the more grandiose reform plans conceived in the capital of the country.

II. Woman in History

Certain problems tend to reoccur in literature at different historical periods, each time proposing a new way to look at an issue. In every one of these changes, the woman character's role is expanded and modified to include anxieties about the social and political issues important at that moment. One important development in the beginning of the twentieth century, when the nations were already established as independent entities, was that women writers emerged on the literary scene, moved by the urgency to become active participants in the national discourse.

In RoseAnna Mueller's discussion, the woman character, now, not simply the product of the imagination of a male writer with nation-building intents, appears as the result of a feminine sensibility that can — for lack of a better term — "see the woman's situation from the inside." The work of Venezuelan Teresa de la Parra (1889–1936) is particularly instructive, because through María Eugenia, the protagonist of *Iphigenia: The diary of a young lady who wrote because she was bored* (1924), she shows how the nation is building its capitalist enterprise on the backs of its daughters, who, in the process, must relinquish any individual identity, as well as financial independence.

With *Hasta no verte Jesús mío* (1969) based on the life of Josefina Bórquez (1900–1987), Elena Poniatowska (1932–) tells the life of Jesusa Palancares, a woman who lived and fought during the Mexican Revolution. In Linda Ledford-Miller's discussion, this extremely complex novel illustrates how, in spite of her illiteracy and many difficulties, a woman made history and helped shape the nation alongside men and other women. Another novel that looks back to make connections and shed new light on the Mexican past is *Arráncame la vida* (1985), by Ángeles Mastretta (1949–). The novel is narrated by Catalina, the wife of a strong man who manages to climb the political and social ladder of power through intimidation, torture, and killings. Alice Edwards argues that, as a woman who has access to the most powerful man and does nothing to help the powerless people he persecutes, Catalina can be seen as a projection of La Malinche, the indigenous woman who became Hernán Cortés's translator and lover. Even though Mastretta's novel has been criticized by many, the essay points out that the ambiguity in Catalina's decisions reflects the weight of history and the burden of decisions taken on a personal level by a woman who feels no connection with other women.

But the action need not take place in the grand stage of national politics to refer to the political situation. *La casa de Bernarda Alba: Drama de mujeres en los pueblos de España* (1936) by the Spanish poet and dramatist Federico García Lorca (1898–1936), is set in a provincial home, and the struggles among the three generations of Bernarda Alba's family can be seen as a representation of the Spanish cultural scene on the verge of the Civil War: not only does Bernarda Alba herself represent a political figure whose importance was reaching alarming proportions at the time García Lorca wrote the play *Francisco Franco*, but she also represents the leftover characteristics of naturalism. The conflict among all the women in the story, Jeffrey Oxford argues, is a representation of the literary and cultural ethos of Spain, at a time when different styles competed for predominance.

III. Woman as the Perverse Powers of Race and Sex

The two essays in the next section, by Leonora Simonovis and Linda Ledford-Miller, respectively, deal with the matters of race and sex, and how women's bodies have been appropriated to represent a mixture of both, and how, in one case, the woman has to pay with her life because of how she is seen. In *Of Love and Other Demons* (1994) Gabriel García Márquez (1927–) creates Sierva María de Todos los Ángeles, a white child who embodies the black African culture from the slave quarters where she was raised. Her upbringing makes her black, but she is ethnically white, so Sierva María is seen as a monster who provokes violence and blood thirst among the religious people in charge of "exorcizing" her.

In *Gabriela, Clove and Cinnamon* (1962), Jorge Amado (1912–2001) presents a different type of racialized female body. Here, the woman Gabriela, even though she is illiterate and not versed in the ways of the urban environment where the story takes place — the town of Ilhéus, in Bahia — manages to carve a space in which she can be celebrated both as a sexual being, and as a woman of color. But even here, it is important to observe that Gabriela's supposed liberation is obtained at the cost of what can be seen as an unobtainable ideal of perpetual youth and beauty at the service of the dominating man.

IV. Woman and the Burden of Globalization

What happens to a country when it is mercilessly penetrated by external influences that feed on the population and transform everyone to fodder for a never satisfied globalized machine of capitalist consumption? Aldona Pobutsky discusses precisely this matter, analyzing a novel that opens with the brutal scene of the rape of the young protagonist. The Colombian Óscar Collazos (1942–) addresses this and other questions with the novel *Rencor* (2006), which takes the reader to a Cartagena shantytown and dramatizes the plight of the poor, especially poor females, in the character Keyla, a young, mixed-race woman whose anger — rencor — is the running theme in the novel. Defenseless against her father's incestuous desires, and later defenseless against the fact that the only way she can feed her family is through prostitution, the young character leads a life of abject violence and unrelenting desperation and ends up alone, defeated, orphaned, and locked up. The novel thus reveals how, even in the twenty-first century, the racialized woman's body still continues functioning as a sex commodity, a process through which she is objectified and abjectified.

In the novel *Única mirando al mar* (1993), the Costa Rican Fernando Contreras Castro (1963 —) tells the story of Única, a former teacher who loses her job and ends up in a sea of garbage, living with people who live off the garbage. These people, from different parts of the country, embody those who are discarded when their employers no longer find them useful. Jerry Hoeg writes that, because she embodies a realistic portrayal of human nature, the character Única — a woman who never gives up and never gives in — has become a symbol of ecological devastation, as well as an indictment of consumer society. In spite of its scathing critique of the system that allows the continuation of the depletion of the natural resources, the Costa Rican Ministry of Education made the novel obligatory reading for all ninth graders, and it has been successfully adapted for the stage.

V. Woman as the Unknowable Other

The essays in this last section, by María Fernández-Lamarque, Lisa Merschel, and Marcus V.C. Brasileiro, concentrate on the discussion of woman as Other. Fernández-Lamarque concentrates on the work of Argentinean writer Jorge Luis Borges (1899–1986), and begins with a question about the seeming scarcity of female protagonists in his fiction. Considering the issue through an analysis of the short story "El Zahir," the essay evokes the idea of the thread of the *histos* as it is used by Jacques Derrida. Both the woman character Teodelina Villar and the coin called "El Zahir" coexist in the story and are internally connected, as the narrator "Borges" realizes after receiving the coin after her death. The woman, in this case, is the alter-ego of the narrator, at the same time she is also his obsession.

The work by Chilean writer María Flora Yáñez (1901–1981), although little known outside her native country, constitutes an important moment of women's literature in Latin America. The fact that, even though she belonged to the elite of her country, Yáñez could not initially publish under her own name, shows — as Lisa Merschel reminds us — the kind of obstacles that existed for women at the time. Barred from political life as other women writers of her time, Yáñez herself noted that Virginia Woolf was barred from entering male dominated "turf," and considered the British writer an inspiration. It is no wonder, therefore, that *Cenizas* (1949) concentrates on the psychological life of Irene, the protagonist of the novel. The "positivist world" of her husband does not interest her, and, as a final assessment, the incommunicability among the characters is the most salient characteristic of the novel. Immersed in her interior, domestic life, Irene finally finds the serenity she seeks.

Finally, Marcus V.C. Brasileiro, focusing on *São Bernardo* (1934) by Brazilian writer Graciliano Ramos (1892–1953), and on *The Hour of the Star* (1977), by Clarice Lispector (1920–1977), asks quite simply if it is possible for women to speak. Perhaps today, the essay contends, women may not have to resort to the desperate measures taken by Madalena, the protagonist of *São Bernardo*, who can only be heard through her suicide. It is possible also that with Macabéa, the protagonist of *The Hour*, Lispector was able to call attention both to the suffering and to the means of representing the suffering of migrants from the impoverished Northeast of Brazil, who see their lives consumed in the big urban centers of the south. The essay aligns women with the subaltern, and equates writing as a potential feminist gesture in the sense that it can demonstrate the pitfalls of trying to represent the life and feelings of someone who is other than the middle class, educated writer. In spite of the recent election in Brazil of the first woman president, patriarchal views of femininity and masculinity still prevail, and there is much work to be done.

Throughout the process of thinking about the subjects raised by the many essays that compose this book, our initial conviction of the importance of understanding the representation of women in Latin American and Spanish literature has been expanded and strengthened. Just so, we hope that this collection of essays becomes both an apt demonstration of a fuller and more nuanced understanding of both these literatures, as well as an inspiration for more readings that assume the centrality of female characters in fiction. In Latin American and Spanish literature, the significance of women continues to be neglected, even as women themselves keep rejecting this neglect through their increased prominence in the social and political lives of their countries.

Notes

1. In "Jameson's Rhetoric of Otherness and the 'National Allegory'" Aijaz Ahmad contests Jameson's use of the term "Third World" by asserting that what Jameson calls "essentially descriptive" ignores the fact that description, itself, "is never ideologically or cognitively neutral," and that "to 'describe' is to specify a locus of meaning, to construct an object of knowledge, and to produce a knowledge that shall be bound by that act of descriptive construction." (6) Consult Aijaz Ahmad, "Jameson's Rhetoric of Otherness and the 'National Allegory.'" *Social Text*, No. 17 (Autumn, 1987): 3–25.

2. Anderson proposes this definition of nation: "it is an imagined political community — and imagined as both inherently limited and sovereign." *Imagined Communities: Reflections on the Origin and Spread of Nationalism.* London: Verso, 1993, 6. For the young Latin American countries whose territories were inhabited by people with different languages, the majority of whom lived in almost complete isolation, the "imagining" was done mainly by urban

intellectuals, the writers, after the struggles for independence had in some cases already produced the desired effect. Therefore, the imagination of a nation had the task of consolidating, and not creating the nation.

3. This phenomenon did not stop in the first years of the twentieth century. In our own time, some important names come to mind: Mario Vargas Llosa, who ran for presidency of Peru, and Rosario Castellanos died in 1974, while serving as ambassador of Mexico in Tel Aviv. Octavio Paz was the Mexican ambassador in India, and Gabriela Mistral served diplomatic posts in Spain, Italy, Brazil, the U.S., and Portugal.

Works Cited

Ahmed, Aijaz. "Jameson's Rhetoric of Otherness and the 'National Allegory.'" *Social Text* No. 17 (Autumn, 1987): 3–25. Print.

Anderson, Benedict. *Imagined Communities: Reflections on the Origin and Spread of Nationalism.* New York: Verso, 1993. Print.

Jameson, Fredric. "Third-World Literature in the Era of Multinational Capitalism." *Social Text* No. 15 (Fall, 1986): 65–88. Print.

Nunn, Frederick M. *Collisions with History; Latin American Fiction and Social Science from El Boom to the New World Order.* Athens: Ohio University Press, 2001. Print.

Ramos, Julio. *Desencuentros de la modernidad en América Latina: Literatura y Política en el siglo XIX.* Mexico: Fondo de Cultura Económica, 1989. Print.

Sommer, Doris. *Foundational Fictions: The National Romances of Latin America.* Berkeley: University of California Press, 1991. Print.

I

WOMAN AS NATURE

1

Gender and Nation from Past to Present: From María to Macabéa

HÉCTOR FERNÁNDEZ-L'HOESTE

Growing up in Colombia, like most members of my generation, I was expected at some point of my education to read *María*, by Jorge Isaacs. At the time, the reading of this text, so representative of Romanticism in the Nineteenth century, was a ritual of passage for anyone completing a K–12 degree program in the country. The text had been embraced by other Latin American nations and was repeatedly celebrated as a high point of Colombia's literature at a time yet unaffected by the clout of Gabriel García Márquez and magic realism. I recall little about my first impression of *María*, aside from the fact that I found the protracted descriptions of Colombian landscapes wearisome and demanding of my patience; later on, I would learn that there actually was a stylistic justification for them. Aside from this, the story itself was quite undemanding, and did not exactly inspire much of the curiosity of my easily distracted mind. Around the same time, I was exposed to the latest film adaptation of the book (in 1972, when I was merely nine), with a very young and beautiful — and poorly dubbed — Taryn Power (Tyrone Power's daughter)[1] in the role of María, and an incredibly handsome Fernando Allende in the role of Efraín. Absurdly, casting had emphasized physical appeal to such a degree that both protagonists competed for good looks onscreen. In my eyes and imagination, tainted by years of consuming melodramatic *telenovelas*, which warped once and forever my understanding of things romantic, feeding me with unattainable expectations, I could hardly have imagined a better couple.

Years later, once I worked in the U.S. academe, I reencountered the text. Though it still had not become a favorite of mine, I could now regard *María* with different eyes, valuing its prose in the context of its century. Quite understandably, having embraced a cultural studies approach, I began identifying some of its narrative as troubling and perilously uneven in its management of features of national identity. As a child, the Colombia described by Isaacs was one that I found strangely alien to my Caribbean sensibility, accustomed as I was to the limitations of regionalism. As a graduate student, influenced by my reading of the writings of José María Samper, in which I found many clues for the lackluster implementation of the idea of nation in contemporary Colombia, I began to trace a similar evolution of ideas in *María*, in particular when it came to an assessment of female identity and the concept of nationhood. Beyond its enactment of Colombian identity within the context of a love story, the fact that a female character entirely resulting from the male imagination played such a notable role within the canon of Colombian literature — an almost exclusively male domain up until well into the latter half of the twentieth century — struck me as a little odd. In a way, to me, *María* always felt like a male prescription for femininity.

Along the way, I came across another text that reminded me of *María*: Brazilian author Clarice Lispector's *The Hour of The Star* (1977). At first glance, the Brazilian's narrative, rooted in the haphazard existence of a poor *nordestina* (northeasterner) called Macabéa, bears little in common with Isaacs's novel. Nonetheless, a closer look at both texts reveals more than a few commonalities. For one, both authors were of Jewish descent, trying to operate as outsiders within the constantly evolving construction of their nations in their corresponding centuries. To address this condition, both created texts firmly supported by Judeo-Christian frameworks. To problematize contemporary issues (for Isaacs, the hope to inspire passionate support for emerging constructs of nationhood; for Lispector, the willingness to criticize risks associated with rampant social disparity), both texts center on female characters, suggesting them as national allegories.

In Isaacs's case, male construction of female identity is particularly straightforward (and even brazen). In Lispector's case, even though the writer is a woman, it is a male narrator, Rodrigo S. M., who tells Macabéa's story. Quite skillfully, Lispector uses Rodrigo to evince the travails of male construction of female identity within Brazilian society. Along the same lines, both narratives are based on characters that, for the most part, hardly accomplish any physical actions — aside from turning sick and dying — both are depicted as objects, rather than subjects. Thus, both are fitting examples of the appropriation of female image for literary purposes.

Although chronologically distant, both texts share a general context and operate with a common set of variables (identity, gender, class, nation, marginality, Judeo-Christian tradition, death, etc.). In this sense, both of them can be equally disquieting. Of course, for me, *María* struck closer to home, given its problematization of an emerging sense of Colombianness and its idiosyncratic representation of gender. At the same time, Macabéa, representing the plight of the poor in the middle of Twentieth Century Brazil, also makes a compelling character.

María and Macabéa, Women of and in Their Time

As suggested, not much really happens in *María*. In terms of action, María is a sort of "boy meets girl" account. As a boy, Efraín leaves to study in Bogotá. He bids farewell to his mother, sisters, and María, who is just a child. Men, it seems, are allowed to wander across the geography of the nation, whereas women seemingly know their place, close to the house. Efraín needs to travel far — quite literally — to become a man. At the end of the nineteenth century, when going from Cali to Bogotá involved crossing two branches (*cordilleras*) of the Andes and the valley of the Magdalena River on horseback, his journey must have appeared titanic. Once he finishes school, Efraín returns home, taking the perilous journey in the opposite direction. At home, María (who has transformed into a gorgeous teenager) and his sister Emma anticipate his homecoming, avid to share evenings with him reading French novels. Along the way, Efraín also takes time to visit employees and slaves at their humble abodes, and even goes hunting, like any good master. When María suddenly falls ill, it is Efraín who faces the night and rushes out to get the doctor, in one of the most memorable passages of the story. After a brief interlude in which his love for María becomes explicit, he travels once again: this time around, to London. In the context of the nineteenth century, it must have been akin to a trip to the moon, whether it meant boarding a vessel on the Pacific Ocean, traveling around the southern tip of the Americas (via the Strait of Magellan, the Beagle Channel, or the Drake Passage); going the way of the Caribbean, exiting Colombia through the Magdalena, an epic endeavor in itself; or traveling to Panama, in those days still part of Colombia. Judging from the contents of the novel, this latter route (the way of Panama) was the one favored by Efraín. As if to reiterate his manhood, his lengthy travels confirm him as a man of world. His boundaries are no longer national; instead, they ratify his profile as a being of privilege, a young master of the universe. There are scant limits to where Efraín can travel.

His heart, however, lies in his native Colombia. Once he gets to London, he learns about María's poor condition: she has suffered a new attack. Without hesitation, he returns. His crossing of the ocean pales next to the trip within Colombia, with its treacherous waterways (the Dagua) and improvised roads. Once Efraín gets home, sadly, María has died; he has arrived too late. By then, María is already buried, in close, intimate contact with the single element that equates (and thus honors) her beauty: Colombian land. In short, María's death is the ultimate consecration of hallowed ground. Narratively speaking, she has been sacrificed to augment the virtue of national territory.

Isaacs takes advantage of this aspect, beautifying Colombia at every corner:

Una tarde, tarde como las de mi país, engalanada con nubes de color de violeta y lampos de oro pálido, bella como María, bella y transitoria como fue ésta para mí, ella, mi hermana y yo, sentados sobre la ancha piedra de la pendiente, desde donde veíamos a la derecha en la honda vega rodar las corrientes bulliciosas del río, y teniendo a nuestros pies el valle majestuoso y callado, leía yo el episodio de Atala, y las dos, admirables en su inmovilidad, oían brotar de mis labios toda aquella melancolía aglomerada por el poeta para "hacer llorar al mundo" [38].

One afternoon, an afternoon like those of my country, decorated with violet-colored clouds and gleams of pale gold, beautiful like María, beautiful and temporary as she was to me, she, my sister, and I, seated on a wide rock of the slope, from where we could see, to the right, the ebullient currents of the river roll in the deep meadow, and having the majestic and silent valley to our feet, I read an episode from Atala, and both of them, admirable in their motionlessness, listened from my lips the melancholy gathered by the poet "to make the world cry."[2]

The phrase "tarde como las de mi país" has become part of the vernacular repertoire of Colombian Spanish, encapsulating splendidly the beauty of afternoons along the Andes while simultaneously highlighting the power of literary tradition. In Isaacs's prose, though, María and the afternoon are one (Una tarde … tan bella como María), so a bond between the nature of the countryside and the beloved one is unmistakable. This is a key element in Isaacs's contribution to the concept of nation in *María*: if María, the character, is equated with the country and its nature, then all women replicating María's behavior are reproducing a Colombian way of enacting female identity, honoring the nation, never mind the intricacy of the benchmark.

To imagine the nature of the Americas as a beautiful woman is a common literary device, present in many texts of the period. Mary Louise Pratt has documented this practice well in *Imperial Eyes: Travel Writing and Transculturation*. My point here, rather, is that it was not only foreigners or conquerors that engaged in this practice. Well-celebrated Latin American authors — patriots, according to the common lore — also practiced it widely, as a means of hegemonizing the masses and contributing to a growing sense of nationalism, consciously or not. In the nineteenth century, the nation had to be narrated, to be consumed; and what better text to accomplish this than a tearjerker?

To give some background to this sample of gender construction in favor of a particular notion of nation, let's name a case in point: to equate María's sense of beauty with immobility stands in an almost timid way, within the overall context of Latin American tradition, as a sort of prelude to Pablo Neruda's famous Poem 15, "Me gustas cuando callas" (I like it when you're quiet)—another high point in the history of commodification of female identity in the annals of Latin American literature.[3] Like Neruda's beloved, Emma and María appear "admirable" in their lack of movement. In the very same way, María is at her best when she does not move a finger. For Isaacs's hero, nature appears even more mobile than for women:

> El Amaime bajaba crecido con las lluvias de la noche, y su estruendo me lo anunció mucho antes de que llegase yo a la orilla. A la luz de la luna, que atravesando los follajes de las riberas iba a platear los ondas, pude ver cuánto había aumentado su raudal. Pero no era posible esperar: había hecho dos leguas en una hora, y aún era poco. Puse las espuelas en los ijares del caballo, que con las orejas tendidas hacia el fondo del río y resoplando sordamente parecía calcular la impetuosidad de las aguas que se azotaban a sus pies; sumergió en ellas las manos; pero como sobrecogido de un terror invencible, retrocedió girando sobre las patas [43].

> The Amaime was sweeping down, swollen by the rains of the night, and I could hear its roar long before I reached its bank. By the moon's light, which was struggling through the trees on the shore, I could see how high the waters were; but I could not wait. I had come two leagues in an hour, and it was not much farther. I put spurs to my horse; he thrust forward his ears towards the river, snorting loudly, and seemed to be estimating the swiftness of the current; he stepped in, but then, overcome by unconquerable fright, reared backward [37].

The well known passage, taken from the description of the night when Efraín rushes to locate a doctor for his sickly beloved, features all the necessary elements: a challenging scenery, a flooded river, a noble brute of a horse, and a hero up to the test. In the case of the male protagonist, nature, so ravishing and dynamic, seems to have, for him, the opposite effect it has for women: it is a call to action, an engine of progress, motivating him to advance and conquer. Thus, while the plotline in *María* appears to proceed along a straightforward manner, it is vital to note how surroundings inform the feeling of empowerment or conformity of the corresponding genders.

One need not go too far to realize the disparity in the plot: the fact that, within the majority of the storyline, most of the action is reserved for Efraín, and very little actually concerns María. As a matter of fact, the two greatest

events in her life are actions that befall her, rather than events which she initiates: her disease (a form of epilepsy, the same that her mother suffered), which
comes and goes in harmful attacks, and her death. And it is also in death that
she sets the example, because it mythifies and augments her, the character,
which then becomes the unattainable bar for women of her generation.

On an anecdotal basis, aside from the text's problematic construction of
gender, there were other details I recalled as troubling in *María*. There was
one thing I remembered clearly from my middle school experience with the
novel: my Spanish teacher repeatedly alluded at Jorge Isaacs's predicaments as
an individual of Jewish origin in nineteenth-century Colombia, an enclave so
influenced by Catholicism that circumstances must surely have been challenging
for the romantic author. Like many Latin American nations, Colombia had
gained independence from Spain in the early part of the nineteenth century.
However, just like many others, one aspect of Spanish heritage that remained
unchanged through the tumultuous political process preceding and following
independence was the acceptance of Catholicism as the country's official religion, a feature that persisted until the rewriting of many Latin American con-
stitutions during the latter part of the twentieth century. In a sense, criticism
by my schoolteacher — who clearly did not embrace such prejudice — just served
as a healthy reminder of deeply embedded anti–Semitism in Colombian culture. Since many of my classmates and friends were Jewish, I was particularly
puzzled by this aspect. How was it possible, I surmised, that just a century
ago, people in Colombia — so far from Hitler's Germany, I thought naively —
were not able to recognize what was blatantly obvious to me: that friends like
Reina, Samy, and Raquel were very driven, good-to-the-bone individuals and,
on top of that, quite smart and likeable? Jewish identity, I admit, played a big
role in my benevolent embracement of difference. Home to immigrants from
all over the world, my native town prided itself on its cosmopolitan nature,
quite oblivious to the fallacies of regionalism, so preponderant in Colombia.
Such were the conundrums that the study of *María* guided me to at an untimely
age.

Viewed from afar, with less intimate concerns in mind, a careful, detailed
reading of *María* now leads in more engaging directions, more along the lines
of academic training. These days, what I find disturbing in *María* is its con-
jugation of ethnicity, race, and gender in the context of the manufacturing of
identity of a young Latin American nation. To advance this critique, I rely
closely on what I deem to be a very judicious assessment of Isaacs's work: Germán Arciniegas's *Genio y figura de Jorge Isaacs* (1967). After all, while María,
the character, is the hypothetical heart of Isaacs's novel, it is amazing how little
physicality female identity actually attains throughout the narrative, mostly

focused on lengthy descriptions of the Colombian countryside and social milieu, and on Efraín's propensity for gallantry. Hence, to identify key aspects of Isaacs's understanding of narrative, some biographical insight might prove beneficial.

While Arciniegas's customary style is devoid of theoretical premises — his writing style could be aptly described as "gossipy," condoning an earlier appreciation of the role of history, which sought to destabilize historiographic narratives through the shrewd use of irony — it does contain, in the author's habitual colloquial tone, precious information on the life of Jorge Isaacs, as well as on the general cultural context of a pubescent South American nation desperately seeking an established identity during the latter half of the nineteenth century.

The author can, of course, be understood through his character: Isaacs's *María* is, to say the least, a shining example of feminine passivity and sexual purity. María, the main character, fits remarkably well within the dictates of *marianismo*, the popularly-held construct of female identity shared across many Latin American borders, according to which women are simplistically interpreted along the lines of behavior of two of the Bible's most eminent female characters. Extensively documented and criticized in the twentieth century, given changing mores and tangentially improved conditions of gender, *marianismo* is an old practice, rooted in the virgin-whore dichotomy, juxtaposing Mary, Christ's abnegated mother, and the Magdalene, who emerges from a life of sin (as prostitute) for her love of Jesus. It is not hard to imagine which of these two is the one Isaacs's *María* is more likely to resemble, an aspiration that might have proved plausible in the nineteenth century, though altogether impractical in current times. In addition, the narrative was also meant to settle, once and for all, any of the doubts held by Colombian society with respect to the author's spiritual affiliation. These doubts plagued Isaacs so long that, even at his deathbed, he had to corroborate his belief in Christ, in a manner well beyond the customary response for anyone receiving his last rites.

But gender is not the only troublesome spot of this text, nor its single-handed mainstay. For *María* to work as an effective delineation of national identity during a turbulent historical period fraught with civil wars, several aspects have to come into play and interact vigilantly. As a cornerstone of a provincial social order, gender disparity works better if it is concealed by the illusion of greater accomplishments in the context of ethnicity and race, informed by political difference. For a man of his times, Isaacs's political evolution and travels through Colombia brought him into close contact with disparate sectors of national society and, on many occasions, his Jewish heritage was not exactly appreciated or understood. In fact, as an example of this kind of abuse, Arciniegas points out how, when Isaacs participated in a debate in the Colombian congress, people called him names (Germán Arciniegas 38). "Sí, he pasado de las sombras a la luz"—"Yes, I've gone from darkness to light," the historian claims he stated, alluding to a shift in political allegiance. (Isaacs had started his political life as a *godo*, a Colombian conservative, and gradually mutated into an ardent *radical*, or progressive.) And some characters, like the slave Feliciana who takes conscientious care of the child María, were even included in the novel as progressive acknowledgements of the changing situation of Afro-Colombians, hinting at how the republic was changing for the better, trying to treat its citizens in a more even-handed fashion.

The consideration of these elements informs my general reading of *María*. With them in mind, I contend the following: despite Isaacs's progressive bent, which favors depiction of the nation in a better light, as a place where society was certainly advancing in terms of ethnic and racial disparity, when it comes to delineation of identity, he gives preferentiality to gender as vehicle for the portrayal of nation. That is to say, Isaacs's version of Colombia conforms to his understanding of gender as a provincial, nineteenth-century man. After all, despite repeated criticism of his heritage, Isaacs pursued general acceptance of his work by Bogotá's hyper-traditional social milieu, coding his novel with Biblical connotations. On the other hand, *libertad de vientre*, the rule stating that children of slaves were born free, had become a legal norm shortly after independence; importation of slaves had also been outlawed from the very beginning, though abolition of slavery only took place in 1851. Within this context, María, the suffering cousin of the novel's hero, Efraín, embodies the kind of temperament best suited to endure the trials of nation building. In fact, through most of the narrative, María stands as a passive agent, honoring *marianismo*; it is Efraín, with a demeanor proper of men accustomed to battling endless civil wars, who engages most of the action. Thus, what I wish to argue is that, while ethnicity and race are viewed and problematized as issues of necessary resolution for the successful implementation of a certain construct of nation, gender embraces a more conformist perspective, supporting a predictably rigid construct of Colombian identity, which informed unrealistically the enactment of national female identity for decades. In fact, when it comes to identity in terms of gender, *María* serves as a contradictory forerunner of more contemporary texts.

Well over a century before Latin American female protagonists represented more committed enactments of womanhood, *María* shares its main narrative strategy with Clarice Lispector's *The Hour of The Star*: the use of a female character to expand a certain notion of nation, founding its construction on guidelines influenced by religious tradition. Nevertheless, when it comes to the fiction of this Brazilian author, though her text does share its main narrative mechanism with Isaacs, it does so with a twist.

The plot, again, is extremely simple: a male narrator, Rodrigo S. M., tells the story of Macabéa, a poor girl he happened to see on the streets of the big city. She is almost illiterate, has no friends, and works as a typist. The only person she speaks with is Glória, her office mate who is a local girl, has a family, is well-fed and well treated. One day Macabéa falls in love with Olímpio, a man who comes from the same Northeastern state. But Olímpio does not love her, and ends up with Glória. Macabéa goes to a fortune teller who predicts a brilliant and happy future for her with a foreign man. On the way out of the fortune teller's house, Macabéa is run over by a car driven by a foreigner. She dies on the sidewalk, observed by the passersby, who for the first time pay attention to her.

When comparing the two texts, we see that, true to its title, *marianismo* plays a big role in Isaacs; in Lispector, the same *marianismo* is subverted. Whereas in Isaacs's novel María incarnates purity and sacrifice, in close identification with the Virgin, in the case of Macabéa, her name is more complex: it points at the many biblical figures called Maccabeus and suggests both resistance and martyrdom. In the case of Macabéa, martyrdom is achieved at the end of the narrative for the sake of Brazil's poverty-stricken masses; the aspect of resistance is implied in the text as a metaphor that indicates that she, like the weeds of the world, will not disappear. While María dies to fulfill her role as catalyst for Efraín's heroism (and his corresponding construction of nation), Macabéa perishes to heighten the visibility and — no matter how paradoxical this may seem — to praise the resilience of the poor.

Isaacs and Lispector in Their Time

As I have mentioned, politically speaking, Isaacs was a character of shifting allegiances.[4] His provincial origin, as well as the fact that he was the scion of prosperous landowners, dictated an initial complicity with conservatism. However, by the time he developed friendships in Bogotá and was influenced by mentors, like José María Vergara y Vergara or Aníbal Galindo, he was a declared progressive, or *radical*, as they were known in those days. To sum up, this meant that, when it came to dealing with conflict as part of the state, Isaacs would usually side with Amerindians or slaves, defending their claims to lands or right to freedom, and question the Church's involvement in political matters, a behavior sorely resented by conservative factions. To drive this point across, Arciniegas even describes how Isaacs's participation in congress was once received with stones, with a mob later following him to his home in the capital (62). Having suffered discrimination for his Jewish descent in Bogotá—*María's* success was not enough to contain this feature of the capital's society—it is understandable that Isaacs would lean in favor of the interests of oppressed sectors of the population. Then again, from this point on, his strategy would replicate the tactics of society in the province of Antioquia, a land he had visited and learned to love during his military errands. To eradicate any criticism regarding his spiritual affiliation, Isaacs relied heavily on a Judeo-Christian context and developed a narrative in which Biblical echoes are evident and undeniable. In plain terms, as a reaction to the offensive treatment of his heritage, he tried to out–Christianize Christians, appearing more regimented by religious context than the rest. Thus, *María* alludes to the New Testament and points towards a construction of identity rooted in Christian novelty, rather than Jewish tradition. The text might mention Paradise (the hacienda from the novel, where the idyll takes place, is called "El Paraíso") and favor Jewish nomenclature, but only as long as they both inform notions of Christianity and Catholicism. María, the character, is without a doubt, the unchallenged embodiment of Christian and Catholic virtue:

> Ella, tan cristiana y tan llena de fe, se regocijaba al encontrar bellezas por ella presentidas en el culto católico. Su alma tomaba la paleta que yo le ofrecía, los más preciosos colores para hermosearlo todo; y el fuego poético, don del cielo, que hace admirable a los hombres que lo poseen y diviniza a las mujeres que a su pesar lo revelan, daba a su semblante encantos desconocidos para mí hasta entonces en el rostro humano [Isaacs 38].

> She, so Christian and full of faith, rejoiced upon finding beauties anticipated by Catholic creed. Her soul embraced the palette I offered with the most beautiful colors to embellish everything; and poetic fire, a heavenly gift that renders admirable men who possess it and divinizes women who reveal it to great regret, gave her semblance charms till then unknown to me in the human face.[5]

For the most part, the passage proves my point. The María along these lines is an object of cult, in which the spiritual and the godly combine to grant her an almost unattainable quality. How could any woman, from the past or the present, live up to this model? It demonstrates the intricate nature of the relationship between religious discourse (in response to hateful treatment of ethnicity) and a more complicit demarcation of gender. In it, María is contemplated as an object of religious and bodily desire, but in a manner that appears almost naïve when it comes to commodification of gender. Whether this was a conscious or internalized trait of Isaacs's prose I leave for the reader to decide.

In the case of Macabéa, the poverty-stricken woman from destitute neighborhoods of Rio, the religious context is more up-front. Macabéa is not framed as the incarnation of purity, like María. Rather, to facilitate visibility before the reader, she is sacrificed at the end of the novel (a vehicle runs her over). This sacrifice opens the way to the suggestion of the resistance of the Jewish people, while at the same time it mimics the Eucharist. It is only when Macabéa lies dying on the street that her fellow citizens notice her. According to Lispector, the poor in Rio exist, amazingly, because the privileged classes have learned to live and ignore them, fading them into the background, in the *morros*. The only alternative is to bring one of them into the open and sacrifice her, so she becomes apparent. In this way, the narrator — and Lispector, by way of Rodrigo S. M.— goes beyond acting as a safety valve for the bourgeoisie. Although the overall strategy of the text is based on a Christian notion, it appears thoroughly informed by Lispector's Jewish background.

Then again, Jewishness is not the only factor informing constructs of race or ethnicity. First, let's see the case of *María*. In his book about Isaacs, Arciniegas mentions two aspects as proof of Isaacs's insightful view of Afro-Colombians. On one hand, he points out correctly that Feliciana, the slave who takes care of María in the novel, and Nay, the slave that was freed by Isaacs's real father, are the same (58). While Nay's story appears in *María* as a separate episode, it has usually been identified as a concession to the penchant for exoticism of the literary movements of this period. Having landed in Turbo, the seaport in Chocó that to this day serves as link between the continent and the West Indies, the slave Nay feared she would be bought and shipped to the U.S. Rumors of ghastly treatment in the Jim Crow south poison her soul. Thus, she appealed to Isaacs's father, who paid for her freedom in exchange for her services as a nanny for Ester, the daughter of Salomón, a cousin of Jorge Enrique Isaacs). On the other hand, Arciniegas quotes a lengthy segment of the novel which describes a conversation between the blacks that row up the Dagua River (during Efraín's hurried return from London), comparing their language to the one by Candelario Obeso, a renowned Afro-Colombian author of the nineteenth century (59–62). Typical of the literature of this period, so concerned with laying down boundaries for national behavior, Isaacs's Spanish attempts a close phonetic transcription of the language favored by the oarsmen. Isaacs, it turns out — according to Arciniegas — was writing in the style of Obeso *avant la lettre*. Hence, it is within the general framework of these two passages that the reader shares the Colombian author's paternalistic view of Afro-Colombians. True to his romantic nature, Isaacs idealized blacks, imagining them as the perpetual subordinates of a social order ruled by Colombian *criollos*.

Also, during Isaacs's tenure in the office of the Secretary of Interior, Arciniegas describes an incident with some Amerindians — named Quinitanchala, Tenganan, and Tulcán — who come to the capital to file a complaint (54). Having lost their lands, they seek justice by hand of the white man. What a band of fools, anyone could have claimed; have they learned nothing from history? Isaacs, Arciniegas argues, comes immediately to their rescue (it is unquestionable that they *need* to be rescued), reminding government that General José Hilario López and the glorious Liberal party have proclaimed the emancipation of slaves and indigenous populations all over national territory. With this behavior in mind, it is understandable that his complicity with a certain social order, disguised as a thirst for equality, informs much of the narrative in *María*. The thing is, it does so only as long it does not violate certain preconceptions of gender, which definitely do not conform to aspirations of equality. It is in this sense that I contend that, while Isaacs showed contradictory deference in matters of race and ethnicity, influenced by his experience as an outsider in the capital, he clearly did not apply the same standard in matters of gender, perhaps precisely because his fiction is so firmly grounded on Biblical notions, which, in themselves, do not favor major gender equality. In sum, whether it was because it resulted from the framework of his fiction or because he had internalized a certain amount of prejudice, Isaacs's construction of female identity does not relate to the construct of nation in *María* along the lines of "egalitarianism" saved for matters of ethnicity or race. In Isaacs, the priority for gender is composure, rather than interrogation.

Lispector too, even though she did not exactly try to mask her Jewish origin, she always referred to herself as a Brazilian. As her first biography informs, Lispector herself writes, "Nasci na Ucrânia, terra de meus pais. Nasci numa pequena aldeia chamada Tchechelnik [...] Cheguei ao Brasil com apenas dois meses de idade" (Nádia Battella Gotlib 18)— I was born in the Ukraine, my parents' country. I was born in a small village called Tchechelnik [...] I arrived in Brazil when I was only two months old. The family first arrived in the Maceió, and later moved to Recife, both cities in the Northeastern region of Brazil.[6] In the case of *The Hour of the Star*, Lispector makes it very clear that Macabéa is from the Northeast of the country. Although such information might pass as a mere geographic setting indicating not-Rio de Janeiro, for any Brazilian the Northeast is a place pregnant (to borrow Lispector's own metaphor) with meaning, pointing to both a rich history and a complex racial heritage, as well as widespread poverty.

As one of the regions of the country that received more African slaves, the Northeast of Brazil is also the place whose indigenous peoples were more quickly destroyed or incorporated into the white colonizing enterprise. The people resulting for the mixture of whites, blacks, and Indians, lived in immense hardship due to the inhospitable land and the harsh climate, and was subjected first to the abandon and carelessness of the colonial powers, and later to the indifference of the independent government of the empire of Brazil from 1822 to 1889. And yet, once the Republic was inaugurated in 1889, this same people ("a resistant, stubborn dwarf race" in Lispector's words, 90) stopped the Brazilian army when thousands of soldiers came to destroy the town of Canudos because some believed its leader (the messianic Antonio Conselheiro) wanted the return of the ousted emperor. Lispector is not the first one to refer to the strength of this race: the narrator of *The Hour of the Star*, clearly quotes from Euclides da Cunha's *Os Sertões* (1902), when he says that the *sertanejo* (person who comes from the *sertão*—the backlands) is, above all, patient. To be sure, Da Cunha says that the sertanejo is *strong*. Lispector, because she wants to emphasize *resilience*, uses the adjective patient, because it embodies the characteristic that her female protagonist, Macabéa, displays. The strength that carries the poor, semi-illiterate, and sick young woman from the Northeast is her patience. The country is vast and indifferent. She is patient, and even when she dies the death of a martyr, the text tells us that she is "capim," a mere "weed" growing at the side of the road. But weeds, the text suggests, will thrive anywhere. In sum, it is possible to say that, by far, death is the biggest event in María's short existence, just as in Macabéa's.

It is in this respect that I detect the greatest commonality between María, and Macabéa: they are both sacrificial lambs. Like María, Macabéa does not do much throughout Lispector's narration. To be more precise, events befall her, just like to María. Her male counterpart, Olimpico, just like Efraín, seems more capable of action: he has murdered a man and dreams of becoming a politician (eventually, he ditches Macabéa for buxom, well-fed Gloria). Macabéa's story might be set in modern-day Rio de Janeiro, but her concerns are minimal and almost as trivial as María's, never mind the latter's familiarity with French literature. Unlike María, though, Macabéa is not a child of privilege. Lispector created her with a primordial objective: to promote the social consciousness of the bourgeoisie, exposing her readers to intimate contact with the psychological consequences of poverty. During Macabéa's lifetime her presence is just too easy to ignore. To be noticed, she needs to die, like a modern-day martyr.

To the average visitor in Rio de Janeiro, this must stand as a broad contradiction. How is it possible that someone in Rio, of all places, with its *morros* covered with *favelas*, could fail to notice poverty? Well, it is precisely for this reason, I suppose, because of the radical omnipresence of poverty, that the city's inhabitants choose to tune it out and not problematize it. Otherwise, daily existence in Rio, perhaps the most privileged city in the world in terms of setting, would be unbearable. To tune out poverty is a common defense mechanism of the bourgeoisie, unaccustomed to dealing with reasons for discomfort in life. In fact, were this sizeable poverty located in any other place in the world, its effect on setting would have been entirely detrimental. In Rio, on the other hand, with its heightened contrast between verticality (skyscrapers, *morros*) and horizons (the beaches, the water), and its lush vegetation, it appears almost folksy, becoming one more ingredient in the mix.

Unlike *María*, *The Hour of the Star* is a brief text. Having barely started, *The Hour of The Star* is over. As a matter of fact, its narrative is circular, ending with a phrase that takes us to its beginning. Yet, just like María, Macabéa's greatest accomplishment, it becomes apparent, is her death. That is to say, over a century later, a Brazilian woman writes a story that, by and large, relies on the same basic literary mechanism of the novel by the Colombian author: to take advantage of the melancholy of death as a device that will drive forward a seminal point. In the Colombian's case, the novel alludes to specific qualities of nationhood, appropriating gender to legitimate certain forms of identity: a good Colombian boy/man must behave like this; a good Colombian girl/woman must behave like that: that is what we learned when we read *María* in school. Carlos Monsiváis argues that Mexicans attended cinema to learn how to be Mexicans. I will contend that, as Colombians, we read *María* to learn how to be Colombian, regardless of our gender. In the Brazilian's case, things are simpler but no less significant: to learn about your nation you must first and foremost recognize the acts of the poor as a valid form of enacting *brasilidade* (Brazilianness). The *favelados* are also Brazilians, and the culture they produce is just as relevant as the best piece by Villa-Lobos. A competent reader must *see* poor Brazilians who, in spite of their poverty, embody biblical qualities of perseverance, and resilience at the same time they are usually sacrificed and die without a sound. With this text Lispector leads the reader to acknowledge the presence of the poor, thus stating that they should not fade into the background. In both novels, however, the mechanism that triggers forward the acknowledgement of identity happens to be gender. The main difference between the two is that, for Isaacs, it is a matter of personal reading (there is scant proof that the author was particularly aware of his bias), whereas in Lispector's case there is ample evidence of authorial consciousness.

Some Possible Conclusions

On the whole, despite what is immediately apparent, *María* and *The Hour of The Star* share many similarities, emanating from common strategies — conscious or not — by their authors. Both are immersed in literary projects tied to notions of nation. In Isaacs's case, there is the hope to feature the makings of a land tied to nature. In Lispector's, there is the will to posit some form of lesson: Brazil will only achieve its potential once it manages to include the many dispossessed within the order of the state. Both María and Macabéa are rather passive and seldom engage in action through their own free will. Rather, things happen to them, and, at the end of their corresponding accounts, stands their greatest achievement: death. For *María*, it is a matter of sacrifice and pain, so its hero may learn the risks of life in a bucolic setting, so distant from the benefits of modernity. True to its time, *María* endorses dichotomy of civilization versus barbarism. For Macabéa, the hope is that, as she dies, she will finally gain visibility as the embodiment of the massive poverty drowning Rio and her nation. Lispector compares Macabéa to Marilyn Monroe, not because of her good looks, quite obviously, but for the theatrical bent of her death. María's death, on the other hand, is not even allowed this much. (Pop culture had yet to make its mark in the nineteenth century.) Having determined the full arc of the narrative from its very inception, her demise takes place outside the narration. Both settings are painstakingly beautiful: the valley of the Cauca River and the surroundings of Guanabara Bay. In *María*'s case, to heighten the virtue of being Colombian, the narrative promotes an indissoluble link between nationality and the magnificence of its nature. With such a fertile countryside, it appears to argue, it is impossible not to feel blessed. In Macabéa's instance, although unmentioned, nature is ever-present; if this were the case of any city other than Rio, poverty would have overshadowed its beauty.

Then again, Lispector did not have to suffer her ethnicity (her Jewish heritage) or background (the fact that, as a child, she had lived in northeastern Brazil) like Isaacs. She had the fate of landing in a multicultural enclave, influenced by *branqueamento* (racial whitening) and a myth of racial democracy (and also by her own physical beauty and her marriage to a diplomat who took her outside the country — something quite desirable for Brazilians). Isaacs was born in a country where the white elite from the interior sought to impose its version of identity upon the rest of the population, along the general outline of a pyramidal arrangement, in which whites were at the top, living in the pleasant climate of mountainous plateaus, and Afro-Colombians lagged at the bottom, condemned to the unbearable heat of coastal plains. Gender was not a key consideration for this model, suggested by José María Samper — that is why women did not even figure as a separate concern in its setup. Thus, when Isaacs wrote *María*, he failed to contemplate the implications of gender in his general elaboration of a theory of nation. In it, the role of women, aside from incarnating virtuous objects of desire, served as accomplice to the wider order set in place by men, who were too busy fighting their wars to care for the general well being of the population.

In the end, *María* is less about race and ethnicity than it first appears. Unlike his audience, Isaacs did not wish to add further controversy to the matter of his heritage. In his imagination, blacks and Amerindians were as equal as his circumstances could have allowed. Instead, gender marks the ultimate concern. My critique of the text is not oriented by some misguided, politically correct desire to settle accounts with a nineteenth-century text. Rather, my hope is to inspire readers to revisit the novel and view it with different eyes, and learn from it, so that, as nation, Colombians stop repeating the mistakes of the past and are finally able to implement successful formulas for the future: a world in which the female protagonist — or anyone else, for that matter — does not have to die, figuratively or metaphorically, to convey an effective, plausible way of enacting *colombianidad* (Colombianness). In these times of repressive preparations for World Cups and Olympics, an equal cry goes for the *favelados* and *brasilidade* (Brazilianess).

Notes

1. Tyrone Power (1914–1958) was an American Hollywood star famous for his leading role in *Murder for the Prosecution* (1957), *The Mask of Zorro* (1940), and *Blood and Sand* (1941).

2. For analogous reasons, this translation is mine.

3. Neruda, Pablo. *The Essential Neruda: Selected Poems.* San Francisco, CA: City Light Books, 2004, p. 7.

4. For a very complete discussion of Isaacs's family history and how it influenced the creation of María, see Arciniegas's *Genio y figura de Jorge Isaacs* (1967).

5. This translation is mine as the entire segment is missing in the English translation.

6. See Nádia Battella Gotlib's book for more details about the many inconsistencies in Lispector's birth and exact date of arrival of the family in Brazil.

Works Cited

Arciniegas, Germán. *Genio y figura de Jorge Isaacs.* Buenos Aires: Editorial Universitaria de Buenos Aires, 1967. Print.

Gotlib, Nádia Battella. *Clarice: Uma vida que se conta.* 2nd ed. São Paulo: Editora Ática, 1995. Print.

Isaacs, Jorge. *María.* Madrid: Ediciones Rodas, 1972. Print.

_____. *Maria: A South American Romance.* Translated by Rollo Ogden. New York: Harper & Brothers, 1890. Print.

Lispector, Clarice. *The Hour of the Star.* New York: New Directions, 1992. Print.

Neruda, Pablo. "Me gustas cuando callas." In *Veinte poemas de amor y una canción desesperada.* Madrid: Planeta, 1995. Print.

_____. "I like it when you're quiet." *The Essential Neruda: Selected Poems.* Ed. Mark Eisner. San Francisco: City Light Books, 2004. Print.

Pratt, Mary Louise. *Imperial Eyes: Travel Writing and Transculturation.* New York: Routledge, 2007. Print.

Samper, José María. *Apuntamientos para la historia política i social de la Nueva Granada.* Bogotá: Imprenta del Neogranadino, 1853. Print.

2

Intoxicating Outlaws:
Dominance and Sexuality in
Rómulo Gallegos' *Doña Bárbara*

PATRICIA L. SWIER

When we speak of female icons in Hispanic literature, the sultry, yet foreboding image of Doña Bárbara comes to mind. Her sexuality, her supernatural powers and her limitless authority in the novel defy traditional conceptions of gender during the time period, and under this light she seems to pop off of the page and stand out among the many female characters of Hispanic novels. Interestingly, her character was inspired by the legend of a powerful woman in the *llanos* that Rómulo Gallegos had heard about during his eight day visit to a ranch near San Fernando, the capital of the *llano* area (Donald Shaw 1974: 265). He must have considered her to be such an anomaly that she would be the perfect persona to embody the ominous oppressive rule of the current dictator Juan Vicente Gómez.[1] Through the contradictory character of Doña Bárbara, we see how gender codes are employed, manipulated, and eventually spilled over in this regional anti-dictatorial novel. In fact, Doña Bárbara serves as a pivotal figure in Latin American literature, as she continues to capture the attention of a multitude of generations of readers who cast an array of critical observations onto her, stemming from the atypical characteristics of dominance and sexuality uncharacteristic of women during this and any other time period. This essay will explore both the evolution and the different approaches of this mesmerizing Plainswoman, who has been compared to Medusa and the sphinx, and has been described as "part Amazon, part vampire; the traveler's return; Pygmalion and Galatea."[2] Through the lens of gender and sexuality, I will point out the rich and textured fabric of literary and historical criticism surrounding this unique protagonist and the diverse scope of meaning that this figure projects.

The criticism surrounding this novel is as diverse as it is contradictory. While Donald Shaw (1971) claims that *Doña Bárbara* is one of the most widely read of Latin American texts, producing over 2000 critical articles, 22 books, a film, an opera and several plays; in 1971, he decried that "nothing of real value has [yet] appeared on the development of the text of this major work" (265).[3] Carlos J. Alonso (1989) casts a similar futile approximation towards the analysis of the novel focusing on the overuse of allegory in an outstanding essay broaching a modern and perhaps postmodern reading. Despite his critical perspective, he concludes that any attempt at a single analysis through allegory is impossible, as this trope provides an interpretation so far removed from the signified, that it collapses meaning onto itself (438). Perhaps the most intriguing part of this study is Alonso's theory of Doña Bárbara's adherence to negativity, which he argues, represents the dialectics of meaning within the novel that resists a singular monolithic meaning that most critics grasp on to in their insistence on Domingo Faustino Sarmiento's paradigmatic dichotomy: "civilization and barbarism."[4] Gallegos' intention, therefore, according to Alonso, becomes far reached, unattainable and reverberates within a field of reiterated allegories that could essentially go on forever. Given the more diverse and problematic aspects of the novel by two well respected critics, I will invite my reader backwards in history, into some of the earlier literary critiques that are intricately related with Doña Bárbara's sexuality and power.

Doña Bárbara was written alongside popular regional novels in Latin America including Jorge Rivera's *The Vortex* (1924), the political writings of José Vasconcelos in Mexico, and the Mexican "novel of the revolution," Mariano Azuela's *The Underdogs* (1915), all of which provide a change of perspective from the model of the European ideal to the autochthonous nature of the land. Following World War I, Latin American writers became less enamored with the progressive ideals responsible for the destruction and chaos that emerged from technological advancement of more progressive nations, and were also more skeptical of the imperialist advances of foreign nations in their respective countries. The literary trend of looking inward and celebrating the unique characteristics of the people and the land became more prevalent, as it oftentimes served as a means of political or social protest. The character Doña Bárbara emerges into this setting, and in this novel, she becomes the epitome of the union between land and the Venezuelan people, thereby captivating the nationalist surge of narratives of this type. Moreover, she is seen as a celebrated flashback and/or prototype of Sarmiento's portrayal of the controversial

Facundo Quiroga as she displays dominance over the uncontrollable aspects of the land, and therefore provokes a sense of awe and fascination on both the writer and the reader. *La mujerona* is described as a woman that was "all man riding horses and lassoing wild animals" (*Doña Bárbara* 10) — "una mujer que era todo un hombre para jinetear caballos y enlazar cimarrones." She is further lauded for her ability to toss a lasso and bring down a bull out in the open as well as her most skillful cowboy (45). Finally, through her knowledge of black magic learned from the Indian tribe with whom she lived, Doña Bárbara wielded an uncanny sense of power over the other protagonists in the novel, ultimately making her intoxicating, bewitching, and dangerous.

Early Reception and Revisions (1930–1960)

Many of the early reactions to the novel focus on the intricate relationship between Doña Bárbara and the land. In 1930, S. L. Millard Rosenberg cites Gallegos as the "leading American novelist," proclaiming the land itself as the chief protagonist (333). Muna Lee reiterates this idea in her review of the first English translation of the novel as early as 1931: "A story of the Venezuelan plains, with a fiercely dominant woman, a female embodiment of *caciquismo*, its dynamic center, Doña Bárbara is a portrayal of the *llanero's* turbulent existence" (259). Early critics note the hefty critique of barbarism made evident through the land and the sexual wiles of Doña Bárbara, exemplifying the age-old conflict between good and evil, masculine and feminine, and civilization and barbarism.

Despite the author's intentions to condemn the more barbaric aspects of the land, *Doña Bárbara* enjoyed a very positive reception. The people of the *llano* experienced a sense of pride at seeing their lifestyle portrayed so candidly in literature. According to John E. Englekirk, many of the characters were inspired by people that Gallegos had met, or by well-known characters in the region that the author had heard about from his guide. After only eight days in the *llanos*, critics extolled Don Rómulo as one who "ha vivido, sin duda la vida amplia y libre del inmenso llano" — "has doubtlessly lived the wide open life of the immense plains," and "el que forjara la ficción de la hombruna Doña Bárbara" — "and one who had forged the fiction of the mannish Doña Barbara" (qtd. in Englekirk).[5] Many readers may be aware that the numerous characters of the novel stem from veritable sources, including Doña Bárbara, Melquiades and Antonio Sandoval; however, the other principal protagonist of the novel, the Venezuelan terrain, is also featured in a verisimilar manner. Of the approximately fifty bayous, streams, rivers, ranches, towns, cities, and states mentioned, twenty five or more can be located on maps, while many more are associated with similar places (Englekirk 267). It is not surprising that the Apure Plainsmen fully supported Gallegos, and saw in his novel a mirroring of their lives, daily struggles, and aspirations (Englekirk 268). In spite of the novel's intentional jabs, the dictator Gómez had also been very eager to read the novel, and it is said that he had his limousine driver read it to him under the headlights of the car. His response was none other than positive, as he decries: "Este bachiller sí sabe cómo trabajan los hombres"—"This scholar really knows how men work."[6] The novel had touched a personal cord of pride and nationalism, which may be one of the reasons why Gallegos put forth such a concerted effort to revise it.

Unhappy with the first edition of this work titled *La Colonela*, Gallegos got to work writing and revising key aspects of the novel.[7] Shaw points out that Gallegos made drastic changes in the 1930 edition that emphasized the importance of Doña Bárbara, and brought her "to the forefront" (1974: 266). While initially the novel focused on Santos' ambiguous nature revealing the conflict between civilization and barbarism, the revisions developed Doña Bárbara's character and ennobled her character "until it received parity of importance with that of Santos" (1974: 267). One of the more pertinent changes made is both the title and movement of Chapter 3, initially titled "El recuerdo de Asdrúbal"—"The Memory of Asdrúbal," now changed to "La devoradora de hombres"—"The Man Eater" (266). According to Shaw, this alteration positions Doña Bárbara's traumatic past as a parallel occurrence, contributing to the underlying theme of the novel. Another significant addition is the project of the *cerca*/fence that Santos Luzardo proposes in order to contain the barbarous aspects of the land and to enclose the cattle that drifted onto Doña Bárbara's property. This addition, which will be addressed in detail by future critics, serves as a "symbol of the llano's submission to restraint" (Shaw 1974: 271). Among the many changes made to the original text, Gallegos fine-tunes Doña Bárbara's character, sharpening the symbolic parallels to the crocodile and *El Tuerto*, while suppressing her more feminine qualities (275). Now her character is more sinister, complex, and dark, which are features that are expounded in her overall sense of dominance and her deviant sexuality.

Sexuality and Symbolism (1960–1985)

The *Merriam-Webster Dictionary* defines sexuality in the following ways, all of which have been addressed by various critics in their illumination of Doña Bárbara's character: 1. the quality or state of being sexual; 2. the condition of having sex; 3. sexual activity; and 4. expression of sexual receptivity or interest especially when excessive.[8] In his 1964 conference, "La pura mujer sobre la tierra" ("The Pure Woman on the Earth"), concerning female protagonists in his novel, Gallegos makes reference to the origins of the character of Doña Bárbara as he candidly asks his audience: "¿Quieren un monstruo? Aquí tienen uno" (Gallegos 74)—"Do you want a monster? Here you have one." La *mujerona's* monstrosity, of course, lies in her deviant sexuality, which is developed through her ambivalent gendered characteristics,[9] her sexual attraction, and in her insatiable sexual appetite, which is enhanced in the novel by the aphrodisiac potions she concocts for her lovers. Shaw points out that since the publication of the novel critics have disagreed about this protagonist's fictional creation, the credibility of her character, and the meaning and symbolism attributed to her (*Doña Bárbara* 46). While Ciro Alegría (1953) argues that Doña Bárbara is a character with clear motivation that fails through excess thesis, M. Morínigo (1963) and Waldo Ross claim that she lacks the interior life of a real person.[10] Conversely, Jorge Mañach, Concha Meléndez, Arturo Torres Rioseco, and Ángel Damboriena celebrate the admirable psychological development of this character, which is a tribute that Shaw finds to be lacking in her overall development (Shaw 1972: 43). Despite the contradictory approaches towards this character, most critics would agree on *la cacica's* deviant sexuality in the novel, which has been described for its pathological factors, its mythical origins, its relation to the conquest and colonization of the New World, and is attributed to the emasculating effects suffered by the male characters surrounding her. Because Doña Bárbara's sexuality exceeds that of real life personalities, she is more often cast into the symbolic and allegorical mode, leading to a complex, yet rich array of interpretations.

Sturgis E. Leavitt's "Sex vs. Symbolism in *Doña Bárbara*" is testament to the changing perceptions of sexuality through the years and the interest that it draws to critics. A short four pages, this work offers no reference to a historical or political context, but harbors on *la cacica's* possible desirability for Santos. Leavitt addresses Doña Bárbara's questionable physical appeal due to her rugged activities as a rider and lassoer under the hot Venezuelan sun: "Her complexion must have been anything but that of Elizabeth Arden. Her hands must have been calloused by handling the reins of the troublesome horses" (118). Persistent in Santos' possible sexual arousal for this middle-aged woman, he comments on the former's perceived failed *machismo* if he were to completely reject her. He then alludes to the slim pickings of plainswomen, claiming that *la cacica* must have been "the only woman worth looking at for miles around," especially as Santos had been away for some time from "those flesh pots from Caracas" (119). Despite the clearly misogynist and superficial comments of this critic, Leavitt throws his reader a glimmer of hope when he recognizes Marisela's active role with regard to Santos' salvation. Unable to attract the desired interest from Santos, Doña Bárbara is forced to resort to *brujería*; and Marisela, concerned for Santos, stops her mother from proceeding with these actions. In a somewhat disdainful manner, this critic first states: "we (the readers) are asked to believe that [...] this move (witchcraft) will bring Santos Luzardo to his knees." In a similar incredulous tone, he points out that we are also asked "to accept Marisela's opportune interruption of the witchery of Doña Barbara as the salvation of Santos Luzardo" (120). Any sign of female agency one would care to read of between the lines is quickly debunked as Marisela's efforts and Doña Bárbara's defeat are cast into the literary imaginary of Symbolism. Leavitt succinctly concludes his article saying: "The conflict between Doña Bárbara and Santos Luzardo is not a conflict after all. Symbolism comes first" (120).

André S. Michalski's (1970) analysis also stems from the symbolic; he points out the fusion of the mythical and the realistic in Doña Bárbara, which according to this critic makes her a universal symbol. He sees this work as a type of Sleeping Beauty with Santos as the prince, Marisela as the princess and Doña Bárbara as the *bruja* that relinquishes herself when she loses power (1016). Moreover, the autochthonous background of the Venezuelan plains is highlighted in the *bongos* that serve as the ships or boats of legendary tales and medieval *caballerías*, while the alligators are depicted as dragons. Within this fairy tale setting, Doña Bárbara emerges as a type of centaur, recalling fairy tale ogres, and like this mythical creature, she is only half human. Lethal sexuality and allure contribute to the development of her hybrid character, which is further established by Gallegos' repeated reference to her as the Sphinx and the "devoradora de hombres" (man eater). According to Michalski these epithets are used more frequently with relation to the fallen character Lorenzo, who is the first victim to be devoured by Doña Bárbara. The chapter surrounding Lorenzo's fall, or "ruina fisiológica" (physiologic ruin, 1017) is testament to the deleterious characteristics of the barbarism of the land that are incarnated in this mythical character.

While early readings of the novel focus on the symbolic aspects of Doña Bárbara's sexuality, one in particular gives credence to her more human qualities, which will be the basis of some of the ambiguities in the text addressed by later critics. In his analysis, Glen Kolb refers to the pathological aspects of Doña Bárbara, who was tainted by her past of abuse and violation. *La cacica* not only suffers due to her loss of her first love Asdrúbal and the rape that she endured from the boatmen, but she also suffers, like so many others surrounding her, "de la barbarie que ella misma practicaba" (85)—"of the barbarism that she herself practiced." In fact, in a weak moment of vulnerability, she confesses to Santos: "si yo me hubiera encontrado en mi camino con hombres como Ud., otra sería mi historia." — "If I would have encountered men like you in my path, my story would be different."[11] This critic notes the more fuzzy aspects of this character that do not fit perfectly within the dichotomous scheme of civilization and barbarism. He gives the example of the transformative effects that Santos has on Doña Bárbara, which highlight her femininity from early on. The first encounter between the two is described by the *mujerona* as an "acontecimiento insólito" — "an uncommon circumstance" that induced in her "un respeto que Doña Bárbara nunca había sentido" (86) — "a respect that Doña Bárbara had never felt before."[12] Nevertheless, destined to be the symbol of barbarism, she is subject to the more compulsive aspects of the intoxicating characteristics of the land. Much like the critics before him, Kolb reverts to the dichotomy of civilization and barbarism in his analysis of the protagonists, made evident by the civilizing qualities that Santos acquires in the city and the barbaric aspects of the *llanos*, embodied in the enigmatic character of Doña Bárbara (86). The encounter between the two is inevitably one of good over evil, and the didactics of the novel trump the human qualities initially seen in our female protagonist.

Shaw, who has one of the most comprehensive analyses of the novel to this day, also dedicates much of his investigation to the symbolic aspects of the *mujerona* while emphasizing the dual aspects of her personality. Like many critics before him, he points out that Doña Bárbara symbolizes the Venezuelan *llano* that Gallegos describes as "bello y terrible a la vez" (76) — "beautiful and terrible at the same time." Because Gallegos cannot see the *llano* nor the "alma de la raza" — "soul of the race" as an entirely negative factor, both the woman and the plains in the novel are "reinvested with positive potentiality" (Shaw 1972: 76). This theorization coincides with Shaw's readings of Gallegos' earlier writings and the latter's drastic shift in perspective concerning the Venezuelan "modo de ser" (way of being). In an essay titled "Las causas" (1909), Gallegos describes the Venezuelan national character as amorphous, hybrid and utterly incapable of providing a stable basis for progress. Just one month later in his essay "La alianza hispanoamericana," he criticizes the decadent influence of European races and celebrates "el vigor juvenile de las [razas] que se levantan en nuestro continente" — "the youthful vigor of the races that rise up in our continent" (qtd. in Shaw 1972: 13). This idea is expressed more succinctly in an essay written this same year when Gallegos decries: "Barbarie quiere decir juventud, y juventud es fuerza, promesa y esperanza" — "Barbarism means youth, and youth is strength, promise and hope" (qtd. in Shaw 1972: 13). These contradictory thoughts towards the Venezuelan "alma de la raza" are manifested in Doña Bárbara's character emphasizing both her beauty and savagery, encompassing features of dominance and desirability. After all, according to E. A. Johnson, Doña Bárbara really is only *semi-bárbara* (458).

Writing, Language and Sexuality (1985–1994)

It is important to point out that the term sexuality has shifted significantly in meaning from its connotations of desire, desirability, and sexual preference or activities to its more implicit association with power, language, and knowledge. The rising interest in feminism, postcolonialism, psychoanalysis and Michel Foucault's influential work *The History of Sexuality* (1976) had a profound impact on the field of academia calling attention to the intricate relationship between dominant discourse and the Other, often times expressed through the gendered body. While the next group of critics may not necessarily address these theories in their works, they are certainly knowledgeable of the more insightful interpretations of gender and sexuality and its relation to the political mechanisms of national identity and authority. The articles in this next section expound upon the importance of language and writing that is expressed through the sexual body of Doña Bárbara, and address in one way or another the representation of civilization versus barbarism in Gallegos' text.

Sharon Magnarelli opens her essay asking her reader what more could possibly be said about the novel after over fifty years of criticism (3). Despite the apparent exhaustibility of the topic, she squeezes out a laudable analysis of the significant change in women and nature since the publication of Jorge Isaacs' *María* sixty years earlier when nature was portrayed as *naturaleza* instead of barbarism.[13] She cites the historical happenings of World War I, the findings of Darwinism and "survival of the fittest," and Freud's theories of the antagonistic and castrating essence of women to be influential factors (4–5). Magnarelli recognizes that the dichotomies established in the novel are not so simple; she points out the less than philanthropical motivations of Santos, which, she argues, are driven by his perception of women and his interest in property (8). This critic insists that the mercantile ideals, which are the basis for Santos' journey, are founded on his perceived perception of the superiority of European ideas over Latin America. In this way, *Doña Bárbara* (novel) is the paradigm of the conquest: Santos embraces European ideals, and Doña Bárbara (the protagonist) represents the *mestizo* (10). Following current theories of the barbaric aspects of femininity, Gallegos stresses the masculine project in the novel, which is to define, harness, and codify these aspects of barbarity through the education of Marisela, and more importantly in the installation of the fence.[14]

Magnarelli argues that it is the delimitation, demarcation, and supplementation afforded by the word or language which create the ambivalence of the female (15). If women are defined in relation to men, Doña Bárbara defies this sense of property because she has no surname and is "estranged from the definition and limitation of civilization" (15). Because she resists female sexuality as constructed by Western culture, her character defies fencing and limitations, and ultimately repels that which is related to culture. Thus, she may be defined as the enemy of civilization, which in this case is characterized as the irrepressible aspects of nature (16). This critic further stresses the important role that language has in the power exerted by male protagonists that used the power of the word "to violate or distort the images of women and nature" (16). The real danger, warns Magnarelli, is when we lose sight of the metaphor as these ideas become naturalized into ideologies and practices.

Doris Sommer also addresses sexuality, language, and the dichotomous paradigm of civilization and barbarism in her analysis. Sommer places the novel within populist terms, and also in relation to the more ambiguous interpretations of José Eustacio Rivera's *La Vorágine* (1924) claiming that in *Doña Bárbara* "Gallegos reinscribes those oppositions with a vengeance" (276). While this critic insists upon the implementation of Sarmiento's dichotomous structure that she argues sutures up the leaky meanings that emanated from Rivera's work, much of her investigation is dedicated to the ambiguities of the text that stem from the *cacica's* sexuality. Sommer entertains different approximations and interpretations of the novel that creep forward from these ambiguities, one of which is Doña Bárbara's rape and metamorphosis, notions that harken back to the days of conquest and colonization of the New World. She also recognizes the dual factors, prevalent in the *novela de la tierra* itself, the love for the land, the celebration of autochthonous roots, and the romanticism of the *llano*, all of which contradict the motives of the populist ideals and the need to implement a national industry from within as a sign of progress. Like Magnarelli, she points out the civilizing factors of language, the branding of the cattle, and the education of Marisela in the novel. Sommer, however, stresses that it is Santos' commitment to marry Marisela that echoes all too clearly Sarmiento's claims to fill the empty spaces, as the new found couple will populate the vacant space of the *llanos* with future generations of "educated" people (281). In this way gender and race are refurbished in the consolidation of the national project as Doña Bárbara ineluctably fades into the background.

In a more exacting feminist approach, Claudette RoseGreen-Williams examines concepts of race, class and gender in a novel that she describes as the "epitome of the authoritarian text" (295). She argues that the binary construction used to define civilization and barbarism also underscores discourse through which gender is constructed. Not only are male and female polarized in the novel, but opposing coordinates of women are also reflected through this dichotomy. Contrary to the civilizable Marisela, who reflects stereotypes of femininity as submissive and domesticated, Doña Bárbara embodies the stereotype of strength and dominance. Her overall defiance of rigid sexual categorizations is further accentuated by her lack of maternal instinct, thus classifying her as a monstrous aberration. This critic points to issues of race and class beneath this implicit discourse that lie in Doña Bárbara's representation of non–White sensuality. Her feminization in the novel, made evident by the shift in epithets assigned to her (*mujerona*, *cacica*, etc), marks her disempowerment as well as the subsequent reinstatement of patriarchy (293–5).[15] This analysis differs drastically with that of William Rosa, who just five years earlier argued that women are represented as the more empowered characters of the novel, as they carry out decisive actions that move the narrative forward. First of all, it is Santos' mother who takes her son to the city in order to remove him from the destructive feud and barbarism of the *llano*. And more importantly, it is Doña Bárbara who makes crucial decisions towards the end of the novel that would assure her daughter's future: "Doña Bárbara 'ha enderezado los entuertos' que angustiaban a Santos y sobre todo aseguraban el futuro así como la posición sociopolítica de su hija" (96) — "Doña Bárbara has straightened out the wrongdoings that had tormented Santos and overall she assured the future, as well as the socio-political position of her daughter."

On a somewhat different note, Roberto González Echevarría draws upon the gendered binaries in the text and places the novel within a modern context by pointing out the deconstructive constituents of writing itself. His analysis challenges the legal (masculine) space of law and civilization. As the critic points out, the appropriation of the land by Santos' ancestors is based on violence: "we learn that the origin of writing is impure, that Evaristo's initial violence has left his mark on the land, has made it his and his descendants' property" (50). This fact, however does not prevent Santos from pursuing his claim to legitimacy (50). As a lawyer, Santos specializes in the encoding and interpretation of language in its relation to reality (48). While he is moved by a need to fix meaning in writing (according to the law), Doña Bárbara "is motivated by the contradictory wish to eradicate all marks and thus induce a chaos of marks and boundaries" (49). Her insistence to remain in the center defies all sense of boundaries related to fencing and the law: "I'm satisfied with only a bit of land, enough so that I can be in the middle of my property." In this way, the female character works as a disseminatory force, made up of contradictory desires and given to repetition instead of distinction and difference (56). Instead of emphasizing the dichotomous aspects of civilization over barbarism, González Echevarría stresses the contradictory nature of writing that Doña Bárbara represents, a notion that "invalidates the message contained on the doctrinal level and offers a critical view of literature itself" (56).

Androgyny and Transgendered
Approximations (1994–2011)

Sexuality — and its relentless baggage of ambiguities — takes on more open-ended dimensions related to the national complexities of race, class and gender in the analyses of Julie Skurski, Stephen Henighan, and Wendy V. Muñiz. The rise in homosexual (and transgendered) communities is accompanied by critical and philosophical theories that challenge the dominance of heteronormative reproduction.[16] Judith Butler's *Gender Trouble* provides a means in which critics can separate gender from the biological body and approach identity in a more fluid manner. I have found that more recent critics of the novel focus on the androgynous features of the protagonists, searching for hidden socio-political meanings that lie in these ambiguities. I will begin with Skurski's argument about the ambiguous gendered depictions in the novel, which she believes to mirror Gallegos' ambiguous claims to republican statehood driven by the resurgence of feminine representations of the natural, the instinctive and metaphysical (636). Skurski focuses on the role of ambiguity in the novel and its link to a new authority, referred to as "the discourse of authenticity." She proposes that Gallegos pertained to a more moderate group of elitists that, instead of divorcing themselves from the people, strived to unite with the masses, campaigning for education as a way of consolidating and uplifting the nation. Following the lead of intellectuals of the era, (notably José Ortega y Gassett's *Revista de Occidente* [funded in 1923] and Oswald Spengler's *Decline of the West*, 1918), Gallegos recognized the importance of the telluric and autochthonous aspects of the nation, many of which inspired him to develop the ambiguously female character Doña Bárbara.

Significantly, Skurski also emphasizes that the hybrid status of *la cacica's* sexuality reflects the hybrid racial makeup of Latin America as both a source of creative energy and a threat to civilization (606). As a consequence of colonialism's violence, Doña Bárbara is also split into opposing selves. While before she had been the innocent young girl tutored by her first love Asdrúbal, she was now the feared Doña Bárbara, "a destructive figure of undifferentiated sexual energy, with male and female impulses, mixing in a monstrous hybrid combination driven to conquer men in revenge for her own conquest" (623). Skurski points to the alterations that take place in Doña Bárbara's character following her encounter with Santos. Because Doña Bárbara sees the civilizing qualities of her former love in Luzardo, she undergoes significant transformations in the text that inevitably mirror Gallegos' aspirations for the nation.

The most important transformation, in fact, takes place at the end of the novel when Doña Bárbara cedes to the well-being of her daughter; and instead of fighting her rival for Santos she disappears, thereby marking the end of an era of violence and authoritarianism. Skurski proclaims that the novel is in dialogue with the civil dissent and social protests of the Gómez regime of the group who would become to be known as the "Generation of 28." Accordingly, Gallegos' revisions of the novel following the protests produced "a tightly structured mythic tale" or "an allegory of the nations' rule by despotism and of the projected triumph of the liberal, modernizing state" (619). While the novel ultimately endorses the elimination of the *cacica*, it is important to point out that Doña Bárbara remains as a submerged presence in legend and fantasy, thus celebrating the "primal instincts within leader and pueblo alike" (623).

Stephen Henighan also addresses the importance of gendered ambiguities in the novel, but he sees this as an integral aspect of the narrative that is shaped by the narrator's need to make these two characters conform to conventional gender definitions (29). Barbarism does yield to civilization, but this would be impossible without the erasure of gender identities that blur the boundaries of femininity and masculinity. Henighan addresses the male-female dichotomy in reference to Santos' rationalist project of harnessing the plains with fences, confronted with the borderless gendered aspects of Doña Bárbara, who fails to fit into the neat categories of femininity proposed by Western culture. Her adaptation of the immorality of the male species and her boundless control "tap into an ancient male fear of the power of unbridled female sexuality" (31). Consequently, the novel constructs Doña Bárbara's iconoclastic sexuality not as a rebellion against tradition but as a dangerous vestige of pre-modern backwardness (31). Henighan stresses that Doña Bárbara's refusal to conform to femininity as constructed by Santos Luzardo's modernizing ideology becomes the problem the narrative must solve (34). Persephone Braham also expounds upon an unharnessed femininity in Gallegos' star character that she claims has its origins in early Europeans' fascination with amazons and cannibalism dating back to medieval times. Braham argues that Gallegos and Rivera refer to the monstrous *vagina dentata* as a defining trope for regional identity at a specific historical moment characterized by dramatic epistemological challenges, namely post-war modernization. From early chronicles onwards anthropophagy has been associated with emasculating and libidinous behaviors by women (50).[17] In fact, early reports of the New World tell of female Amerindians' irreverence for domestic duties, their insatiable sexual desires, and the life draining effects they have on men (53).[18] Braham stresses that the stories surrounding the *vagina dentata* emerge into European literary texts, such as Lope de Vega's *La Serrana de la Vera* and Juan Ruiz's *El libro de buen amor*, serving as precursors to *La Vorágine* and *Doña Bárbara*. In the latter, we see how the mythical and the fabricated conjoin with the national as the female monstrous figure of Doña Bárbara threatens Santos with spiritual and even physical emasculation.

César Valverde looks to more contemporaneous explanations of the characters' sexuality in the novel in relation to the role of the male national subject in twentieth-century narrative in Latin America that, he argues, is multidimensional (128). Valverde claims that the prevalence in South America of uprisings, military coups, and diverse levels of social instability provoked the need to create strong masculine characters who could confront these imposing forces (129). I would argue that the novel reflects a pivotal moment in history when writers and intellectuals saw the need to alter more refined and erudite perceptions of masculinity that resonated in Sarmiento's intellectual narrator of *Facundo* (1845) and the helpless and frenzied Unitarian positioned underneath the "*matadero*/butcher" in Esteban Echeverría's "The Slaughterhouse" (1871).[19] With the innovative theorizations of Butler's gender performance, one can see more clearly the ways in which gender is constructed in the novel as a free floating artifice, shifting back and forth between characters. Doña Bárbara's persona maintains the masculine characteristics, and Santos, having been raised in the city, retains former conceptualizations of masculinity that are now almost obsolete in the modern era: "a young man whose strong, though not athletic, stature and decided expressive features gave him an air of almost aristocratic hauteur" (*Doña Bárbara* 4). Instead of an attraction based on sexuality and desirability, Santos seeks to take from Doña Bárbara that which is most vital to him with regard to the revitalization of the national project: her masculinity.[20]

Within the novel, the reader sees the process of a gendered *bildungsroman* of Santos who accrues layer upon layer of masculinity through his relationship with the land and his dealings with Doña Bárbara.[21] Similarly, Doña Bárbara becomes more feminine through her encounters with Santos, as she is gradually divested of power and ultimately dissipates into the Venezuelan landscape.[22] While the process of transgendering is vital to this analysis, it is important to point out the dynamic aspects of gender constituted in the female character of Doña Bárbara that are necessary components of the national project, as well as the indispensable components of femininity that Santos maintains as a stabilizing factor in order to control the more unharnessable aspects of masculinity that had run amuck in figures like Rosas, and in this case Gómez. We see an important shift in gender in this sense, because it is now masculinity that needs to be gauged and placed in check by the residual feminine qualities in Santos, and more importantly by his soon-to-be bride, Marisela.

This investigation represents a limited selection of the abundant criticism dedicated to this novel, focusing on how the evolution of gender and sexuality has produced diverse approximations to this internationally acclaimed work. It does not claim to be a closed reading, nor will it be a succinct reading of all that has been written, and the reader can certainly find overlaps of conceptualizations of gender represented here. Overall, it provides a curious approach to the readers' fascination of the topic of sexuality and power and the fluidity of both concepts that take on different meanings and interpretations throughout diverse historical moments, which is a methodology that undoubtedly will continue to evolve. As Wendy V. Muñiz stresses, this character comes to represent the iconoclastic aspects of Leonardo Da Vinci's "La Gioconda" featured in the 1929 cover of this work, pointing to Gallegos' transformative project on the national spectrum (1). Moving from her former characterization as the "outlaw" of the Plains grounded on the pathological aspects of her aberrant sexuality, her now iconic status in Hispanic literature, alongside more viable conceptualizations of gender and sexuality, positions her as a catalyst for change, accentuating the valuable presence of primal instincts and autochthony to be embraced in the national body of Venezuela, and within the broader spectrum of Latin American identity, in its constant movement towards renovation and renewal.

Notes

1. See "Doña Bárbara, Legend of the Llano." In this article, John Englekirk explains the stories surrounding Doña Pancha, who was the inspiration of the character of Doña Bárbara. This plainswoman was also believed to have never married, is described as *hombruna*, and was notorious for the property disputes with other landowners. Although stories about Doña Pancha provide different elements of the details of her life, including whether or not she had children, her cunning and her physical appearance, do coincide in reference to her frequent boundary disputes, one of which gained much notoriety in the plains.

2. Quoted in Margaret Wilson, 681.

3. These calculations were made in 1971 when Shaw published this article. Since that time period, much more has been written on the subject, including the production of the popular *telenovela* produced by the United States-based television network *Telemundo*.

4. Sarmiento wrote *Facundo* in 1845 as an attack against the dictatorship of Juan Manuel de Rosas. In this work he outlines the conflicts of Argentine society that are categorized in the terms of civilization and barbarism, which also take form in the division of the political factions of the Federalists and the Unitarians. This dichotomous theory became a popular theme for later writers who employed this model in the diagnosis of the social and political ills of their respective nations.

5. Quoted in Englekirk, 262. The first quote is made by Manuel Pedro González (1930) and the second by Loreley (1937).

6. Quoted in Alonso, 418. Unless otherwise noted, all translations in this work are mine.

7. In his book on *Doña Bárbara*, Shaw points out that Gallegos stopped the printing of the first draft in 1928 shortly after the student rebellion of 28 February broke out. After revising and rewriting much of the first work titled *La colonela*, the first edition was published in Spain in 1929. Gallegos returned to Spain and made several extensive revisions before finally publishing the novel that we know today in 1930 (16–17).

8. The *Merriam-Webster Dictionary*.

9. In "La pura mujer sobre la tierra," Gallegos alludes to the ambiguous characteristics of his lead character: "que no es hombre, que no parece mujer"—"that is not a man, that does not seem to be a woman" (70).

10. Quoted in Shaw, *Gallegos: Doña Bárbara*, 48.

11. Quoted in Kolb, 85.

12. Ibid, 86.

13. Magnarelli points out that nature is no longer viewed as the *locus amenus* of classicism and romanticism. In this novel nature, like the female and barbarism, is viewed as a threat to mankind and civilization (4)

14. Magnarelli refers to the fencing of Altamira and concludes that "To civilize is to define, highlight and glorify the self" and to "impose a degree of homogeneity" (11–12), which she points out is economic as well as egocentric (14–5).

15. Rosegreen-Williams concludes that while the novel seems to just exalt civilization and deplore barbarism, it also disseminates the theory of white supremacy and explicitly depreciates non-White races, legitimizes dominance of ruling over peasant class, and affirms the notion of male over female (295).

16. In a recent lecture on academic literary criticism at Yale University, Paul Frye opens his discussion with the seemingly innocent task of defining sexuality, only to conclude on the impossibility of this undertaking. In this lecture, Fry points out the discursive nature of sexuality with regard to Foucault and Butler. While Foucault sees sexuality as the effect of power-knowledge, power as knowledge, Butler sees it as the effect–"insofar as it's visible, insofar as it is acted out"—sees it as the effect of performance (Yale Literary Theory, transcript 23).

17. Early associations of emasculation with the New World can be seen during Columbus' second voyage in 1493 when Dr. Álvarez Chanca documented accounts of man-eating Caribs who preferred to eat the flesh of grown men instead of that of women or little boys (Braham 49–50).

18. World renowned explorer and naturalist Alexander von Humboldt justifies these fabricated findings in his account (not witnessed) of a city of female warriors who accepted male visitors annually to procreate (Humboldt 1995).

19. Esteban Echeverría's *The Slaughterhouse* (written in exile in 1839 and published in 1871) also employs the theme of civilization and barbarism in its harsh critique against the Rosas' regime in Argentina. In this short story, the refined and educated Unitarian is bullied by the primitive and uncivilized Federalists. Gender codes become slippery in this work as the macho Federalist *Matasiete* towers over the helpless and more feminized Unitarian until the latter ultimately dies in resistance to this brutally depicted mob.

20. See Patricia Lapolla Swier, *Hybrid Nations: Gender Troping and the Emergence of Bigendered Subjects in Latin American Narrative* (Madison, NJ: Fairleigh Dickinson University Press, 2009) and "Transgendering and the Emergence of Ambiguous National Subjects in Rómulo Gallegos' *Doña Bárbara*," *Hispanic Journal* 29.1 (2008): 91–105.

21. Ibid.

22. Ibid.

Works Cited

Alonso, Carlos J. "'Otra sería mi historia:' Allegorical Exhaustion in *Doña Bárbara*." *Modern Language Notes* 104.2 (March, 1989): 418–38.

Azuela, Mariano. *The Underdogs (Los de abajo)*. Trans. Sergio Waisman. New York: Penguin Classics, 2008.

Braham, Persephone. "Anthropology, Anthropophagy and Amazons." *Letras Hispanas: Revista de Literatura y Cultura* 5.2 (2008): 49–62.

Butler, Judith. *Gender Trouble: Feminism and the Subversion of Identity*. New York: Routledge, 1990.

Englekirk, John E. "Doña Bárbara, Legend of the Llano." *Hispania: A Journal Devoted to the Teaching of Spanish and Portuguese* 31.3 (1948): 259–270.
Eustasio Rivera, Jorge. *La vorágine* (*The Vortex*). Buenos Aires: Editorial Losada, 1959.
Foucault, Michel. *The History of Sexuality*. New York: Pantheon Books, 1978.
Gallegos, Rómulo. *Doña Bárbara*. 1929. Madrid: Cátedra, 1997.
_____. *Doña Barbara*. Trans. by Robert Malloy. New York: J. Cape and H. Smith, 1931.
_____. "La pura mujer sobre la tierra." *Cuadernos Hispanoamericanos* 675 (2006): 63–77.
González Echevarría, Roberto. *Voice of the Masters: Writing and Authority in Modern Latin American Narrative*. Austin: U of Texas P, 1985.
Henighan, Stephen. "The Reconstruction of Femininity in Gallegos' *Doña Bárbara*." *Latin American Literary Review* 32.64 (2004): 29–45.
Isaacs, Jorge, and Donald McGrady. *María*. Madrid: Cátedra, 1986.
Johnson, Ernest A. Jr. "The Meaning of Civilización and Barbarie in *Doña Bárbara*." *Hispania* 39.4 (December, 1956): 456–61.
Kolb, Glen L. "Dos novelas y un solo argumento." *Hispania: A Journal Devoted to the Teaching of Spanish and Portuguese* 46.1 (1963): 84–87.
Leavitt, Sturgis E. "Sex vs. Symbolism in Dona Barbara." *Revista de Estudios Hispánicos* 1 (1967): 117–120.
Lee, Muna. "*Doña Barbara* by Rómulo Gallegos." *Robert Malloy The Americas*. 6. 2 (1949):259.
Magnarelli, Sharon. "Woman and Nature in *Doña Bárbara* by Rómulo Gallegos." *Revista de Estudios Hispánicos* 19.2 (1985): 3–20.
Michalski, André S. "Doña Bárbara: Un cuento de hadas." *PMLA: Publications of the Modern Language Association of America* 85.5 (1970): 1015–1022.
Muñiz, Wendy V. "Entre Doña Bárbara y 'La Gioconda': Un estudio paratextual sobre la novela cumbre de Rómulo Gallegos." *Espéculo: Revista de Estudios Literarios* 44: (2010). Web. 25 Mar. 2011.
Rosa, William. "'*Doña Bárbara*': Sexualidad y dominación política." *Escritura: Revista de Teoría y Crítica Literarias* 12.23–24 (1987): 89–97.
Rosegreen-Williams, Claudette. "Rómulo Gallegos' *Doña Bárbara*: Toward a Radical Rereading." *Symposium: A Quarterly Journal in Modern Literatures* 47.4 (1993): 279–296.
Rosenberg, S. L. Millard. "Reviewed Works: *Doña Bárbara* by Rómulo Gallegos." *Books Abroad* 4.4 (1930): 333.
Sarmiento, Domingos Faustino. *Facundo: civilización y barbarie*. Garden City, NY: Doubleday, 1961.
"Sexuality." *The Merriam-Webster Dictionary*. 26 Mar. 2011. Web.
Shaw, Donald. Shaw, Leslie. *Gallegos: 'Doña Bárbara.'* London: Grant & Cutler, 1972.
_____. "Gallegos' Revision of *Doña Bárbara*, 1929–1930." *Hispanic Review* 42.3 (1974): 265–78.
Skurski, Julie. "The Ambiguities of Authenticity in Latin America: *Doña Bárbara* and the Construction of National Identity." *Poetics Today* 15.4 (1994): 605–64. Sommer, Doris. *Foundational Fictions: The National Romances of Latin America*. Berkeley: University of California Press, 1991.
Valverde, César. *Masculinidad en la narrativa hispanoamericana: Hegemonía, transgresión y Desconstrucción*. Ph.D. diss., University of California, 1997.
Wilson, Margaret. "Review: *Gallegos*: Doña Bárbara by D.L. Shaw and Calderón de la Barca: *El alcalde de Zalamea* by P. Halkhoree." *The Modern Language Review* 69. 3 (1974): 681–682.

3

Through the Eyes of the Child: The Narrator of *Balún Canán*

JEANIE MURPHY

For the first half of the twentieth century, Mexico was a nation undergoing profound social, political and economic change. The violent upheaval of the Mexican Revolution forever altered the nation's political institutions and began a reevaluation of its indigenous past as well as its collective identity. A new constitution was written as a first step in the restructuring of society; an emphasis was placed on national control of natural resources, on limits to the power and privileges of the clergy and on expanded educational opportunities. Additionally, one of the basic tenets of the Revolution, since Zapata's Plan of Ayala in 1911, was land reform. It was not until the 1930s, however, with the socioeconomic policies initiated by the government of Lázaro Cárdenas, that a serious attempt was made to follow through on many revolutionary promises. The Cárdenas presidency (1934–1940) redistributed millions of acres of land, reassigned land titles in order to allow the traditional indigenous *ejidos* to have access to farmland, and set up banks and other agencies to provide credit and machinery to poor farmers. In addition to the agrarian reform, the Cárdenas administration undertook a reorganization of the public education system by endeavoring to offer free, compulsory education throughout the country and, in this way, to integrate the most marginalized sectors of society into the national panorama.

The six-year term of Cárdenas, particularly with respect to his promotion of the interests of the indigenous population, can be considered the culmination of the Mexican Revolution and its goals. Nevertheless, the agrarian and educational reforms he proposed were not completely successful nor were they embraced by all. Some of the redistributed lands were of poor quality and corruption on many levels often affected the process of attaining credit. Literacy and other educational campaigns did not always meet with full compliance. Furthermore, ladino society, comprised in part of the families of the landholding elite, did not passively accept the new Cárdenas policies. The ladino opposition to agrarian and other reforms would lead to unrest and violent confrontations in much of rural Mexico, including the southeastern state of Chiapas, the childhood home of Rosario Castellanos.

Castellanos' first novel, *Balún Canán* (1957), captures the atmosphere of apprehension, uncertainty, and anger on all sides as the government began its efforts to institute agrarian as well as political and educational reforms on behalf of the indigenous population. The novel, following the story of the Argüello family, begins in the city of Comitán. César, a wealthy landowner and patriarch of the clan, decides to return with his wife and two children to Chactajal, their ranch in southern Mexico, in an attempt to prevent its expropriation. Their stay at Chactajal ends in a violent confrontation; César loses all authority as the patrón, a sugar mill is set afire, and the Argüellos are forced to abandon the ranch in the interest of their own safety. They must go back to Comitán.

In terms of narrative structure, the novel is divided into three parts. The first and third sections are narrated by the seven-year-old daughter of the Argüello family and correspond to the family's time in Comitán. The second section, in which the incidents of Chactajal are recounted, employs a third person omniscient narrator and, in this way, allows for multiple points of view ranging from that of César to his wife, Zoraida, from Felipe, a leader of the indigenous peasants, to Ernesto, the illegitimate son of César's deceased brother.

In this essay, we will be paying particular attention to the voice of the young daughter as she observes the events that will forever alter her world and her place in it. Her role in the recounting of the Argüello family's story is noteworthy and fundamental to the development of the narration, given that her perspective presents an additional challenge to the traditional social patterns and rules under attack in the novel. She is able to view and participate in both the ladino and the indigenous sectors of her society, yet, in one way or another; she is also barred from both worlds. While her comprehension of the events is restricted, the very innocence with which she tells her story provides the reader with a portrayal of the limitations and separations, based on gender and race, inherent in early twentieth century Mexico.

As Jean Franco has noted, Castellanos' literature in general, and the novel *Balún Canán* in particular, demonstrate a concern for the ways in which the indigenous and ladino communities connect and permeate each other, especially in the Chiapas region of southern Mexico (252). As a result, the com-

plexity of intercultural conflict is a key element of the novel as it underscores
the heterogeneous nature of Mexican society. María Elena de Valdés, commenting on the social conscience present in the works of Castellanos, affirms
that the author's evaluation of Mexican society is observed through the "textual
situation of interethnic relations" (94). Furthermore, the novel is informed in
large part by the actual experiences of Castellanos as a young child. The author
herself declared that her childhood heavily influenced the text when indicating
that "*Balún Canán* es la narración de mi infancia; es, además un testimonio
de los hechos que presencié en un momento en que se pretendió hacer un cam-
bio económico y político en los lugares donde yo vivía entonces..."—"*Balún
Canán* is the story of my childhood; it is, as well, a testimony to the events
witnessed at a time in which attempts were made to create economic and political change in the places where I was then living..."[1] (interview with María
Luisa Cresta de Leguizamón, cited in Lorenzano 38). In this way, Castellanos
affirms that both the private and the public spheres are present; childhood
memories become part of a larger national narrative and, as such, autobiography
informs history. Although the accuracy of the literary label "autobiography"
has been questioned with respect to Castellanos' text, it is important to note
that the details of the author's childhood experiences as a young girl perceiving
great social change in 1930s Mexico are consistent with certain circumstances
presented in *Balún Canán*.[2] Perhaps more important, however, is the text's
contribution to the process of producing a national identity. Through its fusion
of real and imagined events, the novel becomes what Laura Beard refers to as
a hybrid text in which "private interests (the realm of autobiography) assume
public significance (the realm of narratives on the nation...)" (65). The child
and her family become the focal point of a story that has much greater implications for the sociopolitical structure of the country as a whole. *Balún Canán*
is, indeed, a work of fiction, but the fictionalized account of an actual family
history cedes a space to the author in which she can explore a moment of
violent rupture in the history of Mexico. To use a term coined by Beard, it can
be argued that *Balún Canán*, represents a "natiobiography" given that its fictionalized accounts expand the usual self/life context of autobiography in order to
include stories of family/life and nation/life (71). Furthermore, this act of
fictionalizing her own recollections as a young girl allows Castellanos to add
her own voice to that of the Mexican collectivity. As Beard also notes, women
writers have often worked from the notion that "the official stories of their
nations do not include them [and they therefore] write themselves into the
national imagination through autobiographical writings" (99). Daniel Challener makes a similar assertion, noting that a "writer's sense of being marginalized is a powerful impetus to write ... and be heard" (8). Thus, the writers

can create a sort of historical dialogue that challenges the more traditional socio-political norms that would determine their peripheral place in the larger story.

The sense of exclusion to which Beard alludes would be felt all the more strongly by a young female child in a traditional family. The narrator of *Balún Canán* does not even name herself nor claim an identity within the family beyond that of daughter and sister. Although from the opening passages of the text she asserts herself by establishing her voice and insisting on her importance as a young girl, she also subverts her own significance. Her perspective is very limited and this becomes abundantly clear as she presents herself early on.

> No soy un grano de anís. Soy una niña y tengo siete años. Los cinco dedos de la mano derecha y dos de la izquierda. Y cuando me yergo puedo mirar de frente las rodillas de mi padre. Más arriba no. Me imagino que sigue creciendo como un gran árbol y que en su rama más alta está agazapado un tigre diminuto. Mi madre es diferente. Sobre su pelo—tan negro, tan espeso, tan crespo—pasan los pájaros y les gusta y se quedan. Me lo imagino nada más. Nunca lo he visto. Miro lo que está a mi nivel [9].

> I'm not a seed of anise. I'm a little girl and I'm seven years old. All five fingers of my right hand and two of the left. And when I stand up straight I can see my father's knees just in front of me. But not higher. He must, I suppose, go on growing like a big tree, and in its topmost branch a very small tiger is hiding. My mother is different. Birds wander through her hair — so black and thick and curly — and they like it there, and they linger. I'm only supposing that's how it is, that's all; for I've never seen it. I see what's as high as myself [13].[3]

The young narrator cannot see beyond the confines of her own personal space. She is not a part of the adult world and, as a consequence, can only imagine what that world holds in store. She can only see "as high as [her]self." From this first affirmation on the part of the child narrator, we are confronted with the problematic of point of view. Although the young girl is recounting her story, a story with national implications, she undercuts her own authority; she makes plain that her knowledge of the events is restricted and laced with ambiguities. At the same time, her voice as an outsider gives her story a perspective that creates a challenge to the hegemonic discourse at a time of profound and far-reaching social change.

Certainly, her youth prevents the narrator from understanding the larger events as they unfold around her. Yet, it is her gender that also precludes her from being entirely included in the family unit. Although she is the eldest, as the female child, she cannot participate in certain games, such as the running of the kites. She and the other girls on the outing must "mira[r], apartadas de los varones, desde [su] lugar" (22)—"watch from [their] places" (25), apart from the boys. Her place and her role are determined by her femininity and she is scolded when she does not pay close enough attention to the exploits and triumphs of her younger brother. Even more telling, however, than this gendered assignment of play, is her mother's reaction when the young narrator discovers a small booklet in her father's study. The papers are a history recorded by the indigenous Elder Brother. The information contained in the pages confirms the long-standing presence of the Argüello family in the lands of Chactajal, in essence accepting this presence as the fate of the land and its people, while at the same time documenting the forced labor, violent punishments and other abuses suffered by the indigenous once the "cashlán" (58) — "men of Castile" (57) arrived. When Zoraida catches her young daughter with the pilfered manuscript, her response is immediate and to the point, "No juegues con estas cosas.... Son la herencia de Mario. Del varón" (60) — "You mustn't play with these things.... They are Mario's inheritance. The male child's." (59).

There can be no question about the fact that the girl will be excluded from the larger family plans. As María Luisa Gil Iriarte has affirmed, *Balún Canán* is a novel that traces the growing self-awareness of the young narrator; it is her *toma de conciencia* (304) or moment of awareness. As such, and in terms of her place within the Argüello family, she is clearly learning that as the female child she will not have the same claim to the family's holdings as her male sibling. She will not be able to learn the full history of her family and their lands; likewise, she will not be permitted the same agency as her brother in that history. The loss of the papers also suggests her circumscribed access to knowledge in general and, more specifically, to the power of language and expression. A book taken from her hands, literally, signals her own symbolic privation, the fact that the use of the written word is out of her reach. This restriction or prohibition is, of course, in the end, rejected by the young girl. Not accepting the established norms, the Argüello's girl child will in fact eventually take up the pen. The story we have is, at least in part, hers; she has given voice to her experiences. Regardless of the limits placed on her, she will not completely abide by the more passive role that her traditional society would have expected of her and, in fact, the family history she was prohibited from reading will now become hers as she writes it.

The narrator shows no immediate reaction to her mother's insistence that the papers, and therefore history, belong to the male heir. The narrator does not respond to her mother's assertion; rather, in the next scene, she is reduced once again to the role of the observer as the family and their multitude of servants prepare for the journey from Comitán to the ranch in Chactajal. As a witness, rather than a participant, her perspective is beginning to change. Having read the accusatory papers and earlier, having seen her father, lying in his hammock, receiving the goods brought to him by his indigenous workers, the young girl realizes the role her family has played in the inequality of the society she inhabits. She understands that her father is "el que manda, el que posee" (16)—"the one who gives orders and owns things"(19). Similarly, she watches as he shouts orders and brings down his whip as he leads the long train of horses and indigenous porters out of Comitán on the way to Chactajal. Although this is the world into which she was born, it is not one with which she completely identifies. She is beginning to look more critically at the order of her microcosm. Recalling her father's treatment of the indigenous, she states, "no puedo soportar su rostro" (16)—"I can't bear the look of him" (19).

The indigenous nanny, the woman to whom she refers as her "nana," plays a fundamental role in the young girl's life and, by extension, in the narration of events. The Argüello girl has a very intimate relationship with her nana; she listens to her stories, heeds her warnings and feels her presence when she is not there. The bond she shares with the nana represents the other, opposing aspect of her worldview. The first section of the narration includes the voice of the nana and several anecdotes that clearly show the affection between the two. They go on an outing to the Fair of San Caralampio together and the nana arranges with the Lotto-man that her young charge, tired of her losing cards, win a prize; they sit together by the light of the kitchen fire and speak of Mayan beliefs and customs; they visit the chapel so that the nana can pray over the girl before she departs with her family for Chactajal. What is particularly consequential about these anecdotes and the other interactions between the young girl and her nana is the fact that, despite the tender attachment they share, despite the assertion by the narrator that "cuando quiero saber algo, voy a preguntárselo a la nana" (27)—"when I want to know anything, I go and ask Nana" (29), there is always a very clear separation of the two worlds they both inhabit. At the Fair of San Caralampio an indigenous man nearly falls out of his seat on the Ferris wheel and the girl does not understand the heated exchange and looming brawl that follows. She cannot ask her nana about what has happened, however, as she notices that "[tiene] sus ojos arrasados en lágrimas" (40)—"her eyes are cloudy with tears" (41) as they rush through the crowd. Along a similar vein, a part of the nana's existence will never include the young narrator. One evening in particular she goes to the kitchen to seek solace in the embrace of her nana:

> Cuando termina de servirles [los indígenas venidos de Chactajal] la nana también se sienta. Con solemnidad alarga ambas manos hacia el fuego y las mantiene allí unos instantes. Hablan y es como si cerraran un círculo a su alrededor. Yo lo rompo, angustiada.
> Nana, tengo frío.

Ella, como siempre desde que nací, me arrima a su regazo. Es caliente y amoroso. Pero tendrá una llaga. Una llaga que nosotros le habremos enconado [16–17].

When she's finished serving them [the indigenous who have come from Chactajal], Nana sits down too. Solemnly she stretches both hands to the fire and holds them there a while. They talk, and it's as if a circle had closed around them. I break it in my suffering:
"Nana, I'm cold."
She draws me to her lap, as she always has done ever since I was born. It is warm and tender, but it has a wound. A wound and it's we who've opened it [20].

The girl is clearly not an included member in this group; she is considered an outsider and she acutely feels a sense of exclusion as a circle seems to close around the others. Once again social constraints will define her place: as a child and, more importantly, a ladino child, she has no place in the conversation. In fact, the responsibility for the suppression of the native inhabitants, the collective guilt in which she shares as a member of her social class, is underscored by the figurative wound even as her nana, in a generous gesture, brings her into her lap. Nevertheless, it is here, rather than within her own family, that she makes the effort to be included and her childlike plea, an appeal to the affection of her nana, allows her to enter the circle.

It is necessary to contrast here the reaction of the young girl to her mother's act of exclusion (taking back the family papers) and her nana seeming to shut her out. Whereas there is no attempt to contradict her mother's assertion that the papers are a part of her brother's patrimony, the narrator very much wants to maintain her connection with her nana. The papers represent the harm her ancestors have caused to the land and its original inhabitants and she, perhaps still only unconsciously, repudiates that history. However, feeling abandoned by her nana, she plays on the emotions of her caretaker and she is able to gain, at least temporarily, access to that other realm. The two situations and the resulting attitude of the narrator illustrate the fundamental conflict of the novel: that of inclusion versus exclusion.

While it is certain that *Balún Canán* captures the interconnected nature of the indigenous and ladino cultures in southern Mexico, it is equally true that there is a constant textual tension between what it means to be a part of a dominant social group and, by contrast, the significance of being forced to remain on the periphery. The young narrator is simultaneously an insider and an outsider at all times. She is a member of the privileged class, and yet, as a child and as a female, many aspects of that social status are proscribed to her. Likewise, she is deeply attached to her nana and has some insight into her protector's belief system, yet she will never be fully integrated into that world. In reading the novel as a "natiobiography," the inevitable conclusion is that, despite official policies and programs, it will be difficult, if not impossible, to overcome long-standing prejudices as well as gendered and racialized oppression.

The middle section of the novel, the account of the family's time spent in Chactajal, further creates a sense of alienation and separation. As mentioned above, the narrative voice shifts in this segment as the young child is silenced and an omniscient, third person narrator takes over the story. In fact, the Argüello children almost completely disappear from the narration as the social and racial conflict associated with the time period comes to the forefront. The young girl, whose age and gender have already limited the scope of her participation in and understanding of the occurrences she has witnessed, is now all but erased, suggesting that the coming confrontations are completely beyond her comprehension. As the society in which she has grown up undergoes profound change, the protections and guarantees that would have been hers based on social class are also vanishing. The fact that she plays so little a role in this segment of the story, in addition to signaling her own inability to grasp the import of the events, also reflects the futility of the ladino struggle against the proposed reforms and the violence that will usher them into Mexican society. César, Zoraida and the other adults in her world are preoccupied with defending their position and privileges, arguably for the future generation. Yet, significantly, the representatives of that future are barely noticeable. In this way, the young narrator's lack of voice in the Chactajal section of the narration underscores the change and displacement that is going to affect her place in Mexican society, a situation that will deeply alter the advantages of the landowning class. The narrative "I" disappears in order to emphasize the loss of power and prestige of the entire group.

In "*Balún Canán*: A Model Demonstration of Discourse as Power," Sandra Messinger Cypess has commented on the alternating narrative perspectives in the novel. As Messinger Cypess argues, the narrative structure of *Balún Canán* is a function of form reflecting content and, therefore, works well with the overall meaning of the novel. She notes that the second section of the text, while seeming intrusive for its dissonance with the other two sections, is a narrative structure that "reflects the divisiveness within the social structure that the class in power wishes to maintain" (6), and demonstrates an imbalance of discursive power throughout the novel. In other words, while the narrative voice's transformation from the first person to the third person can signal the inevitable loss of authority, it also captures the overall atmosphere of conflict and rupture. This argument can be expanded to take into consideration the narrative voices that do contribute to the second part of the novel. The thoughts and impressions of the indigenous leader, Felipe, for example, represent one of several perspectives included in the Chactajal section. Having spent time in Tapachula, he returns to Chactajal to organize the workers and preside over the institution of the Cárdenas policies. It is he who shows the most interest in seeing that the workers' children receive an education and, once the school is constructed, he records its founding "para los que vendrían" (126)—"for those who [would come] after" (121). Likewise, the readers are privy to Felipe's newly formed views on the equality between the ladinos and the indigenous as well as his concerns for the future. The presence of his perspective in the narration further emphasizes the rift with past authority and social norms that Cypess Messinger studies. The challenge to authority is further impressed on the readers by the burning of the sugar mill. As César notes after the destruction, "Felipe no tenía necesidad de hacerlo con sus propias manos. Bastaba con que lo hubiera mandado. Los demás le obedecen como nunca me obedecieron a mí" (1985: 203)—"Felipe needn't have done it with his own hands. He could quite as well have ordered them. The others obey him as they've never obeyed me" (189). Allegiances and influence have shifted and those who had held the power for so many generations must now recognize the inescapable force of change.

With the Argüello's return to Comitán, the voice of the young narrator also returns to the story. She is briefly reunited with her beloved nana; however, more tragedy will bring about their permanent separation and will add to the inevitable decline of the longstanding ruling class. The nana shares with Zoraida the frightening news that sorcerers have placed a curse on Mario:

> Los ancianos de la tribu de Chactajal se reunieron en deliberación. Pues cada uno había escuchado, en el secreto de su sueño, una voz que decía: "que no prosperen, que no se perpetúen. Que el puente que tendieron para pasar a los días futuros, se rompa." Eso les aconsejaba una voz como de animal. Y así condenaron a Mario [...] Los brujos no quieren dinero. Ellos quieren al hijo varón, a Mario. Se lo comerán, se lo están empezando a comer [231–232].

> The ancients of the tribe of Chactajal have gathered in conference. For each of them has heard, in the secret of his dreams, a voice saying: 'May they not prosper or be perpetuated. May the bridge they have thrown into the future be broken.' A voice like an animal's counseled them so. And they have marked Mario for condemnation [...] The sorcerers want no money. They want the male child, Mario. They'll eat him, they've begun to eat him already [216–217].

The hope for the future that Mario represented for his parents, the future they vainly attempted to defend, will never be realized. The male heir will not be able to carry on the family name nor expand the family's influence in the region; the family history that the narrator had been prohibited from reading will not be continued. As the narrator discovers, "[su] padre ya no tiene por quién seguir luchando ... ya no [tiene] hijo varón" (283)—"[her] father has nobody to go on fighting for ... [He no longer] has a man-child" (263).

Zoraida, in her anger over the information she has learned, beats the children's nana and banishes her from the house and, in her desperation, seeks any type of help for her son, supernatural or otherwise. A card reader, the local doctor and the Catholic Church cannot protect Mario. In fact, it is as the narrator and her brother study the catechism in preparation for taking their first communion that Mario becomes very ill and dies. In this way, a mother's desire to preserve her young son's life seems to play itself out as a confrontation between the two opposing sides of the larger social struggle, ladino institutions on one side and indigenous resistance on the other. Zoraida's last recourse is the Church and the young narrator, frightened by stories of hell and mischievous devils, stages her own rebellion in order to oppose the will of her mother. She steals the key to the chapel where the first communion mass is to take place and, significantly, hides it among the forgotten belongings of her nana. She knows that she must look out for herself, in spite of the trouble the loss of the key could cause: "¿Quién iba a defenderme? Mi madre no. Ella sólo defiende a Mario porque es el hijo varón" (279)—"Who would come to my rescue? Not Mother. She only protects Mario because he's the male child" (259). In her growing awareness of herself and the vulnerability of her position in a changing world, she feels abandoned and must think of her own survival. She will not return the key even though she fears that its disappearance has contributed to Mario's illness. Furthermore, the narrator's actions once again demonstrate her condition as simultaneously having a connection to and being alienated from two distinct and mutually hostile worlds. In the absence of her beloved nana, she can only dream that the two of them will someday "[estar] sentadas, cogidas de la mano, mirando para siempre"(247)—"sit there hand in hand and go on looking forever" (230). At the same time, as she adjusts to life without her protector, she must prepare herself for a more complete entry, via the Church and its doctrine, into ladino society, a society that has made clear her inferior and marginal status as a female.

In examining the voice of the young narrator in *Balún Canán*, it becomes clear that the text creates a point of contact between the different and politically unequal cultures of Latin America. The Argüello's daughter has insight into two oppositional worldviews, that of the Tzeltal indigenous community and that of her family's ladino heritage, and is a witness to their sociopolitical struggle in 1930s Chiapas. Throughout the narration, she presents herself as a type of bridge between these two worlds, able to enter each one yet not completely penetrating either side. She remains on the periphery in both instances, simultaneously feeling both inclusion and exclusion. Yet, keeping in mind that *Balún Canán* can be read as the story of the growing social and cultural awareness of the young narrator, we also see by the end of the novel a rejection of the indigenous world she had so valued and appreciated. Walking through the streets of Comitán, the narrator believes she sees her departed nana and runs to greet her.

> ¡Es mi nana! Pero la india me mira, impasible, y no hace un ademán de bienvenida. Camino lentamente, más lentamente hasta detenerme. Dejo caer los brazos, desalentada. Nunca, aunque yo la encuentre, podré reconocer a mi nana. Hace tanto tiempo que nos separaron. Además, todos los indios tienen la misma cara [292].

> It's my Nana! But the Indian watches me quite impassively, making no welcoming sign. I slow up — slower and slower till I stop. I let my arms drop, altogether discouraged. Even if I see her, I'll never recognize her now. It's so long since we've parted. Besides, all Indians look alike [271].

As many critics have affirmed, this scene captures the child's casting aside of her intimate contact with the indigenous world.[4] To a certain extent and up until that moment, the narrator had identified with both aspects of Mexican society. However, with time and distance between her and her nana, she has more easily learned the attitudes and internalized the belief system of the dominant cultural group.

As a principal caregiver, the role of the nana was, in part, to instruct and socialize the young girl. The narrator was drawn to the world of her nana and came to understand much of the indigenous customs and beliefs and, in this way, an inchoate integration of the two competing social systems within the worldview of the narrator had begun to emerge. In the end, however, without the guiding influence of her nana, the possibility of maintaining established connections seems to be gone. She did not have the time to assimilate real racial tolerance. Returning to Beard's notion of "natiobiography," the young narrator's ultimate dismissal of the world of her nana can be read as a questioning of the feasibility of the Cárdenas plan for a more integrated Mexican state. The reforms and other attempts to bridge both social and political inequalities at that time were met by resistance that then increased tension and instability, as seen in the story of the Argüello family. Although the narrator stood apart from that tension and had begun to look critically at her family's history, in the end, the ladino cultural paradigm imposes itself. The indigenous mass has become largely invisible to the narrator as she concludes that "all Indians look alike." The nana's departure and the subsequent change in the young girl's outlook suggest that the Cárdenas initiatives will not accomplish the hoped for national integration. Rather, the future will also be marked by racial division and distrust.

The history of struggle and discord of early twentieth century Mexico is presented in the story of the Argüello family through the observations and written expression of a young girl living in the midst of the upheaval. That the child narrator is able to inhabit two distinct worlds, in spite of being a marginalized figure in both, is a reminder of the interconnected, though far from equal, multicultural society she describes. From her marginalized space, the narrator is able to examine and question the norms of a racialized society and the obstacles that prevent real change. Significantly, she does this by challenging the patriarchal expectation of meek docility on the part of women. Disregarding her mother's admonition that history — family or otherwise — is the domain of men, the narrator achieves her own voice and asserts her own agency through the story of her family and, by extension, that of the country as a whole.

Notes

1. The translation is mine.
2. See for example the article by María Luisa Gil Iriarte, "*Balún Canán*: La voz de una Antígona Mexicana," in which the author refers to Castellanos' text as "pseudo-autobiografía." Gil Iriarte argues that, although the text does not meet specific criteria for autobiography put forth by the theorist Philippe Lejeune, it can be considered an autobiographical act.
3. This and subsequent quotes from *Balún Canán* in English are from the Irene Nicholson translation.
4. See for example texts by Carol Clark D'Lugo, "Fictions of Apprenticeship: Following the Growth of Narrative Strategies and Cultural Ideologies in Rosario Castellanos." *Hispanofila*. 156 (May 2009): 101–112, Myriam Yvonne Jehenson, *Latin American Women Writers: Class, Race and Gender*. Albany: SUNY Press, 1995, and Wendy Woodrich, "Rosario Castellanos' *Balún Canán*: A Testimony to the Search for Belonging." *Chasqui: Revista de literatura latinoamericana*. 29.2 (2010): 133–153, in which the child's words are shown to reflect her acceptance of the racist norms of ladino society.

Works Cited

Beard, Laura J. *Acts of Narrative Resistance: Women's Autobiographical Writings in the Americas.* Charlottesville: University of Virginia Press, 2009.

Castellanos, Rosario. *Balún Canán*. Mexico, D.F.: Fondo de Cultura Económica, 1957.

_____. *The Nine Guardians*. Trans. Irene Nicholson. London: Readers International, 1992.

Challener, Daniel. *Stories of Resilience in Childhood*. New York: Garland Publishing, 1997.

Franco, Jean. *An Introduction to Spanish-American Literature*. 3d ed. Cambridge: University of Cambridge Press, 1994.

Gil Iriarte, María Luisa. "*Balún Canán*, la voz de una Antígona mexicana." *Anales de Literatura Hispanoamericana* 27 (1998): 297–310.

Lorenzano, Sandra. "La mirada sobre Chiapas de Rosario Castellanos: *Balún Canán* y la heterogeneidad narrativa." *Celehis: Revista del Centro de Letras Hispanoamericanas* 4.4–5 (1995): 27–57.

Messinger Cypess, Sandra. "The Narrator as Niña in *Balún Canán* by Rosario Castellanos."

El niño en las literaturas hispánicas. Ed. J. Cruz Mendizábal. Indiana, PA: Indiana University of Pennsylvania Press, 1978.

_____. *"Balún Canán*: A Model Demonstration of Discourse as Power." *Revista de Estudios Hispánicos* 19.3 (1985): 1–15.

Valdés, María Elena de. *The Shattered Mirror: Representations of Women in Mexican Literature.* Austin: University of Texas Press, 1998.

Woodrich, Wendy. "Rosario Castellanos' *Balún Canán*: A Testimony to the Search for Belonging." *Chasqui: Revista de Literatura Latinoamericana* 29.2 (2010): 133–153.

II

WOMAN IN HISTORY

4

María Eugenia Alonso: The Modern Iphigenia Sacrificed to Society[1]

ROSEANNA MUELLER

At a time when Venezuelan literature was concerned with criollismo, romanticism, and naturalism, Teresa de la Parra's *Iphigenia: The diary of a young lady who wrote because she was bored* (1924), burst upon the scene with its charming, literate, and unforgettable first person narrator, María Eugenia Alonso.[2] De la Parra's groundbreaking novel introduced readers to the reality of female repression in a time when such ideas were so radical that, as Ana María Caula notes, "for years critics have misunderstood the meaning of her work and underestimated the power of her discourse" (391). Douglas Bohórquez concurs with Caula, adding, "Antes de Teresa de la Parra la mujer no existe en nuestra narrativa sino como estereotipo y convención: no habla, es hablada" (11) — "Before Teresa de la Parra, woman does not exist in our narrative except as a stereotype and a convention: she doesn't speak, she's spoken about." Indeed, one can say that De la Parra created a space for other Venezuelan women writers such as Antonia Palacios (1915–2001), Antonieta de Madrid (1939–), and Milagros Mata Gil (1951–), among others.

However, in spite of De la Parra's recognition in the literary scene, both the writer and her work have been doomed to live in the shadows of Rómulo Gallegos (1884–1969), who, to this day, is considered the country's most representative author. Besides being the author of *Doña Barbara*—a regionalist novel whose protagonist, Doña Bárbara, embodies the man-eating, untamed land — Gallegos was also a renowned politician and one-time president of

Venezuela. Although *Doña Bárbara* can be seen as critical of the *status quo* that did not accept women in positions of power, the novel clearly presents the male character as the domesticator of the "barbarie" and as the civilizing impetus of the story. *Iphigenia,* on the other hand, questions and mocks the conservatism of Venezuelan upper class through a young heroine who — at least in the beginning — rebels against the strict codes of conduct and mores of patriarchy.

In the first edition of *Iphigenia*— dedicated de la Parra's mother, Ana Teresa Sanojo (1889–1936) — the author states that the novel is based upon personal experiences and acquaintances. In fact, María Eugenia, the narrator, is considered a composite of several young women De la Parra had met in Caracas. De la Parra's representation of women's subjectivity broke new ground by articulating the oppressive discourse of a society that coerced women into marriage and restricted them to the domestic realm.

Disgusted with the current values and mores in Caracas in the 1920's, De la Parra launched into writing the novel that gave her an outlet for her "moderately feminist" views; a stance that she would later take up and redefine when — as one of the first female Latin American intellectuals — she delivered *Influencia de las mujeres en la formación del alma americana* (Women's Influence in the Form-ation of the American Soul) in Colombia in 1930. Four years after the publication of *Iphigenia*, De la Parra confessed to her friend Elena Maderos Gonzales that writing *the novel* was therapeutic and it kept her from "screaming from every street corner" (Luis Antoine Lemaitre 89).

The plot of *Iphigenia* narrates the adventures of María Eugenia Alonso, the eighteen year old narrator, who returns to Caracas after studying at a Catholic school in France. While visiting Paris with her father, she becomes a fashionable and chic mademoiselle. Upon the death of her father, María Eugenia returns to her grandmother's home in Caracas.[3] Now orphaned, she arrives in the city a conspicuous consumer, only to find out that her paternal Uncle Eduardo has appropriated her inheritance — the Hacienda San Nicolás — leaving her penniless and dependent on her family. Feeling trapped under the supervision of her prudish maiden aunt Clara and her matriarchal grandmother Eugenia, the protagonist writes a long letter to her school friend Cristina describing her Parisian adventures as well as the family restrictions imposed on her. In the letter, she also makes fun of the outdated habits, mores, and values of contemporary Creole aristocracy in Caracas.

The male components of the family are her avaricious uncle Eduardo — whose mean-spirited wife dislikes her immediately — and her uncle Pancho, a bohemian bachelor who takes María Eugenia under his wing. Her outings are restricted to wherever he takes her, since she is not allowed to leave the house unchaperoned. Most of the time she is forced to stay at home with Grand-mother Eugenia and Aunt Clara, two conservative and prudish women, whose daily lives consist of making lace and reciting the rosary. The black laundress Gregoria becomes María Eugenia's confidante. Gregoria reveals family secrets to the eager young woman, and she also goes to the circulating library to borrow forbidden books that later María Eugenia proceeds to devour in the solitude of her room.[4]

In the cathartic letter that María Eugenia takes four months to write, the narrator positions herself as an intellectual and as a romantic heroine who denounces the lack of options women are offered. Lonely, bored, and poor, she is constantly reminded by her grandmother that all she has left is her good family name and her irreproachable character. Yet, in spite of her grandmother's efforts to tame the young woman's spirit, María Eugenia is not only proud of her transformation from a Catholic school girl to an educated and sophisticated young lady, but she is also confident about of her own blonde good looks and her charm. Little by little, however, she becomes aware of the patriarchal ide-ology that both oppresses and forces her into considering marriage to a man who will, as she says, do "the immense favor of placing himself beside me as a whole number, elevating me by an act and benefaction of his presence to a round and respectable sum that would acquire a certain real value before society and the world" (62).

The long opening letter is followed by Part II, "Juliet's Balcony." Here, María Eugenia has finally sent her letter to her school friend Cristina, and, since she has become used to writing, she decides to keep a diary. In this new writing venue, she describes both her friendship with the exotic Mercedes Galindo, a woman María Eugenia adores and wishes to emulate, and Gabriel Olmedo, a man who will soon become the object of her affection. Mercedes is unhappily married, and she confesses her dissatisfaction to María Eugenia. Grandmother disapproves of Mercedes as well as of María Eugenia's outings with Uncle Pancho. As a punishment, the grandmother banishes María Eugenia to the Hacienda San Nicolás. Once there, María Eugenia flirts shamelessly with her 13-year old cousin Perucho, much to the chagrin of her Aunt María Antonia.[5] The pastoral interlude of the hacienda is interrupted by Cristina's brief and boastful letter describing her impending marriage to a rich man. Although the letter triggers memories of their school days, at this point, the narrator realizes that with this new development in Cristina's life, their friend-ship has ended.[6] To add insult to injury, Aunt María Antonia announces during dinner that Gabriel Olmedo has married María Monasterios, a wealthy young woman with connections to the oil industry.

Part III takes place two years later. Now having been made fully aware of her limited choices and her relative worth on the marriage market, María Eugenia has stopped writing and has instead mastered the domestic arts. No longer a rebel, she sits at the window to display herself, like an object for sale: "... my person acquired a notable likeness to those luxury items that are exhibited at night in store windows to tempt shoppers.... I am for sale! ...Who will buy me? Who will buy me? I am for sale! ...Who will buy me?" (218). When César Leal — a wealthy lawyer, senator, and minister — appears on the scene, María Eugenia agrees to marry him; however, after reuniting with Gabriel at the bedside of the dying Uncle Pancho, her love rekindles as he confesses his love and begs her to elope with him. His letter — the only part of the text in which another character narrates — reveals an unhappy and insecure married man begging, beseeching, cajoling, and finally commanding her to run away with him. If the young protagonist's character portrays the challenges of an intelligent woman living in a patriarchal world, Gabriel's character — as revealed in his own words — is full of the contradictions that will impede their ever being together. Readers are left to wonder whether María Eugenia's future would have been any brighter had she eloped with him.

After a bungled attempt to keep her tryst with Gabriel, María Eugenia realizes she has no choice but to marry Leal for the material comforts he can offer, a choice made because she lacks female role models other than her aunt, the unhappily married Mercedes, and her conservative grandmother. By Part IV, the last section of the novel, María Eugenia presents herself as the Greek heroine Iphigenia on her way sacrifice. Time speeds up in nine chapters spanning one week. On Monday night, when María Eugenia panics and realizes she can't elope with Gabriel, Aunt Clara offers her a sedative and suggests she sleep in her grandmother's bed. From this point on, María Eugenia's destiny is sealed. In the final pages, the protagonist accepts her fate as it has been determined by society, and contemplates the sacrificial offering she is about to become. When Aunt Clara asks her to try on her wedding dress, she refuses, setting it against a chair, and muses, "The chair seems like a sadistic lover embracing a dead woman" (353). Readers are left to imagine her future, as she becomes fully aware of the enormity of her compromise and her self-betrayal. And yet, at the same time the troubled protagonist appreciates what her husband-to-be can offer her in material comforts: "My behavior, my cowardly behavior, criminal to myself, was at the same time horribly disloyal to the man who in one week was going to give me a luxuriously appointed home, filled with everything I needed, and his name and his support, and a position in society, and a secure future sheltered from want and humiliating dependency" (348).

In the last chapters, María Eugenia undergoes a physical change. She tones down her lipstick, adopts a more subdued way of dressing, and no longer expresses herself using foreign words. She immerses herself in domestic chores, cooking, sewing, and taking charge of the laundry. She rubs Elliman's ointment (the smell of which she once detested) on her grandmother, gives her injections, and prays the rosary with Aunt Clara. She is aware of the passage of time; it has been two years since she has last written in her diary. Gradually she becomes a young replica of her grandmother; a survival tactic and an example of the behavioral and emotional changes women have to undergo in order to survive in a patriarchal society.

A Humorous or Tragic Character: or, on Becoming a Hat

Throughout the novel María Eugenia's discourse assimilates, appropriates, and reflects many genres, voices, ideologies and characters drawn from French, English, German, Spanish, and Italian literature. María Eugenia has read, refers to, and identifies with impossible and tragic lovers: Hero and Leander, Ophelia and Hamlet, Tristan and Isolde, the lovers of Teruel, pale Werther, and in her sonnet, she identifies with Juliet. These references reflect her traditional, strict, Catholic education, as well as her love of reading "subversive texts" in her room. There are many intertextual literary allusions, such as the Shakespearean reference to Juliet's balcony, and others that allude to Dante, Cervantes, and Bécquer. While she is confined to the hacienda, she writes a passionate letter to Gabriel; the text is full of biblical allusions, and in it she addresses him as "the sweet Messiah of my soul" (174). Later she writes, "Gabriel, in the burning desert of your absence, you are my glorious Solomon, and I am your adoring Shulamite" (175).

But, in spite of all her literary models, as her life progresses, she compromises her plans for an independent life and ultimately betrays her initial ideals. For example, when she becomes aware that she must please César Leal, her husband-to-be and a man who believes that "a woman's head was a more or less a decorative object, completely empty inside, made to gladden men's eyes, and equipped with two ears whose only function was to receive and collect the orders that men dictated to them" (250), María Eugenia denies knowing Dante's works, stops reading novels in French and English, and lies to her uncle Pancho by saying that all her former writing consisted of copying recipes. Even before the wedding, Leal lays down the rules: his wife will not wear low-cut dresses, attend balls, or read novels or poetry. In other words: aided by the pressure to secure her financial stability, the conservative side of her family molds María Eugenia into one of their own, thus turning her into a docile, subservient wife who will remain behind the scenes.

Iphigenia has been read in different ways since it was first published. Most critics have interpreted it as a tragic comedy, one in which María Eugenia's marriage to César Leal is presented as the tragic finale of the story.[7] Through her protagonist, de la Parra injects humor in the narrative to call attention to social issues. Humor was a rare feature in Venezuelan literature at the time and, although some readers found María Eugenia's attempts to be a naughty adolescent quite funny, others — the majority, to judge from the criticism of the time — completely missed the irony and humor. Indeed, it is not too difficult to see María Eugenia's fashion choices as hilarious when placed against the background of turn of the century Venezuela. Significantly, she herself does not seem conscious of how inappropriate her clothes may be. Instead, she acts as if she lives in a much higher ground, so she mocks her family's morals and customs, and is proud to be able to express herself elegantly, and with good taste, in three languages. Appearances are important to her, and contemplating her future as a wife and mother, she ponders how she would react if she were to bear unattractive children, "I might have a daughter, who instead of looking like me, might look like her aunts, an irreversible disaster, which would probably leave me forever inconsolable" (227).

On the other hand, some critics see the heroine's identification with her sacrificial end as a mockery. Whereas Edna Aizenberg treats the novel as a failed *Bildungsroman* because the heroine does not achieve self-realization, Maria Fernanda Palacios' long monograph (longer than the novel itself) analyzes the protagonist as the archetype of the *doncella criolla*—Creole maiden — and the novel as an allegory of the social and political situation in Venezuela, even to this day (467).

One important aspect of the novel is that, through María Eugenia, de la Parra exposes the mechanisms of a system that forced women to be financially dependent on men who do not hesitate to spend their fortunes. Aunt Clara, for instance, has nothing because she gave her money to her brother, Uncle Pancho. Grandmother has next to nothing because Eduardo, her second eldest son, lost her money on a mining venture. Mercedes Galindo, María Eugenia's friend and mentor, is unhappily married to a libertine and a gambler who spends her fortune and treats her badly. María Eugenia recognizes the irony of her own situation: "the frightful fact: my absolute poverty, without any remission or hope other than the support of the same ones who perhaps had robbed me!" (59). But she is not alone in her musings about the unfair lot women have to face; her own Uncle Pancho says that "For women without a dowry or a fortune of their own, as almost all women are in our society, it is always men who are obliged to totally support them [...] a woman's worth is whatever value a man takes it into his head to place on her" (75). In other words, the victims of the robbery — women — have to turn around and put themselves in the hands and at the mercy of the robbers themselves; therefore, for María Eugenia the solution is to find a man who will place a high value on her, no matter what his social background. As the text makes clear, the family needs an infusion of cash, and María Eugenia becomes her grandmother's prized object, as Uncle Pancho points out: "You are her pride now, rather like what a new hat brought from Europe must have been in her youth" (79).

It is not clear, however, if María Eugenia ever understands the depth of her objectified situation, as we see in her letter to Cristina, for instance, where she writes: "You and I — all of us who, moving through the world, have some talents and some sorrows — are heroes and heroines in the novels of our own lives, which is nicer and a thousand times better than written novels" (10). In a certain way, one can agree that she is the heroine of her own story, and goes through various stages associated with fairy tales, myths, and various literary genres. She begins as Cinderella, an orphaned girl who has been touched by the magic of Paris. She then becomes the captive princess waiting to be freed, and like Penelope, she weaves and unweaves her thoughts while she reads, writes, and expectantly waits for a man to rescue her from a life of boredom. Much later, she compares herself to Juliet, pining or yearning for her Romeo. Later, while waiting to embark on her marriage of convenience, she feigns resignation before the man who will rule her life. And finally, her last and most tragic role is that of the ancient Iphigenia, sacrificed for the well-being of her family. In all these roles, María Eugenia appears almost as a spectator to her circumstances, in spite of her juvenile attempts to show contempt for the norms represented by her older relatives.

Another important aspect of the novel relates to the fact that, because María Eugenia is presented as a conspicuous consumer who reflects Creole tastes, *Iphigenia* might be read as a forerunner of the contemporary genre known as "Chick Lit," in which the heroine becomes "branded" according to what she wears and what she does. Throughout the novel, de la Parra introduces commercial references to products her protagonist must have, such as makeup by Guerlain and Faber, 100 gauge stockings, hairstyles and clothing as seen in *Vogue*, (first published in 1916), perfume by Bichara, Bossier chocolates, and a trousseau of Milanese and Parisian silk. María Eugenia's friend and confidante Mercedes represents fun, travel, fashion, and all things exotic, and, in true imitation of European taste, she smokes Egyptian cigarettes and serves Medoc wine. In fact, many of the products named were consumed by bourgeois Venezuelan households at the time, to the point that the novel becomes an exposé of the frivolous and materialistic vein of Venezuelan upper class.[8] In addition to the poignant critique to Venezuelan consumerism, the naïve, yet very perceptive narrator levels her criticism on institutions and customs the landholding Creoles were not ready to give up. María Eugenía depicts the city she returned to in a less than favorable light; as a result, de la Parra was taken to task for her heroine's description of a Caracas street:

> And as if the [telephone] lines were not enough, the intruding telephone posts opened their arms and, feigning crosses in a lengthy Calvary, stretched one after another, until they were lost in the remote confines of the horizon. Oh! yes, Caracas, of the delightful climate, of gentle memories, the familiar city, the intimate and distant city, turned out to be this flat town ... a kind of Andalusian city, like a melancholy Andalusia, without a shawl or castanets, without guitars or music, without flowerpots and flowers on the balconies ... a drowsy Andalusia that had dropped off to sleep in the sultry heat of the tropics! [38].

Not surprisingly, European readers and critics found the novel and its protagonist charming and funny, while Venezuelans — mostly conservative and male — called it "Voltaireian" and, therefore, "revolutionary" (in a negative way). For many of her contemporary Venezuelan readers, the novel was too realistic and hit the spot in its depiction of their society. María Eugenia's caustic commentaries about respectable marriages of convenience and her descriptions of Caracas society were taken for de la Parra's own unmediated opinions, and this put the author in the position of having to defend her name and reputation in letters, editorials, and in her lectures. In these lectures, delivered to standing-room audiences in Bogotá in 1930 (published in 1961), de la Parra continued to demand changes in women's position within the nation by critiquing its social order and emphasizing their economic independence.[9]

To be sure, De la Parra wrote fiction to amuse, entertain, and challenge the mores of a highly hypocritical society halfway between the colonial and modern age. Her stance, however, was apolitical. It is important to keep in mind that de la Parra wrote during the Juan Vicente Gómez repressive dictatorship.[10] According to Velia Bosch, "Teresa's work was produced at the most difficult moment in Venezuela's history, with no democratic tradition, with associations, unions and political parties being founded ... only much later, intellectuals [would be allowed] the possibility of political debate" (134).

De la Parra, however, wanted to chronicle her times faithfully, revealing the circumstances under which many Latin American women lived. She was convinced that middle and upper class women were at a disadvantage when compared to women from the lower classes, because they lacked the freedom to choose their marriage partners. The text dramatizes this belief when, during one of her conversations with the black laundress Gregoria, María Eugenia suggests, "In your youth, Gregoria, you must have been really wild" (288). To which the black woman responds laughing, "Yes, I may be really black, and really ugly, and everything else, but I always had someone interested in me" (288). But even for the lower classes, marriage at that time was not an unqualified blessing, as Gregoria clarifies, "Black women who are married put on airs, and they're ashamed of their color and they have to put up with insults and beatings from their husbands" (288). White women of María Eugenia's class, even though they are supposedly better off and will not be physically abused by their husbands, have to resign themselves to becoming a mere embellishment in their husbands' careers, a hat with a European flavor.

Race, Class, and the Betrayal of Women

Unable to voice her own opinions openly during the Gómez dictatorship and its censorship in Venezuela, de la Parra portrayed societal attitudes towards racial mixing through the observations and attitudes of the characters in her novels. Through María Eugenia's conversations with Gregoria, or through the table talk at Mercedes' soirees, or through her educational field trip to the port, the reader learns about attitudes towards race relations as María Eugenia witnesses them while living in a Creole Caracas household. The discourse reflects attitudes towards racial mixing as Venezuela was transitioning from an agrarian society to an economy based on oil. Social hierarchy was still based on skin color, and Creoles (which in this case means the landed aristocracy who were the descendants of the first Spanish settlers and conquerors) were proud of their "white" lineage. For example, in her visits the port of Caracas, María Eugenia notices the racial mixtures of the dockworkers; she is forced to reflect on the difficult lives led by people of color on the waterfront. Even in her visits to Mercedes, María Eugenia must defend her friend from her grandmother's and her aunt's disapproval reminding them that Mercedes Galindo is "white on all four sides," because she knows that this will boost her status in their eyes.

Interestingly enough, the novel presents the lower classes as freer than the upper (white) classes, or at least free enough to choose their partners, whereas a poor white Creole like María Eugenia cannot marry a poor ambitious young man like Gabriel Olmedo, while his own ambitions force him into a loveless marriage to a woman with connections and money. Regardless of her feelings and interests, the protagonist is expected to marry a rich man — albeit a mixed-race one allied with the government — in order to improve his social standing. She has the aristocratic last name and irreproachable character; he has the money. During de la Parra's lifetime, economic affiliation to the oil industry and political affiliation to the government were becoming important connections, and they were beginning to displace and challenge established racial hierarchies. One example of such changes reflected in the novel occurs when María Eugenia's grandmother, confronted with the fact that Leal's family originated a long way from first-class, says, "It's true that things have changed today and exceptions must be made" (225). While the Creoles seem comfortable with the presence of "pure black" servants and descendents of slaves like Gregoria, the racial mixing that lies in the middle between "pure black" and "white on all four sides" causes discomfort and anxiety among the Venezuelan elite. The "exception"—in the grandmother's words—is made so that a "pure white" young woman can have her financial security assured.

De la Parra's gift for describing defects and prejudices in Venezuelan society, all the while employing tongue-in-cheek humor and subtle irony in the letter, diary, and reflections of an engaging character, made her an outstanding social critic. After all, the heroine's decision to marry Leal is brought about by a network of women who protect and coddle their men, and who had, in one way or another, sacrificed, and impoverished themselves to men while continuing to enforce this practice on their daughters. Rebellion, in the end, gives way to resignation, and the young girl who was once pleased with herself, who peppered her talk with French, and was a voracious reader, is left with two choices: she can either become a soul without a body for Gabriel, or a body without a soul for her husband-to-be, César Leal.

Critic María Fernanda Palacios points out how the element of sacrifice enters abruptly in the novel, frustrating the expectations of the reader (439). In the linguistically overcharged and dramatically rhetorical declamatory conclusion to the novel, the heroine submits to the "Sacred Monster with seven heads that are called society, family, honor, religion, morality, duty, conventions and principle" (353). The marriage amounts to a business deal meant to grease the wheels of society, much as the mythological Greek Iphigenia's sacrifice allowed the favorable winds to blow.

In a letter in response to Colombian critic Eduardo Guzman Esponda's unfavorable review of María Eugenia's inconsistent behavior, de la Parra explains that we all have within us a mysterious duality and conflicts that surprisingly arise to prove that we are not what we believe to be. She termed this "su huésped desconocido" or the "unknown guest" that drives María Eugenia towards her future motherhood. Ultimately, de la Parra states, the heroine is ruled by the voice of her ancestors (*Obra* 596).

While most readers sympathize with the heroine's plight, Angélica Palma jokingly suggests that we should be more worried about Leal's fate: instead of sighing "poor María Eugenia," we should be thinking, "poor Leal" (203). Palma also asks the readers to contemplate what this unfortunate marriage would be like from Leal's point of view. Readers are so caught up in the story that they assume the marriage *will* take place. But, as Annis Pratt reminds us, "The woman's novel asks questions, poses riddles, cries out for restitution, but remains in itself merely rhetorical, an artifact or idea rather than an action. It is the reader, who, having participated in the narrative reenactment, must put its message into effect in her own life" (177). No matter how disappointing María Eugenia's final "capitulation" might have seemed to de la Parra's contemporary readers, one can ask how else she could finish a novel that tried to be faithful to the real conditions of the first decades of the twentieth century in a rapidly developing country of South America, ruled by a dictator who crushed the opposition, from within a society in which women would only obtain the right to vote in 1946.

Women did not engage in downright rebellion or revolution at the time. In fact, although María Eugenia's grandmother thinks she is rebellious, and she acts out in petty ways to annoy her aunt and her grandmother, there is no final rebellion or rejection of the societal code. As the story shows, María Eugenia is angry when she discovers that her uncle has taken over the hacienda meant to be her inheritance, but she never questions the decision or confronts the man. Rather, she stews about her diminished prospects and writes in her diary to vent her anger and disappointment. There is never any hint that María Eugenia realizes that her rights have been violated. Her writing becomes a search for a much more restricted, personal self-knowledge, during which she eventually accepts her weakness and inability to rebel.

If it is not a novel about a young woman's gradual understanding of how her destiny is tied up with the destiny of other women in her country, we can at least see *Iphigenia i*s a novel about generalized betrayal. First, her late father betrayed her by living a spendthrift life in Paris, a pattern María Eugenia blithely repeats. Then, the uncle betrays her by taking over the hacienda she was to inherit. After writing a long, heartfelt letter to her friend, the only reply she receives is a short and superficial message informing of her impending marriage and changing lifestyle. Maria Eugenia's own true love Gabriel marries another woman out of expediency. And yet betrayal is not just María Eugenia's lot, because other women are also betrayed: Aunt Clara never marries because she is betrayed by her first love; grandmother does not have any money because her own son took what she had, and Mercedes is abused by her husband. And, even though there is a pressure for all women to marry, all marriages in the novel prove to be unhappy ones. Furthermore, neither sons nor siblings feel any hesitation to take over their own mothers' and sisters' money. In the end, on the eve of what she foresees as her own unhappy marriage, the heroine betrays herself.

However, lest we think that these fictional situations are illustrations of de la Parra's *uncompromising* belief in women's political importance, it is crucial to clarify that de la Parra's lectures show that she at the same time highlighted *and* denied women's political importance. That is to say, even the writer herself, in full possession of her mature faculties, had to tread lightly. This is not to say that she did not use her fame as a way to intervene in the Venezuelan cultural scene and call attention to the situation of women. As Luz Horne writes, on her study of de la Parra's *Influencia de las mujeres en la formación del alma Americana* (*The Influence of Women in the Formation of the American Soul*), "De la Parra ... sale del papel asignado a la mujer como simple literata e interviene en el terreno del pensamiento" (13)—"De la Parra ... steps out of her assigned role as a literary woman to step into the realm of thought." In other words, in the lectures de la Parra took advantage of her role as a renowned and admired novelist to affirm herself as a historian and an intellectual, while at the same time trying to highlight women's historical and political participation, pointing out how women had provided the support for men who were "doing history."

In her lectures, de la Parra also used the opportunity to defend her novel, and *Iphigenia's* subject matter, as the sign of the current crisis affecting modern young women (Horne 9). There is, in fact, a performative aspect to the lectures. The speaker contradicts herself by saying she will not talk about herself, yet does so by ironically claiming that women should not be "doing politics" all the while providing examples of how women had played important roles and had influenced Latin American history. "Este modo de intervención de la Parra lo encontrará en la actuación de las mujeres que recupera del pasado" (Horne 10)—"De la Parra will find this method of intervention through the actions of the women she recuperates from the past." De la Parra thus actively recuperates the past as a defender of women as important historical/political subjects worthy to be included in "the official history."

However, in the novel *Iphigenia*, María Eugenia cannot have such comprehensive thoughts about history. Enclosed in a tight familial circle, surrounded by men who prey on women, she can only be a victim, a sacrificial victim, a scapegoat to the ills of her society, standing in for all the other betrayed women. But, although she is a victim, she does not accept her fate quietly: as we see, in the end Maria Eugenia ultimately puts on a final performance, the last of many roles she has played throughout the novel.

Indeed, as James Scott correctly points out in his discussion about subordination and resistance, "In the short run, it is in the interest of the subordinate to produce a more or less credible performance, speaking the lies and making the gestures he knows are expected of him" (4). What is expected of

María Eugenia is, in sum, that she continues to support and ascribe to the *status quo*. Whether she wants it or not, or even whether she even understands it or not, María Eugenia is a piece of the machinery that moves her society. The many roles she plays throughout the novel, the many masks she wears, are simply a hindrance to a final act that was, in a sense, designed from the very beginning of the life of a white woman born into the Venezuelan elite.

In conclusion, we can say that, in spite of its humorous vein, de la Parra did not create a comforting fiction. By adapting for her contemporary time the ancient myth of Iphigenia, de la Parra shows how her young heroine is forced to fulfill a debt to society by entering a marriage that will subject her to follow on the footsteps of women like her grandmother. De la Parra shows that her heroine's happiness is certainly neither relevant nor the main subject of her novel. But in so doing, the author lifts up a mirror to the face of Venezuelan society for her contemporary readers to see themselves as well as the huge sacrifices being demanded of Venezuela's women.

Notes

1. I was able to write this chapter thanks to a sabbatical granted by the department of Humanities, History and Social Sciences at Columbia College Chicago. I also want to acknowledge the assistance of my Undergraduate Research Mentorship student, Samantha Blattner.

2. All translations from the Spanish are from *Iphigenia: The Diary of a Young Lady Who Wrote Because She Was Bored*. Trans. Bertie Acker. Austin: University of Texas Press, 1993.

3. In 2005 dollars, the 50,000 francs María Eugenia spent in three months in Paris amounts to between $32,280 and $36,010 (*Ifigenia*, Doral: Stockcero, 2008). In the second edition, de la Parra more than doubled María Eugenia's disposable income. See Elizabeth Garrels, Las Grietas de la ternura: Nueva relectura de Teresa de la Parra. Caracas: Monte Ávila, 1985, p. 8.

4. See the excellent discussion of the figure of Gregoria in the novel in Elizabeth Russ, "Intersections of Race and Romance in the Americas: Teresa de la Parra's *Iphigenia* and Ellen Glasgow's *The Sheltered Life."* Mississippi Quarterly 58. 3–4 (Summer/Fall, 2005): 737–759. For Russ, "Gregoria's darkness, repeatedly described by María Eugenia in terms of its "brilliance" and "purity," transforms her into a symbol of the Venezuelan elite's longing for a stable, unmixed racial order" (741).

5. Annis Pratt describes the need for the female protagonist's "retreat into the green world" and how women find a place of solace, companionship and independence in nature" (21). At the hacienda, María Eugenia communes with nature, enjoys a pastoral idyll and writes a love letter and a sonnet to her beloved.

6. The secrets and shared experiences of the two girls were described in the prize-winning short story originally published as "Mama X" in 1922, and were later incorporated into the novel.

7. The novel is by turns ironic and melodramatic, which makes it difficult for some readers to take María Eugenia's final decision to marry Leal seriously; the ambiguous ending also left many readers hoping for a sequel. Iván Feo directed the film *Ifigenia* (Venezuela, 1986), based on Teresa de la Parra's novel. His solution to the open-ended and problematic ending of the novel is to have the actress who plays María Eugenia contemplate her wedding dress, disrobe, and walk off the movie set at the end of the film.

8. Under Gómez, the exploitation of petroleum led to unprecedented economic prosperity for some and an overriding spirit of materialism. This spirit of consumption in reflected in *Iphigenia*.

9. Indeed, as we can see in her lectures, de la Parra believed that Venezuelan women needed more independence. For a discussion of De la Parra's lectures, see Luz Horne's essay "La interrupción de un banquete de hombres solos: una lectura de Teresa de la Parra como contracanon del ensayo latinoamericano." Pp. 7–23.

10. "Juan Vicente Gómez." *Encyclopædia Britannica. Encyclopædia Britannica Online.* Web. 07 Aug. 2011. Juan Vicente Gómez (1857–1935) was a dictator who seized power in 1908 and ruled either as president or through puppet figures until his death. He ruled during a controversial period in Venezuela's history after the discovery of petroleum in Venezuela in 1918.

Works Cited

Aizenberg, Edna. "El Bildungsroman fracasado en Latinoamérica: El caso de Ifigenia de Teresa de la Parra." *Revista Iberoamericana* 51/132–33 (1985): 539–46. Print.

Bohórquez, Douglas. *Teresa de la Parra: Del diálogo de géneros y la melancolía* Caracas: Monte Ávila Editores Latinoamérica, 1997. Print.

Bosch, Velia. *Esta pobre lengua viva: relectura de la obra de Teresa de la Parra: A medio siglo de la* Memorias de Mama Blanca. Caracas: Ediciones de la Presidencia de la Republica, 1979. Print.

Caula, Ana María. "Parra, Teresa de la." *Latin American Women Writers: An Encyclopedia,* Eds. María Claudia André and Eva Paulino Bueno. New York: Routledge, 2008. 390–393. Print.

Horne, Luz. "La interrupción de un banquete de hombres solos: Una lectura de Teresa de la Parra como contracanon del ensayo latinoamericano." *Revista de crítica literaria latinoamericana.* Año XXXI, 61. Lima-Hanover, 1er. Semestre de 2005. 7–23. Print.

Lemaître, Louis Antoine. *Between Flight and Longing: The Journey of Teresa de la Parra.* New York: Vantage Press, 1986. Print.

Palacios, María Fernanda. *Ifigenia: Mitología de la Doncella Criolla.* Caracas: Fondo Editorial Angria Ediciones, 2001. Print.

Palma, Angélica. "La novela de una venezolana: Ifigenia, por Teresa de la Parra." *Epistolario íntimo.* Caracas: Eds. Línea venezolana aeropostal, 1953. Print.

Parra, Teresa de la. *Obra: Narrativa, Ensayos, Cartas.* Ed. Velia Bosch. Caracas: Biblioteca Ayacucho, 1991. Print.

_____. *Ifigenia: The diary of a young lady who wrote because she was bored.* Trans. Bertie Acker. Austin: University of Texas Press, 1993. Print.

_____. *Ifigenia.* Ed. Elizabeth Garrels. Doral, FL, Stockcero: 2008. Print.

Pratt, Annis. *Archetypal Patterns in Women's Fiction.* Bloomington: Indiana University Press, 1981. Print.

Scott, James C. *Domination and the Arts of Resistance: Hidden Transcripts.* New Haven: Yale University Press, 1990. Print.

5

Jesusa in the Context of Testimonios: Witness to an Age or Witness to Herself?

LINDA LEDFORD-MILLER

Jesusa Palancares is one of the most studied figures in Mexican literature, yet she remains one of the most enigmatic. A poor *campesina*, or woman from the country, Jesusa first made her appearance in 1969, when Elena Poniatowska published *Hasta no verte Jesús mío* ("Until I See you, my Jesus; *Here's to You, Jesusa!* 2001), which became one of the foundational texts for the genre of testimonial writing.[1] Although the idea of giving testimony in itself is not new, testimonial writing became a very important form in Latin America from the middle of the Twentieth Century, arising from periods of unprecedented social unrest — the Cuban Revolution (1959), the civil wars of El Salvador, Guatemala, and Nicaragua (1970's and 1980's), and the Mexican student movement of 1968 which Poniatowska immortalized in *La noche de Tlatelolco* (1971) or *Massacre in Mexico* (1975).

Testimony as a genre was officially recognized when the Casa de las Américas added it to its prize categories in 1970, but the form resists absolute definition. Testimony may contain elements of autobiography, history, and ethnography. True testimony differs from other forms of documentary literature by the presence of a witness, normally illiterate or nearly illiterate, a subaltern by class and perhaps race, and very often by gender, who testifies about events to an educated mediator of her story, creating a mediated oral history. Testimony is thus always a "*collaborative* mode of production [...] produced through voluntary collaboration between a metropolitan intellectual and a subaltern or grassroots individual" (Marie Louise Pratt 65). Though the testimony typically comes from a single individual, the life and context of that individual is taken to represent, as John Beverly says, a "collective social situation [...] representative of a social class or group" (1992: 95).[2] In addition, Georg Gugelberger and Michael Kearney comment that "testimonial literature is powerfully gendered by the voices of women" (8). Beverly goes a step further: "Where literature in Latin American has been (mainly) a vehicle for engendering an adult, white, male, patriarchal, 'lettered' subject, testimonio allows for the emergence — albeit mediated — of subaltern female, gay, indigenous, proletarian, and other identities" (1993: 98). Testimonio is not exclusively narrated by women, but it is predominantly female. Testimonio thus provides a means of making the subaltern voice heard, and in particular it enables women to have a voice in a patriarchal system that often silences them.

In "Can the Subaltern Speak," Gayatri Spivak writes that "the ideological construction of gender keeps the male dominant. If, in the context of colonial production, the subaltern has no history and cannot speak, the subaltern as female is even more deeply in shadow" (82–83). In Latin America, to date, the most influential text authored by a person embodying several of the categories of subalternity is *Me llamo Rigoberta Menchú y así me nació la conciencia* (My Name is Rigoberta Menchú and This is How My Consciousness Was Born, 1983), translated into English as *I, Rigoberta Menchú: An Indian Woman in Guatemala* (1984). A K'iché Mayan Indian, Menchú traveled to Paris in 1982 as part of a European tour to raise awareness of the Mayans' armed resistance and its causes. Over the course of several days Menchú narrated her story of Mayan oppression in Guatemala to a Venezuelan anthropologist in Paris. Menchú explicitly states that her testimony represents a collective:

> Quisiera dar este testimonio vivo que no he aprendido en un libro y que tampoco he aprendido sola ya que todo esto lo he aprendido con mi pueblo ... es la vida de todos. La vida de todos los guatemaltecos pobres [...] Mi situación personal engloba toda la realidad de un pueblo" [21].

> I want to give this living testimony that I didn't learn in a book and I didn't learn alone because I learned all this with my people.... It's the life of all of us. The life of all poor Guatemalans [...] My personal situation encompasses the reality of a whole people [my translation].

In 1992, the quincentennial of the European "discovery" of the Americas, Menchú was awarded the Nobel Peace Prize "in recognition of her work for social justice and ethno-cultural reconciliation based on respect for the rights of indigenous peoples" (Press Release). Due to her fame and in part precisely because she claims to represent all poor Guatemalans, Menchú's testimony gave rise to a vigorous academic controversy. The anthropologist David Stoll critiqued and challenged her testimony, indicating inconsistencies and claiming that Menchú had falsified some of her facts (though he also demonstrated the truth of many of her statements).[3] Indeed, the "truth" or lack of truth in this non-fiction genre is a pivotal conundrum. The testimonial text is purported to be an account by a witness to the events recounted, yet the story told may itself be an adjustment or interpretation of events from the perspective of the witness, who perforce depends on recollections and memories. On the other hand, the mediator clearly serves as an editor of the text and may alter, edit, eliminate, or embellish events as well. There is thus a kind of double mediation in any testimony: the mediation of memory and the mediation of the author/editor of those memories.

In addition, a number of ethical questions surround testimonial literature. For instance, the educated mediator typically profits from the testimony of an uneducated witness whose own material conditions may not change. Awards are given to "the author or *gestor*, not to the interviewee or narrator" (Elizabeth Burgos, xiii).[4] The author receives recognition and royalties that most probably do not accrue to the witness.[5] Poniatowska produced and sold *Hasta no verte Jesús mío*, for example, while Jesusa/Josefina Bórquez continued to live, and eventually died, in a tenement housing on the very margins of the Mexico City metropolis. Poniatowska herself is quite aware of the conflict. To be sure, Poniatowska gives "voice to the voiceless" by publishing her testimonial novel, and, as Beth Jörgensen notes, "we can appreciate the combination of empowerment (giving voice) and appropriation (taking interpretive control of the other's voice) entailed by such a project" (65). On the other hand, Beverly believes that testimony "is not a form of liberal guilt" but "an appropriate ethical and political response [that suggests] more the possibility of solidarity than of charity" (1992: 99). Pratt sees a clear political purpose in testimonio, because in her view "the two subjects are linked by shared commitments to social justice and the radical transformation of capitalist society" (65). Spivak's essay suggests that a voice, once heard, is no longer voiceless. That is, once heard in the language of the majority and by the majority, the marginalized subaltern enters into the mainstream of the society. This may be true of Menchú, who is internationally known and undoubtedly more Westernized than the collective of the Mayan people she represents in her testimonio. In addition, it is important to keep in mind that Menchú's testimonio also exemplifies the political purpose of the genre, in this case to inform the West of the brutal repression of the indigenous of Guatemala with the hope that the West (particularly the United States) would cease funding the Guatemalan military responsible for that repression. As Pratt comments, "the assumption is that educated metropolitans, as committed as they might be to values of justice and democracy, must be compelled to become aware of the realities of grassroots life and struggle and take responsibility" (65).

Poniatowska was aware of her status as an intellectual metropolitan and Jesusa's status as a subaltern, though neither of them used that term: "I always tried to maintain a balance between the extreme poverty I shared in the afternoon and the glitter of the receptions. My socialism was two-faced.... I have never gotten so much from anyone; I have never felt more to blame" (1988: 152). In other words: while Poniatwska enoyed the social results of the work she did with a subaltern woman, the subaltern herself continued where and as Poniatowska first found her. Unlike Menchú, Jesusa's status did not change. In fact, Jesusa became more marginalized over time. To her poverty, race, and gender were added the many tremendous disadvantages of age. Through her testimony, Jesusa Palancares, participant and witness to an age, enables the reader to experience, from a woman's perspective, one of the greatest upheavals of the Americas in the beginning of the Twentieth Century, but she also testifies to life as a member of her collective: the marginalized, poverty-stricken masses.

The Mexican Revolution (1910–1920) began in great part as a response to the people's fatigue with the dictatorship of President Porfirio Díaz, whose thirty-one year reign, the Porfiriato, created an ever increasing gap between the powerful and wealthy few and the impoverished and disenfranchised many. It is a very complex period in Mexican history, with a dizzying cast of characters struggling for power, including most famously Pancho Villa and Emiliano Zapata among them. The disruption caused by the revolution cannot be overestimated. Men left their towns and villages to fight first with this leader and then with that one. Many women accompanied their men, becoming *soldaderas*, or camp followers, literally carrying their camps on their backs and leading their children by the hand. These women were mothers, wives (legal or common law), and lovers, and they sometimes even took on traditional male roles, dressing like men, and learning to "load and shoot rifles, and take part in battle [...] thereby creating a new type of *soldadera* who was not merely a camp follower (the original nineteenth-century connotation) but a combatant in [their] own right" (Victoria McCard 44).

Perhaps the most famous fictional example of the new *soldadera* is Gertrudis, a character of *Como agua para chocolate—Like Water for Chocolate,* Laura Esquivel's ground-breaking novel. Gertrudis escapes the oppression of her mother's tradition-bound life by running off with a rebel soldier. She later returns in full revolutionary kit, including cartridge belts across her chest, the general of a regiment of fifty men. But Gertrudis, of course, never existed in a real world. Jesusa, however, did. The circumstances surrounding Jesusa's and

Poniatowska's meeting are in themselves very indicative of not just how women have been portrayed in literature, but the kinds of work a woman academic has undertaken.

Jesusa's Reluctant Testimony

Poniatowska was working as a journalist when she first overheard a woman arguing vigorously with someone in a laundry space and was impressed by her frank and energetic language. While visiting the infamous Lecumberri prison weekly to interview political prisoners, Poniatowska saw the same woman again, not as a visitor to the prison but as an inmate in the women's section.[6] Based on a series of interviews beginning in 1963 and occurring over a period of two years, *Hasta no verte Jesús mío* garnered the Mazatlán Award for Literature in 1971.[7] The book has been translated to English, French, Dutch, German, Italian, and Polish, and has appeared in at least forty-three editions in Spanish.[8]

Jesusa initially rejects Poniatowska's interest in her:

— What do you want? What business do you have with me?
— I want to talk to you.
— To me? Listen, I work. If I don't work, I don't eat. I don't have time to hang around chatting [2001: viii].[9]

Jesusa eventually, and reluctantly, agrees to allow Poniatowska to visit her each Wednesday from four to six P.M., the only time Jesusa is not either working or traveling to and from work. After early attempts to use a borrowed tape recorder, Poniatowska settles on taking notes during the two hour interviews, and from her notes reconstructs each day's conversation.[10] Poniatowska describes the work as a "testimonial novel," and admits to using great latitude in her reconstruction:

> Since I am not an anthropologist, my work may be viewed as a testimonial novel and not an anthropological or sociological document. I made use of the anecdotes, the ideas, and many of Jesusa Palancares' expressions, but I would never be able to assert that the narrative is a direct transcription of her life because she herself would reject that. I killed off the characters who got in my way, I eliminated as many spiritualist sessions as I could, I elaborated wherever it seemed necessary to me, I cut, I stitched together, I patched, I invented.[11]

Born in rural Oaxaca at the turn of the century, Jesusa's life story (1900–1987) is the story of Mexico during a period of tremendous change, including the Mexican Revolution (1910–1920) and its aftermath; the Cristero rebellion (1926–1929), and the rapid urbanization of Mexico City.[12] But it is also the life story of a member of "the other Mexico," as Octavio Paz calls it, the "underdeveloped Mexico," whose members are the subaltern, "the other," those living in what anthropologists have called "the culture of poverty" (284–86). With *Hasta no verte Jesús mío* Poniatowska, a member of the developed Mexico, the elite Mexico, came to know the other Mexico and made that impoverished, struggling Mexico manifest.[13]

After a short chapter in which the older Jesusa (age sixty three) explains her beliefs in reincarnation and the "Obra Espiritual," or "spiritual work," based on spiritualism, *Hasta no verte Jesús* mío follows Jesusa's life chronologically in twenty-eight chapters, beginning with the death of her mother. She has a very difficult life, with many "mothers" as her father brings women home to serve his needs and care for his children. By the time she is fifteen she is an orphan who is married off against her wishes to a seventeen year old soldier in the revolution. Like her father's women, her husband beats her often and sometimes severely. Widowed by the war, still a teenager, she resolves never to marry or be controlled by a man again.

The revolutionary period disrupted normal life and created an internal migrant population, as soldiers and *soldaderas* wandered from place to place. Jesusa, orphaned and widowed, had no home to return to, so her final great migration is Mexico City, where she works as a servant, waitress, laundress, cleaner, wood varnisher, and nurse's aide — anything to survive. Illiterate, without even a grade school education and no family support system, Jesusa has few options available to her. As the metropolis of Mexico City expands, Jesusa is pushed farther and farther to its periphery, literally marginalized by metropolitan society.

Jesusa and Elena: An uneven friendship

Despite the differences in their social and economic circumstances, Jesusa and Elena Poniatowska share the same sense of alienation — Jesusa due to poverty, illiteracy, and frequent migration; Poniatowska due to coming to Mexico quite literally as an outsider, a French-speaking child in a Spanish-speaking country. Ironically, Jesusa is partly responsible for minimizing Poniatowska's alienation. Recalling the experience of working with Jesusa, Poniatowska writes:

> When I'd get home I'd say: "Something is being born inside me, something new that wasn't there before, but no one answered me.... What was growing, although it may have been there for years, was my Mexican being, my becoming Mexican; feeling Mexico inside me, the same one that was inside Jesusa [...] My grandparents and my great-grandparents always repeated a phrase in English that they thought was poetic: "I don't belong." Maybe it was their way of distinguishing themselves from the rabble, not being like the rest. One night, before sleep over-

came me, after identifying strongly with Jesusa and going over all her images one by one, I could finally say to myself in a quiet voice: "*Yo sí pertenezco,*" "I do belong" [2001: xiv–xv].

But Jesusa had other, more pressing issues, as we see when, near the end of *Here's to You, Jesusa!* she says, "not dying on time is really hard" (2001: 302). She also tells Poniatowska in no uncertain terms to get lost: "Now fuck off! Go away and let me sleep. One day when you come by I'm not going to be here anymore.... It's a lie that you'll miss me. What the hell is there to miss? You don't need me anymore" (2001: 303)—a clear reference to "taking a life" for fame and profit (Doris Sommer 147). But Jesusa lives on for many more years, and she and Poniatowska maintain what grows to be a fond, if still slightly uncomfortable, friendship. While on an extended stay in France, working on her testimonial novel, Poniatowska sends Jesusa regular postcards; Jesusa dictates the occasional letter in return (2001: xv). When Poniatowska is in the hospital, Jesusa stays the night, but refuses to share Poniatowska's hospital bed because "the only bed we both fit in is mine because it's a poor person's bed" (2001: xix). Jesusa lives until 1987, and dies at the advanced age of eighty-seven. She dies in her "last dwelling," built "with sticks, bricks, pieces of cloth" (2001: xxi) on the margins of the ever-expanding metropolis, in utter poverty, in an area without sewage, water, or electricity, no trees, no grass, just "bald plains" (2001: xxv).

Even early in young Jesusa's life we see some of the themes that will mark her until her death: poverty, loss, migration, and abusive relationships between men and women. Mexican history serves as the backdrop for, and sometimes the impetus behind these themes. Violence is ubiquitous in Jesusa's early life, in her family, in her marriage, and particularly in the events and actions of the Mexican Revolution and the Cristero uprising. Solitude and silence are equally prevalent for Jesusa. A veritable indentured servant, she has no one with whom to talk as a child; her husband "uses" her as a vessel of his sexual desire, without affection or conversation; throughout her life she does not communicate her mistreatment at the hands of others because she assumes it will gain her nothing.

Jesusa: Pícara, Proto-Feminist, or Witness?

Critical views of Jesusa tend toward two camps: those who see her as a *pícara*, and the novel as picaresque, detailing the episodic adventures of a cunning rogue, and those who see her as a kind of heroine, or a proto-feminist.[14] I believe neither view is fully accurate. Although the episodic nature of her story and the frequent change of "masters" or "mistresses" are in keeping with the genre of the picaresque novel, the picaresque is typically a satirical critique of society, and its "hero" is actually a villain who takes advantage of his employers in order to rob them or to advance himself socially and economically. Jesusa does not steal from anyone, and the trajectory of her life is from poverty to more poverty to destitution, the clear opposite of the typical picaresque character. Her critiques of society, though frequent, are far from satirical, ranging from annoyance at the cost of eggs to a biting commentary on the failure of the Mexican Revolution:

> Zapata ... just wanted us to be free, but we never will be, that's what I think, because we'll be slaves all our lives. You want me to make it clearer? Everyone who comes takes a bite out of us, leaves us maimed, toothless, crippled, and they make their homes out of the pieces that they bite off. And I don't go along with that, especially now that we're worse off than ever before" [2001: 76].

Nor is Jesusa "a liberated female hero" (Joel Hancock 357). Indeed, there are enormous differences between her and women of similar class and condition. She participates in the Mexican Revolution, yes, but she is a fighting soldier rather than the more typical *soldadera* camp follower accompanying the troops. She marries young, but she has no children, and once widowed, refuses the servitude and abuse she considers typical of a woman's alliance with a man. But Jesusa is not a woman whose stubborn independence makes her either a new hero or a protofeminist. Rather, as Deborah Shaw points out, "Jesusa cannot be made into either a feminist or a socialist, despite her occasional adoption of elements of both discourses. Her politics, like that of so many poor people, are a politics of necessity and survival. Her fight is not for women or the poor, but for herself..." (193–194).

For Poniatowska, Jesusa is one of the innumerable women who are an invisible part of the history of Mexico. "But Mexico doesn't welcome them, it doesn't even acknowledge them" (2001: xxi). Poniatowska has said that she writes "para dar voz a los que no la tienen, a los que están siempre silenciados"—"to give voice to the voiceless, to those who are always silenced" (Teresa Méndez-Faith 57; my translation). In this regard, Jesusa is a witness who gives testimony to the lives of the invisible underclass of Mexico, the maids and workers who make comfortable, even possible, the lives of Mexicans like Poniatowska . But unlike such witnesses as Rigoberta Menchú, she is a reluctant witness who does not see herself as speaking for a collective. She has no political agenda; she is not a political activist desirous of making her story known. In fact she is a reluctant witness whose primary goal is simply to survive. Though *Here's to You, Jesusa!* may be "un texto claramente subversivo que contiene una dura crítica al sistema patriarcal y clasista, a la educación que recibe la mujer, y a las instituciones y mitos mexicanos, sobre todo a la Revolución"—"a clearly subversive text that contains a harsh critique of the classist and patriarchal system, of the education that women receive, of Mexican institutions and myths, and especially of the Revolution" (María Inés Lagos-Pope 250, my translation), Jesusa remains a unique individual whose life is a window on the "other Mexico," the Mexico of the impoverished masses.

Notes

1. Elena Poniatowska. *Hasta no verte Jesús mío.* Mexico: Ediciones Era, 1969. Print. The Cuban writer Miguel Barnet's *Biografía de un cimarrón (The Autobiography of a Runaway Slave.* Trans. Jocasta Inness. London: Bodley Head, 1966) is considered the first example of *testimonio.*

2. Poniatowska's own *La noche de Tlatelolco (testimonies de historia oral)* (Mexico: Ediciones Era, 1971) is a famous exception, containing multiple voices to create a kind of collective testimony. For major critical works on the genre see also Georg M. Gugelberger, ed. *The Real Thing. Testimonial Discourse and Latin America.* Durham, NC: Duke University Press, 1996; John Beverly and Marc Zimmerman, "Testimonial Narrative." *Literature and Politics in the Central American Revolutions* (Austin: University of Texas Press, 1990): 172–211; Naomi Lindström, Testimonial Narrative—Whose Text?" *The Social Conscience of Latin American Writing* (Austin: University of Texas Press): 1998, 70–91; and the special issue of *Latin American Perspectives, Voices of the Voiceless in Testimonial Literature, Part I* and *Part II.* 18.3–4 (Summer/Autumn, 1991).

3. For more on the controversy, see Stoll's *Rigoberta Menchú and the Story of All Poor Guatemalans* (Boulder, CO: Westview Press, 1999, and expanded edition, 2008); Arturo Arias' *The Rigoberta Menchú Controversy* (Minneapolis: University of Minnesota Press, 2001), and the "Forever Menchú" section of Arturo Arias, *Taking Their Word: Literature and the Signs of Central America* (Minneapolis: University of Minnesota Press, 2007): 83–162.

4. Burgos indicates that *"gestor"* is the term Miguel Barnet uses to refer to the writer of *testimonio.* Burgos received the Casa de las Américas prize in 1983 in the Testimonio category. In her recent "Foreword" to the expanded edition of Stoll's critique, Burgos states that when Menchú was soon to receive the Nobel Prize for Peace in 1992, a folder from the Committee in Solidarity with Guatemala in Paris eliminated Burgos' name as author and as prizewinner, substituting Menchú's name for both, apparently at the behest of Menchú. The Casa de las Américas site has not changed authorship: http://www.casadelasamericas .com/premios/literario/busquedapremios.php?pagina=busquedapremiados.

5. In the case of *I, Rigoberta Menchú,* which has been translated into more than twenty languages, it seems that though Burgos may now be listed as "editor," as in the Verso paperback edition, she "registered all the copyrights in her own name" (Arturo Arias, "Rigoberta Menchú's History within the Guatemalan Context." *The Rigoberta Menchú Controversy,* 7). Given the number of editions and translations and adoptions for classroom use, the royalties may be substantial and ongoing.

6. The prison served as a penitentiary from 1910 to 1976, and was known popularly as "the Black Palace of Lecumberri." Activists such as the railroad strike organizer Filomeno Mata and artists such as the Mexican muralist David Alfaro Siqueiros were among those imprisoned there. Jesusa seems to have been arrested a number of times for drunkenness and disorderly behavior.

7. The dates remain confusing. Poniatowska has stated that she first met Jesusa in 1964 ("Introduction" to *Here's to You, Jesusa!,* viii), in 1963 ("A Question Mark Engraved on My Eyelids" [*The Writer on Her Work, Volume II: Essays on New Territory.* Janet Sternburg, ed. New York: Norton, 1991]) and 1968 ("Testimonios de una escritora: Elena Poniatowska en

micrófono," [*La sartén por el mango: encuentro de escritoras latinoamericanas.* Patricia Elena González and Eliana Ortega, eds. Río Piedras, Puerto Rico: Ediciones de Huracán, 1985.]. Cynthia Steele comments on interview notes that Poniatowska shared with her, dating interviews from 1963 to 1964 (*Politics, Gender, and the Mexican Novel, 1968–1988: Beyond the Pyramid.* Austin: University of Texas Press, 1992). Steele's comments suggest that there were drafts of the novel *prior* to the interviews themselves, which is impossible: "During September 1988 and April and May 1989 Elena Poniatowska gave me access to transcriptions of some of her interviews with Bórquez, the first of which is dated March 4, 1964, as well as several early and late drafts of the novel. The first one is from 1963 ... and the last one is marked 'penultimate version' and is dated December 1967" (34). I have chosen 1963 as the most probable date of their first meeting. There is similar confusion about the length of the interview process, stated as a year or up to two years. In the "Introduction" to the English translation, Poniatowska quotes Jesusa: "— Listen, you've been coming here and screwing around and annoying me for two years..." (xii).

8. A translation entitled "Here's Looking at You, Jesusa," was done by Magda Bogin, but never published. The translation by Deanna Heikkinen published in 2001 as *Here's to You Jesusa!* captures the same reference to drinking and toasting as Poniatowska intended when using a "bottoms up" kind of toast for her original title. According to Mary Kiddle, who interviewed Poniatowska in August of 1979, "the toast is a challenge to the drinker to continue drinking until he or she sees the image of Christ painted on the bottom of the glass" ("The Non-fiction Novel or Novela Testimonial in Contemporary Mexican Fiction." Diss. Brown University, 1984. 185–186).

9. All quotations not otherwise identified are from the English translation, *Here's to You, Jesusa!*

10. Jesusa complained about the cost of the electricity the tape recorder would use, and reprimanded Poniatowska for using something that did not belong to her. Poniatowska was also unskilled in using the large apparatus and often would not record the conversation and have to repeat her questions, which annoyed Jesusa nearly as much as the financial concern.

11. Poniatowska, "And Here's to You, Jesusa," 151. One of the scenes Poniatowska admits to inventing paints a flattering image of Zapata as a true gentleman: Jesusa and four married women accompanying the troops were sent on ahead as usual, and were caught by Emiliano Zapata's troops. No harm came to them, and Zapata himself took them back to their camp, with no soldiers to escort or protect him (72–75).

12. Mexico City is the third largest city in the world, with an estimated population of 20,450,000 (2010). According to Sergio Campos Ortega Cruz., "During the 20th century, Mexico City's population has grown from 345,000 in 1900 to 1,029,000 in 1930, 3,136,000 in 1950, 9,045,000 in 1970, and 15,785,000 in 1990. The most rapid growth occurred in 1930–70, when the population grew by more than 5% annually. The growth rate declined to 3.65% between 1970–80," an according to growth has continued to decline to "1.92% in 1980–90." See Campos Ortega Cruz, Sergio. English abstract of "Demography of Mexico City. The same problems with less population" "Demografía de la ciudad de México. Los mismos problemas con menos población." *DemoS* 4 (January 1991): 23–24. English abstract: http://www.ncbi.nlm.nih.gov/pubmed/12158039 Article in Spanish: http://www.ejournal .unam.mx/dms/no04/DMS00413.pdf Web.

13. Poniatowska was born in Paris in 1933 to a Mexican mother and a French father of Polish origin. Her mother's family was landed gentry who lost their lands after the Mexican Revolution; her father's family was noble, descendents of the last king of Poland. Poniatowska came to Mexico in 1942 or 1943, and learned Spanish from the maids and nannies in her household.

14. For Jesusa as a pícara, see Edward Friedman, "The Marginated Narrator: *Hasta no verte Jesús mío* and the Eloquence of Repression," (*The Anitheroine's voice: Narrative Discourse and Transformations of the Picaresque.* Columbia: University of Missouri Press, 1987, 170–

186); Didier Jaén, "La neopicaresca en México: Elena Poniatowska y Luis Zapata," (*Tinta* V [Spring, 1987]: 23–29); and Charles M. Tatum, "Elena Poniatowska's *Hasta No Verte, Jesús Mío"* [Until I See You, Dear Jesus], (*The Latin American Women Writers, Yesterday and Today. Selected Proceedings from the Conference on Women Writers from Latin America, March 15–15, 1975.* Pittsburgh: *The Review*, 1977. 49–58). For interpretations of Jesusa as heroine or proto-feminist, see both Monique Lamaître, "Jesusa Palancares y la dialéctica de la emancipación femenina.*" (Revista Iberoamericana* 51 [July, 1985]: 751–763) and Joel Hancock.

Works Cited

Beverly, John. "The Margin at the Center: On *Testimonio.*" 1989. *De/Colonizing the Subject: The Politics of Gender in Women's Autobiography.* Minneapolis: U of Minnesota P, 1992. 91–137. Print.

_____. "'Through All Things Modern': Second Thoughts on Testimonio." In *Critical Theory, Cultural Politics, and Latin American Narrative.* Eds. Steven M. Bell, Albert H. Le May, and Leonard Orr. Notre Dame, IN: University of Notre Dame Press, 1993. Print.

Burgos, Elizabeth. "Foreword: How I Became Persona Non Grata." In David Stoll, *Rigoberta Menchú and the Story of All Poor Guatemalans.* Expanded edition.Westview Press, 2008. ix-xvii.

Esquivel, Laura. *Como agua para chocolate: novela de entregas mensuales con recetas, amores, y remedios caseros.* Mexico: Editorial Planeta Mexicana, 1989.

_____. *Like Water for Chocolate: A Novel in Monthly Installments, with Recipes, Romances, and Home Remedies.* Tran. by Carol Christensen and Thomas Christensen. New York: Doubleday, 1991. Print.

Gugelberger, Georg, and Michael Kearney. "Voices for the Voiceless: Testimonial Literature in Latin America." *Latin American Perspectives* 18.3 (Summer, 1991): 3–14. Print.

Hancock, Joel. "Elena Poniatowska's *Hasta no verte Jesús mío*: The Remaking of the Image of Woman." *Hispania* 66.3 (Sep., 1983): 353–359. Print.

Jörgensen, Beth. E. *The Writing of Elena Poniatowska: Engaging Dialogues.* Austin: University of Texas Press, 1994. Print.

Lagos-Pope, María Inés. "El testimonio creativo de *Hasta no verte Jesús mío.*" *Revista Iberoamericana* 56 (1990): 243–253. Print.

McCard, Victoria L. "*Soldaderas* of the Mexican Revolution." *Philological Papers* 51 (2004): 43–51. Print.

Menchú, Rigoberta. *I, Rigoberto Menchú: An Indian Woman in Guatemala.* Ed. and Intro. Elisabeth Burgos-Debray. Trans. Ann Wright. London: Verso, 1984. Print.

Méndez-Faith, Teresa. "Entrevista con Elena Poniatowska." *Inti* 15 (Spring, 1982): 54–60.

Paz, Octavio. "Critique of the Pyramid." *The Labyrinth of Solitude and Other Writings.* New York: Grove, 1985. 284–326. Print

_____. "Here's to You, Jesusa." Trans. Gregory Kolovakos and Ronald Christ. In *Lives on the Line: The Testimony of Contemporary Latin American Authors.* Ed. Doris Meyer. Berkely: University of California Press, 1988. 136–155. Print.

_____. *Here's to You, Jesusa!* Trans. Deanna Heikkinen. New York: Farrar, Straus and Giroux, 2001. Print.

Pratt, Mary Louise. "*Me llamo Rigoberta Menchú*: Autoethnography and the Recoding of Citizenship" In *Teaching and Testimony: Rigoberta Menchú and the North American Classroom.* Ed. Allen Carey-Webb and Stephen Benz. Albany: University of New York Press, 1996. 57–72. Print.

Press Release. http://www.nobelprize.org/nobel_prizes/peace/laureates/1992/press.html 8/17/2011. Web.

Shaw, Deborah. "Jesusa Palancares as Individual Subject in Elena Poniatowska's *Hasta no verte Jesús mío. Bulletin of Hispanic Studies* 73 (April 1996)2: 191–204. Print.

Sommer, Doris. "Taking a Life: Hot Pursuit and Cold Rewards in a Mexican Testimonial Novel." 1995. *Proceed with caution, when engaged by minority writing in the America.* Cambridge: Harvard UP, 1999. 147–172. Print.

Spivak, Gayatri Chakravorty. "Can the Subaltern Speak?" In *Colonial Discourse and Postcolonial Theory: A Reader.* Eds. Patrick Williams & Laura Chrisman. London: Harvester Wheatsheaf, 1993. 66–111. Print.

6

La cómplice oficial:
Catalina in Angeles Mastretta's
Arráncame la vida

ALICE EDWARDS

"... if we do not know our own history, we are doomed to live it as if it were our own private fate."—Hannah Arendt

The publication of Angeles Mastretta's first novel, *Arráncame la vida* (1985), situated its author clearly in the forefront of the new wave of writers that emerged in Mexico in the 1980s.[1] With this book, Mastretta won the Mazatlán Literary Prize and gained both critical and popular recognition in Mexico and abroad. Like many Latin American women writers of her generation, Mastretta's works examine, through the portrayal of male-female relationships, the mechanisms in place geared to perpetuate the institutionalization of women's subjection, alienation, and sexual repression. The female condition and the deconstruction of canonic patriarchal structures have been indeed recurrent themes in feminine/feminist literature; in fact, most women writers tend to project and portray their own personal experiences through the lives of their female characters. As Cynthia Steele notes: "The first wave of these new women authors, most of whom are currently in their 40s and early 50s, tends to portray middle-class female subjectivity from a first person point of view" (14).

Set in the Mexico of the 1930s and 40s, *Arráncame la vida* tells the story of Catalina Guzmán de Ascencio, a young woman married to the governor of Puebla, a man whose ruthlessness, machismo, and corrupt use of power serve as the key fact in his wife's sentimental education. Her bildungsroman also tells her husband's personal story, revealing the private, unofficial life of a public figure, and exposing the lies and abuses of his government. Catalina's growth and exploration of her self and her world is often sharply critical and scathingly honest, continually evaluating her own subaltern position outside of the circle of power. She is privy to the details and secrets of government corruption because, as a wife, she is considered harmless, a fly on the wall. Her memoir, however, reveals that she cannot be "trusted" and examines the ways in which she resists her husband's hegemony through multiple private rebellions.

Yet, in spite of Catalina's strength, intelligence, and resistance strategies, she fails in any profound way to establish an identity and a life for herself that is not predicated on that of her husband. Her story is one of passivity, and while it is interrupted by flights into romance and occasional defiance, Catalina does not, and perhaps cannot, separate herself from the people and institutions that seek to constrain her sexuality and identity.

Marriage and Violence

At fifteen, Catalina marries Andrés Ascencio, a character loosely based on Maximinio Avila Camacho, real-life former governor of Puebla (Kay García 73). Franco Moretti notes that in the typical bildungsroman, personal freedom must eventually submit to the limits of socialization, which is best accomplished through marriage, a pact between the individual and the world (22). Marriage, Moretti maintains, is in many ways the opposite of freedom and the end of becoming as it "marks the end of all tension between the individual and the world: all desire for further metamorphosis is extinguished" (23). Women's view of marriage, however, is usually quite different. In *Writing a Woman's Life*, Carolyn Heilbrun states that "[m]arriage is the most persistent of myths imprisoning women, and misleading those who write of women's lives" (77). *Arráncame la vida* explores this myth; marriage is indeed central to the story; however, for Catalina, the act of marriage does not solidify her identity as a consenting adult, like in the standard in the classic bildungsroman, but it becomes the catalyst for her growth and personal search (Claudia Schaeffer 95–96).

In her analysis of *La muerte de Artemio Cruz* and *Pedro Páramo*, Sharon Magnarelli describes the marriages in both novels as a kind of sacrifice performed for social unity. Magnarelli refers to the work of René Girard, who, in *Violence and the Sacred*, mentions that sacrifice is a socially acceptable outlet or diversion for the basic violence inherent to mankind (81). Sacrifice does not have to be a concrete killing, it may also be a symbolic death. "Like the animal and the infant, but to a lesser degree, the woman qualifies for sacrificial status by reason of her weakness and relatively marginal social status. That is why she can be viewed as a quasi-sacred figure, both desired and disdained, alternately elevated and abused" (Girard 141–142). For Sharon Magnarelli marriage not only functions as a means to avoid overt violence, but it is also an act that solidifies the social group. In *La muerte de Artemio Cruz*, for instance, Catalina is given up by her wealthy father to forestall a forcible taking of his property by the younger Cruz. In *Arráncame la vida*, Catalina is also given up (although she does go quite willingly) by her family to a man whose past is strewn with episodes of abduction, illegitimate children, and abandoned women. Her marriage is a means to avert the violence that would be forthcoming otherwise and provides the sacrifice that links Andrés to the poblanos.[2] Yet, as Magnarelli points out — and the novel demonstrates–"can violence ever be truly forestalled? Or do we simply (as Girard suggests) redirect it in a more suitable (read, socially acceptable) form, so that it becomes more covert and *appears* less violent?" (94). Andrés' violence is thus expressed in acceptable patriarchal terms inside the marriage: he is legally allowed to control almost every aspect of Catalina's life.

Catalina's identification with Andrés is enforced even more given the weakness of her relationships with other people. While she is not technically an orphan, Catalina is removed from the protection of her family at an early age. Although the relationship with her father is emphasized, her mother is at best a shadowy figure who does not offer even the rudiments of maternal education to her young daughter; for much of the sexual education, the young woman must depend on a gypsy woman and on her new, insensitive husband. The absence of a "female role model" in the narrative is not an isolated case, as Heilbrun notes: "The heroines of most novels by women either have no mothers, or mothers who are ineffectual and unsatisfactory [...] As a rule, the women in these novels are very lonely; they have no women friends, though they sometimes have a sister who is a friend" (118). Indeed, Catalina has some superficial friendships and her sister serves as her personal secretary, but she virtually has no female bonds of support and solidarity.

Arráncame and Mexican Cultural Identity: The Official Accomplice and the Malinche Paradigm

The novel opens with the line: "Ese año pasaron muchas cosas en este país. Entre otras, Andrés y yo nos casamos" (9) — "That year, many things happened in this country. For one, Andrés and I were married."[3] The frame of the novel is a call to link the personal story of Catalina Guzmán de Ascencio with the larger, national story. According to Schaeffer, the decades of the 1930s and 40s serve as a backdrop to Catalina's own coming of age as a woman in modern Mexico "and at the same time, on another level, parallel or echo her process of development and self-discovery" (89). As the story progresses, Catalina matures, has children, learns the lengths her husband will go to in order to consolidate his power (including robbery, bribery, and murder), and examines the world she moves in with a critical eye. She also falls in love and has an affair; her extramarital relationship suddenly makes her the target of her husband's violence; violence she had been willing to overlook when it did not affect her. Catalina is continually confronted with the choice either to ignore her husband's activities — allying herself with Andrés to benefit from his crimes — or to break away from him, and to side with those oppressed by him, refusing to profit from their losses. Interestingly enough, in her own way, she is willing to admit, she is his accomplice. In addition to performing the role of the perfect governor's wife, Catalina helps her husband by willing herself not to see things, preferring to ignore, forget, and overlook certain connections. The word *olvidar* (to forget) appears with startling frequency throughout the novel, as Catalina chooses to dispense and overlook anything that will conflict with her interests. Furthermore, she is supported by friends and family members who, in the same fashion, would rather remain ignorant of Andres' ruthlessness. Significantly, her ignorance keeps her in an extended childhood. Jerome Buckley notes the importance of memory in the bildungsroman, since it is the memory of vital impressions that binds child to youth to adult (5). In other words, it is memory that creates a coherent identity through time. Catalina's refusal to remember points to a potential crisis in her development of identity, a crisis averted because she obviously has, at some point, remembered, at least enough to record it in the text we are now reading. In her critical analysis of the novel, Alicia Llarena sees this memory recuperated by the more adult, narrating Catalina: "Cabe señalar también que la mujer adulta y liberada que Catalina es cuando nos confía los secretos de su vida, añade a la narración el punto necesario de distancionamiento que explica toda flexibilidad en la rememo-ración de su pasado, toda ironía" (470) — "It is important to note that the adult, liberated woman that Catalina is when she confides her life's secrets adds to the narration the necessary distancing, which explains all of her flexibility in remembering her past, all of her irony."

Catalina, however, cannot defend herself by simply saying she was unaware of her husband's dealings or that she does not care. There are moments in the narrative when not only she admits her implication in his crimes by her acts of omission, but that she also pleased with the way people react to Andrés' abusive behavior. At a certain point, for instance, speaking of her husband, the governor, she comments: "Tenía unas manos grandes. Me gustaban tanto como les temían otros. O por eso me gustaban. No sé" (63) — "He had big hands. I liked them as much as others feared them. Or maybe that's why I liked them. I don't know." In fact, she has learned to negotiate with her husband in his own terms, as when she wanted to recover her horse after a bad deal, she bartered with Andrés, threatening to publicly reveal his involvement in the murder of a group of peasants, thereby using this information to her advantage rather than working to right an injustice. In spite of this, Catalina does not fully endorse her husband's regime. For as much as she his official accomplice, she is in continual conflict with his lack of scruples and his authoritarianism.

Such inner conflict corresponds to the relationships between dominant and subordinate groups described in James C. Scott's book *Domination and the Arts and Resistance*. Scott writes that public deference and approval shown by subordinates (what he calls the "pubic transcript") is countered by a "hidden transcript" of resistance that occurs "off stage": "Subordinates offer a perform- ance of deference and consent while attempting to read the intentions and mood of the potentially threatening powerholder" (3). Read in this way, Catalina's narrative presents us with a kind of hidden transcript that traces the extent of her acceptance of or resistance to Andrés' control. Scott points out that this process does not mean that the public transcript is false and the hidden transcript true; what is important is the *difference* between what is performed in front of the powerholder versus what is expressed within the safety of the subordinate world (5).

As a Novel of the Revolution, *Arráncame la vida* is a view from the under- side, or through the looking glass, the mirror that Catalina is to Andrés. The wife's perspective allows us to see the main actors in this post-revolutionary drama with all their blemishes. While Andrés, the great orator and man of the people, goes out to give a speech, we stay behind the scenes with a cynical Catalina who reveals how hollow his words are. Her viewpoint is especially interesting given the fact that she admits that her formal education is lacking:

> Aprendí los nombres de las tribus de Israel, los nombres de los jefes y descendien- tes de cada tribu y los nombres de todas las ciudades y todos los hombres y muje- res que cruzaban por la Historia Sagrada [...] Total, terminé la escuela con una mediana caligrafía, algunos conocimientos de gramática, poquísimos de aritmé- tica, *ninguno de historia* y varios manteles de punto de cruz [13, italics are mine].

> I learned the names of the tribes of Israel, the names of the chiefs and descen- dents of each tribe and the names of all the cities and all the men and women that passed through the Sacred History [...] All in all, I left school with passing penmanship, some knowledge of grammar, very little arithmetic, *no history*, and various cross-stitched tablecloths.

Her untutored gaze here is a benefit to herself and to the reader. She presents herself as a clean slate, an observer of what goes on in the inner sanctum of the highest levels of Mexican government, with virtually no previous expectations or knowledge through which to filter what she witnesses.

Mastretta gives us an additional take on the Novel of the Revolution, the story Andrés tells Catalina in order to justify the appearance of his two children from a previous relationship. It is the account of a young man from the provinces, arriving in Mexico City during the heat of the Revolution. He meets young Eulalia and her idealistic father, and works delivering milk for them. She is the ideal woman, hard-working, even-tempered, and devoted, happily content with her lot in life. In his story, Andrés becomes frustrated with a life of poverty, and when he encounters his childhood friend, Rodolfo, now a successful military man (he will later become President, patterned after Miguel de Alemán), he senses that his opportunity has arrived. Eulalia, however, becomes sick with typhus and dies. Later we find out that such touching and sentimental version of his youth, is merely a fabrication. Catalina admits that she believed it for quite some time: "Veneré la memoria de Eulalia, quise hacerme de una risa como la suya, y cien tardes le evidié con todas mis ganas al amante simplón y apegado que mi general fue con ella" (43)—"I venerated Eulalia's memory, I tried to laugh like she did and for a hundred afternoons I envied how simple and devoted my general was with her." Eulalia is, in other words, the perfect Mexican revolutionary wife, held up as an example for Catalina to emulate. When Catalina discovers that this perfect woman has never existed and that she was only a figment of her husband's imagination, it casts a doubt on the rest of Andrés' claims, and also serves to disillusion the reader regarding the rhetoric of the Revolution. That potentially grand and noble period in Mexico's history is reduced to propaganda, and the men who participated to crass opportunists. Catalina's reaction is particularly instructive: as the reader of Andrés' bildungsroman, she is only briefly distressed by the lie, but she quickly discards any ideals, and accepts his opportunism and cynicism because she ultimately benefits from it. The unproblematic presentation of this scene invites the reader of the novel to do the same, that is, to forget about trying to find something honorable in the story and instead just enjoy the ride.

Andrés' story echoes that of another revolutionary "hero," Artemio Cruz. In Fuentes' *La muerte de Artemio Cruz*, the main character also invents another past for himself in order to avoid the harsh truth about who he really was and what he did. In Cruz's case, it also concerned a woman, Regina, whose first encounter with Cruz, in reality a kidnapping and rape, becomes a shared lie of a romantic moment at the beach (Fuentes, *La muerte*, 82). Regina, the idealized, self-sacrificing woman, also dies; her memory will contrast with Cruz's later relationship with his official wife, curiously enough also named Catalina. Fuentes' Catalina does not pardon her husband for his actions, however; she refuses to help him whitewash his life, in contrast to Mastretta's Catalina who, passively, helps conceal all of Andrés' limitations and atrocities.

Along with the Revolution, Mastretta takes on another Mexican cultural paradigm in this novel. Catalina's relationship with Andrés suggests a re-inscription of the Malinche legend of Mexico. Like Malinche, she is denied her primary identification with her people (poblanos, other women) and is handed over (by her father) to Andrés, with whom she allies herself; although he will eventually betray her as well, not only with multiple infidelities, but with the murder of her lover, Carlos. Like La Malinche is supposed to have done with Cortés, Catalina acts as her husband's intermediary with his constituents who are first and foremost Catalina's peers; she is a poblana and he is not. Time and again people come to her asking to intercede on their behalf; she "translates" their requests to the governor. He is generally regarded as a despot, usurping indian lands and raping women, killing all opposition and enjoying the material rewards of his various crimes.[4]

In *La Malinche in Mexican Literature: From History to Myth*, Sandra Messinger Cypess discusses the presence of the Malinche paradigm as sub-text in Mexican novels, showing the extent to which she has become "part of the Mexican subconscious":

> When a woman is used as an object of exchange or is raped by an "invading" male figure and then abandoned or willingly consorts with newcomers and betrays her people or accepts a different cutlure and rejects her own or is blamed without reason for the evils that befall her people — such elements of characterization relate that woman to the popular configuration of the Malinche paradigm [153].

Messinger Cypess also notes how the paradigm has changed over time: "[...] with each generation, La Malinche has added diverse interpretations of her new identity, role, and significance for individuals and for Mexico" (5). While colonial views of Malinche were positive, independence movements saw her changed into what Messinger Cypess calls a "desirable woman/terrible mother," a negative figure who betrayed *la patria* (10). The 1950s, with the publication of Octavio Paz's *Labyrinth of Solitude*, La Malinche is presented as a woman suffering passively, restricted by patriarchy. More contemporary versions use Malinche as an antecedent of the Chicana woman or as an active participant in the Conquest, who accepted Christianity and rejected the tyranny of the Aztecs (143). Messinger Cypess continues: "Re/formation and re/visions of the meaning inherent in the sign La Malinche signal the development of real structural changes in social relationships" (13). If so, then *Arráncame la vida*, which presents a Malinche sub-text whose protagonist is not silent, who resists, however modestly, and who outlives — happily — her conquistador, can be seen as a reflection of societal changes for women's lives in the end of the twentieth century Mexico.

Domestic Rebellions

Besides her family, Catalina has had to give up other things in order to live with Andrés. First, for her there is no question of work outside the home that is not connected to her husband's career. In this, her situation is not different from that of most of her peers. Her formal education has been elementary; there is little indication that she has any interest in intellectual or professional pursuits, so her energy is spent on pleasing her husband and having children. Moreover, even her relationship with her children must be forfeited. When one day her five year old son tells her that his father has told him "matar es trabajo" — "killing is work," Catalina makes a decision; rather than trying to protect the children from the harshness of their father's life, she withdraws from them (66). As opposed to other subordinate groups, Scott notes that, because of the nature of family life, women often lack an extensive "off stage" social existence from which to develop "a shared critique of power." (21) Indeed, as we see in the novel, Catalina must rely on Andrés as her sole guide. He himself recognizes that he serves this purpose when he says:

> Son un desastre las mujeres, uno se pasa la vida, educándolas, explicándolas, y apenas pasa un loro junto a ellas le creen todo.... Le hubieran conocido ustedes a los dieciséis años, entonces sí era una cosa linda, una esponja que lo escuchaba todo con atención, era incapaz de juzgar mal a su marido y de no estar en su cama a las tres de la mañana [161].

> Women are a disaster, you spend your whole life teaching them, explaining to them, and a parrot goes by and they believe everything he says ... you should have met her when she was 16, she was a lovely thing back then, a sponge that listened to everything carefully, she was incapable of judging her husband badly or of not being in bed at three in the morning.

As the incarnation of ruthless power and ambition, Andrés is far from simple. Not only is he condescending and insulting with Catalina, but he is also the barrier between her and her lover, between her and her children, between her and the truth, self-actualization, and freedom. Yet, in spite of all these negative qualities, she presents him as warm with his friends and family in a rough, simple way. He is the "common man" — a man of humble origins who has bought his poor mother a lovely home, who organizes family car trips, and who gives in to Catalina's whims in an indulgent, albeit paternal fashion. Andrés is a surprisingly complex character who is at times almost likeable. Indeed, on some levels, he deeply understands and appreciates his wife. As he prepares to die, he reveals that he is aware that he does not know her well enough:

> Te jodí la vida, ¿verdad?—dijo—Porque las demás van a tener lo que querían. ¿Tú qué quieres? Nunca he podido saber qué quieres tú. Tampoco dediqué mucho tiempo a pensar en eso, pero no me creas tan pendejo, sé que te caben muchas mujeres en el cuerpo y que yo solo conocí a unas cuantas [214].

> "I fucked up your life, didn't I?" he said. "Because the others are going to get what they wanted. What do you want? I've never known what you wanted. I didn't really spend too much time thinking about it, either, but don't think I'm stupid, I know that you have many women inside of you and I have only gotten to know a few.

Catalina's rebellion, like most women of her generation, is constant, but limited in scope; it consists of the small rebellions of the powerless. In an interview with Reinhard Teichmann, Mastretta explains that this character does not confront her husband neither in a feminist way, nor like a liberated woman, but with the tools she has, the ones that life has given her, "with her body, with her intelligence, with her emotions, with shouting, falling in love with another man, criticizing him, not obeying him, raising her children as she wants to, or not raising them" (509).

After relinquishing her maternal role, Catalina's inner strength and intelligence must be focused on the emotional arena, particularly on romantic love, which, given the nature of her marriage and the character of her husband, will obviously be problematic.[5] Her relationship with Carlos Vives, the director of the new national orchestra, turns Catalina—her body and her emotions—into a battleground between the opposing political forces. Claudia Schaeffer writes that "Carlos is a threat to the stability and permanence of the world Andrés and his political pals have sought to impose on Mexican women, families, and institutions in general" (95), but Alicia Llarena sees the focus on Catalina's lovelife as one of the ways Mastretta offers liberation to her protagonist: "Es la emancipación emocional, sin duda alguna, la que logra romper con el modelo, y promover en la protagonista la 'desacralización' del general..." (473)— "It is emotional emancipation, without a doubt, that allows her to break with the model and inspire in the protagonist the 'desacralization' of the general." For Llarena, the novel resides on the margins, showing a feminine perspective and focusing on the realm of the domestic, as opposed to the social and public sphere (474). According to the critic, Catalina retreats from a personal situation of patriarchal oppression — and from the larger scene of political repression — into a private space where she can experience desire and emotion, where she can be free.

One image of freedom recurrent in the novel is that of the sea, it is a symbol for all that contrasts with Catalina's husband and her traditional, circumscribed life in the arid landscape of Puebla. It is significant that Andrés hates the ocean, element that he strongly identifies with women: "Me molesta el mar, no se calla, parece mujer" (213)—"The sea annoys me, it's never quiet, it's like a woman." Not surprisingly, he prefers Puebla, Mexico City, Zacatlán — his native town in the mountains — all inland, and, perhaps more important, all places where he is in control and where he has recognized power. For Catalina, the sea refers only partially to a physical place; it is a woman-space outside of male control. After fifteen years of forgetting, she is willing to remember — albeit only "good things" — at the safety of the sea Here, Catalina points to essential conditions for the possibility of her bildungsroman; remembering is dependent upon freedom.

The novel ends with Andrés' death and with the suggestion that Catalina may have engineered it by giving him an addictive and slow-poisoning tea. Although the ending has been read in different ways, it seems clear that Catalina does assume some responsibility for her husband's demise. Significantly, the tea was given to Catalina by Carmela, a peasant woman whose husband was killed by Andrés, and who unexpectedly returns to talk to her after Carlos, Catalina's lover, is killed: "Se sentó junto a mí, puso la canasta en el suelo y empezó a platicarme *como si fuéramos amigas y yo la hubiera estado esperando*" (191, italics mine)—"She sat next to me, put her basket on the ground and started talking to me *as if we were friends and I had been waiting for her.*" Their coded conversation underscores the fact that, while Catalina may have a difficulty in identifying with the other people who are oppressed and abused by the governor, those others clearly understand that, for all her privilege, Catalina is "one of them."

In the lineage of women's bildungsroman in Latin America, *Arráncame la vida* suggests few new options for women's lives, as it fixes the drama firmly in romantic love and centers the female protagonist's growth and identity around that of the men in her life. Indeed, Catalina's situation echoes Scott's argument that : "[...] joint procreation and family life have meant that imagining an entirely separate existence for the subordinate group requires a more radical step than it has for serfs or slaves" (22). The heroine's ability to create an independent and adult self would depend on her willingness to resist the control of her husband and of confining institutions, and of taking the more daring stance of identifying herself in opposition to them. Yet, too often Catalina refuses information and action that could lead to greater clarity about her own life.[6] Catalina's story ends in limbo, with neither the reader nor the writer being able to imagine exactly what happens after the last page. The author herself indicates that there is some doubt about Catalina's destiny. Mastretta says that "After her husband died, I wrote four more chapters, but I didn't know what to do with her to make her credible [...] So I decided to just end the book to see what everybody else does with her" (Kay García 79). The personal growth we have seen in Catalina has been at best superficial. She has learned to play the game, cry at the appropriate moments, continue the farce she married into, move on into pleasant widowhood — another ready-made container for female energy — and she never overtly challenged the roots of her oppression. Even the most hopeful sign that she has indeed woken up — the possibility that she may have killed her husband — is cloaked with ambiguity and side-stepping. Not even the brutal butchery of her lover, the usurpation of her children and their futures, the belittling of her desires and intelligence could make Catalina *do* anything. She receives by default, by virtue of Andrés' death and the convenient Mexican institution that protects widowhood as an honorable state. Till the end, passivity and indecision are Catalina's most notable qualities. Even Mastretta notes her character's essential flaw, "Pero para ser una mujer feminista ella tendría que haber dicho también 'yo quiero aprender a mantenerme, yo quiero bastarme,' cosa que ella no aprendió a hacer" (Teichmann 509) — "But to be a feminist woman she would have had to say also, "I want to learn to support myself, I want to rely on myself," something that she didn't learn to do."

Given the Mexico of the 1940s, another, more openly feminist version of the story might be impossible. Catalina's passivity might be the only realistic portrait Mastretta could give us. Without female role models, Catalina breaks with the traditional life of her foremothers and moves into this new, unstable social space that Mexico itself is entering. The distance between Catalina and her mother is significant if we remember that, according to Moretti, the bildungsroman appeared at a time when modernity was "dismantling the continuity between generations," allowing youth to differentiate itself from the generations that preceded it (4). By removing the link between Catalina and her foremothers, the novel ensures that she will have to reinvent her role in marriage and in her society without the benefit (or detriment) of a model or guide. Catalina's rebellious nature, her refusal to define herself solely in terms of her husband, and her insistence on exploring her own desire, point to an incremental change (rather than a full-blown revolution) in her own life as an individual and in the general situation of Mexican women. Andrés himself recognizes that the gender rules and roles are changing: "Ah, las mujeres. No cabe duda que ya no son las mismas. Algo las perturbó" (161) — "Oh, women. There's no doubt that they're not the same anymore. Something has gotten into them."

Feminism and the Marketplace, the Character and the Writer

Another possible reason for the novel's limits in projecting a fully self-actualized heroine may lie elsewhere. In "Are Women's Novels Feminist Novels?" Rosalind Coward notes the preponderance of novels with commercial success and popular appeal claiming allegiance to the women's movement (226). In such narratives — frequently written as confessionals, or with a quasi-autobiographical structure — the central character undergoes an experience or a series of experiences that radically affect her life or transform her attitudes:

> The effect of this structure is to create a distinct ideology of knowledge and indeed life — that experience brings knowledge and possibly wisdom. But where women have been, and are, the central focus of the novel, a variation occurs. That variation is that the only space where knowledge or understanding for women is produced is across sexual experience — love, marriage, divorce, or just sex [234].

Catalina's limited rebellions are focused on the romantic and sexual. Perhaps, they are the only avenues left open to her, the only aspects of her life over which she has some control and authority. But turning this bildungsroman into a love story displaces the critique of the government, the denunciation of violence, the revelation of the suffering of other marginalized peoples to a mere colorful background for the "true" story that constitutes Catalina's doomed romance. The emphasis on the love story de-politicizes the book and shifts attention to the personal and away from the political, and asks the reader to understand the novel as a personal drama rather than a discussion of larger issues. If Catalina's story and Mexico's story do indeed parallel each other, as Schaeffer and others have suggested, then the failure of the Revolution is also written here, as we are told that the dramas that matter are the individual ones, the romances that we pursue against a backdrop of violence, injustice, and oppression. Such realities are not the story itself, but a suitably dramatic landscape that can be used to sell Mexico on the international literary marketplace.

Although Mastretta approaches moments of potential conversion for Catalina, she is aware that her character must pull back just in time. A white, middle-class protagonist can challenge her machista husband without upsetting the delicate balance that the white, middle-class reader has constructed in her own life. If the protagonist identified with other oppressed groups against that husband and the power structure he represents, the reader would be put in a decidedly uncomfortable position. Reading about slow-poisoning teas and furtive affairs is nothing more than an afternoon of daytime television; divorce and vengeance fantasies are mild compared to proposing that women align themselves with the peasant on the street or the woman doing the laundry.[7]

In many ways, Mastretta's novel reflects an ambiguity in regard to feminism that is expressed directly by the author herself. In her interview with Reinhard Teichmann, Mastretta seems to misapprehend the import of the feminist movement when she says, "Pero yo creo que mientras en este país haya mano de obra que haga el trabajo en las casas de las mujeres de la clase media, no hay mucho que pelear. Tú no tienes que exigir que tu marido tienda su cama y lave sus trastes para poderte ir a trabajar tú" (510) — "But I believe that as long as this country has a labor force that does the housework in the homes of middle class women, there isn't much to fight for. You don't have to demand that your husband make the bed or wash the dishes to be able to go to work youself."

Yet, Mastretta does not face the issues directly. Instead, she has neither decided to abandon issues of justice or women's solidarity, nor has she simply decided to focus on other subjects. The image of the middle class writer behind the glass of her expensive car, struggling to understand her relationship with the poor woman is a profound metaphor to describe what is most touching and most disturbing about *Arráncame la vida*. These issues are constantly at the perimeters of her work, hinted at, glanced away from different angles. In an essay in her collection *Puerto libre*, "La mujer es un misterio," Mastretta touches on two basic themes in her writing: identity and gender issues: "Aún no sabemos bien a bien quiénes somos, mucho menos sabemos quiénes y cómo son las otras mujeres mexicanas..." (107). "We don't yet really know who we are, much less who and how other Mexican women are." Mastretta's discomfort with feminist labels, perhaps because much of her audience is the same privileged, educated class of Mexicans from which she emerged, may be the reason why she is still working out her role as a Mexican woman writer, defining her responsibilities, reaching out to that "other woman" but, just like her character Catalina, hesitating and pulling back before true connections have been made.

Writing about the women's movement in the U.S. in the 1960s, Carolyn Heilbrun helps us see what is missing in Catalina's — and perhaps also in Mastretta's — search for identity and recognition: "What became essential was for women to see themselves collectively, not individually, not caught in some individual erotic and familial plot and, inevitably, found wanting" (46). In

Arráncame la vida, Mastretta reflects on the self-evolutionary process followed by women in the deconstruction of a patriarchal system that seeks to suppress women's intellectual development. Joining in the common preoccupation of her contemporaries, she explores identity issues that clearly relate to gender, politics, and history. By opening the novel's interpretation to a whole realm of possibilities, the feminist writer is making room for new female imagery while creating a locus in which feminine desire might be allowed to manifest in a plurality of forms and remain free from patriarchal and ideological restrictions.

Notes

1. Mastretta wrote a previous book of poetry entitled *La pájara pinta,* published in 1975 without her consent (García 68).

2. The main female characters in both novels are named Catalina, in an interesting and suggestive intertextual coincidence.

3. Unless otherwise noted, all English translations are mine.

4. As Jean Franco points out in *Plotting Women,* referring to the work of Elena Garro, "Yet ... women's plotting is undermined because power seduces them. This finally is for her the lesson of La Malinche" (138). Perhaps the same can be said about Catalina.

5. As with the Victorian heroines Elaine Showalter writes about, Catalina has no other creative outlet for her energies. According to Showalter: "Denied participation in public life, women were forced to cultivate their feelings and to over-value romance. In the novels, emotion rushed in to fill the vacuum of experience." In *A Literature of Their Own: British Women Novelists from Bronte to Lessing.* Princeton, NJ: Princeton University Press, 1999. 79–80.

6. In her afterword to *Latin American Women's Writing: Feminist Readings in Theory and Crisis,* Jean Franco refers to Northrop Frye's comments on the protagonist of the romance as essentially marginal, like the Trickster rather than the Hero. Franco notes: "We should keep in mind that what is seductive about the Trickster's guile is his or her use of the system rather than any desire to destabilize or overturn the status quo." Franco is referring here specifically to Catalina's character in *Arráncame la vida.* In Anny Brooksbank Jones and Catherine Davies, *Latin American Women's Writing: Feminist Readings in Theory and Crisis.* Oxford: Clarendon Press, 1996, 227.

7. Sara Sefchovich offers the following critique of this novel: "... es una propuesta narcisista: la mujer es siempre la más bella, la más inteligente, la más rica, la más poderosa. Se divierte sin culpa, se libra de su responsabilidad sin remordimiento y nunca sufre de verdad, y por si fuera poco un final feliz le augura el mejor de los futuros. Se trata de un personaje que, vestido de mujer, realiza el sueño de todos los clasemedieros de hoy: la riqueza, el poder y la libre sexualidad. La novela resuelve además la contradicción en que se mueve la cultura del día: la de vivir en una época y en un lugar y pensar como en otro" (228–229). "[The novel] is a narcissistic proposition: the woman is always the most beautiful, the most intelligent, the richest, the most powerful. She enjoys herself guiltlessly, she frees herself of responsbilities without regrets and she never really suffers, and as if that weren't enough, a happy ending predicts the best of futures. We're dealing with a character that, dressed as a woman, realizes the dream of the entirety of today's middle class: wealth, power and sexual freedom. The novel resolves the contradiction in which contemporary culture finds itself: that of living in a particular era and place and thinking as if one were from another." In *México: País de ideas, país de novelas.* Mexico: Grijalbo, 1987. 228–229.

Works Cited

Buckley, Jerome Hamilton. *Season of Youth: The Bildungsroman from Dickens to Golding.* Cambridge: Harvard University Press, 1974. Print.

Coward, Rosalind. "Are Women's Novels Feminist Novels?" In *The New Feminist Criticism.* Ed. Elaine Showalter. New York: Pantheon, 1985. 225–239. Print.

Franco, Jean. *Plotting Women: Gender and Representation in Mexico.* New York: Columbia University Press, 1989. Print.

Fuentes, Carlos. *Geografía de la novela.* Mexico: Fondo de Cultura Económica, 1993. Print.

_____. *La muerte de Artemio Cruz* (1962). 4th ed. México D.F.: Fondo de Cultura Económica, 2010. Print.

García, Kay. *Broken Bars: New Perspectives from Mexican Women Writers.* Alburquerque: University of New Mexico Press, 1994. Print.

Girard, René. *Violence and the Sacred.* Trans. Patrick Gregory. Baltimore: Johns Hopkins University Press, 1977. Print.

Heilbrun, Carolyn. *Writing a Woman's Life.* New York: Ballantine Books, 1988. Print.

Llarena, Alicia. "Arráncame la vida: El universo desde la intimidad." *Revista Iberoamericana* 59 (1992): 465–475. Print.

Magnarelli, Sharon. *The Lost Rib.* Lewisburg, PA: Bucknell University Press, 1985. Print.

Mastretta, Angeles. *Arráncame la vida.* Mexico: Cal y Arena, 1988. Print.

_____. *Puerto libre.* Mexico: Cal y Arena, 1993. Print.

_____. *Tear This Heart Out.* Trans. Margaret Sayers Peden. New York: Riverhead Books, 1997. Print.

Messinger Cypess, Sandra. *La Malinche in Mexican Literature: From History to Myth.* Austin, TX: University of Texas Press, 1991. Print.

Moretti, Franco. *The Way of the World: The Bildungsroman in European Culture.* Trans. Albert Sbragia. London: Verso, 2000. Print.

Schaefer, Claudia. *Textured Lives.* Tucson: University of Arizona Press, 1992. Print.

Scott, James C. *Domination and the Arts of Resistance: Hidden Transcripts.* New Haven: Yale University Press. 1990. Print.

Steele, Cynthia. *Politics, Gender and the Mexican Novel, 1968–88.* Austin: University of Texas Press, 1992. Print.

Teichmann, Reinhard. *De la Onda en adelante.* Mexico: Editorial Posada, 1987. Print.

7

Cultural and Literary Ethos as Represented in García Lorca's *La casa de Bernarda Alba*

JEFFREY OXFORD

Much has been written about Federico García Lorca's *La casa de Bernarda Alba: Drama de mujeres en los pueblos de España* (1936; *The House of Bernarda Alba: Drama about Women in the Small Towns of Spain*).[1] Traditional criticism of the work has tended to address Bernarda's aggressive — some say "masculine" — personality, the play's subtitle in reference to the "realist" aspect of the work, and the drama as representative of the polarized social and political situation of the later years of Spain's Second Republic. John P. Gabriele, for example, quotes Carolyn Galerstein as viewing the play as a social and political allegory of the volatile situation in Spain in the months immediately preceding the outbreak of the Civil War (fn. 1). Roberta N. Rude and Herriet S. Turner comment that "Lorca's direction to stage the play as a photographic document points to the underlying presence of something more sinister, more metaphysical than merely the stark realism of the events" (78). Bilha Blum speaks of the realistic element of the stage settings and the social norms of the period, noting that "Lorca's Spanish audience of the 1930s, albeit urban and middle class, could easily identify [with the stage props] as reflecting the peasant population's milieu [... and] the social rules so meticulously obeyed onstage" (73–74). On the other hand, and in opposition to García Lorca's own subtitle of the work, as John Crispin points out, it can be argued also that "*La casa de Bernarda Alba* no corresponde ya a ningún pueblo identificable, ni siquiera al de ninguna región o de ningún país, porque trata, según hemos visto, de espacios y situaciones simbólicos" (183)—"*La casa de Bernarda Alba* does not correspond to any identifiable town, nor to any region or any country, because it deals with, as we have seen, symbolic spaces and situations." John Corbin notes that "*La casa de Bernarda Alba* is not a sweeping condemnation of pre-modern society; what it does is far more subtle. The play probes pre-modern cultural inconsistency and ambiguity, and sounds an alarm to a danger in pre-modern society" (727), further adding that "Repression and the struggle against it are certainly the main theme of the play" (713).

While all of these critics raise valuable points in regards to a general analysis of the work's debt to the society and emerging feminism from which it arises,[2] many of these same critics also allude to the work encompassing more than simply a realist or verisimilar reflection of the society of the day. I likewise argue that—while not denying either the veracity or importance of extant critical analyses of the drama—many fail to realize the true depth of the work in the rush to focus almost exclusively on the characters Bernarda and Adela. Indeed, it is my contention that while individual parts of García Lorca's drama are what many have already contended them to be, when one considers *La casa de Bernarda Alba* on a deeper level and as a synthetic unity, one realizes the much larger critique of the cultural ethos that the author is undertaking: specifically, nineteenth- and early twentieth-century Spain. That is, it is my belief that the dramatist is presenting the three generations of Bernarda Alba's family as representative both of the ongoing battles between the conservatives and the liberals in 1930s Spain and as a cultural study of the nascence and growth of those conflicts and three distinct cultural movements of nineteenth and early twentieth-century Spain: María Josefa (Romanticism and early to mid nineteenth-century); Bernarda (Realism/Naturalism and late nineteenth-century), and Bernarda's various daughters (Generation of 98/Surrealism or early twentieth-century). In my analysis, then, it is not just Bernarda and Adela—the two women most frequently analyzed by the critics—who are important female voices; rather, each of the female members of the family is a powerful figure speaking for the past or future and thereby further illuminating aspects of Spain's literary, cultural, and social tradition which ultimately culminate in the Spanish Civil War. In short, this present study seeks to highlight the relationship between the chronological development of more than a century of Spanish—if not Western—cultural ethos and the representation of the Bernarda Alba family as symbolic of this development; that such is undertaken through the presentation of female characters firmly plants García Lorca's work as a pivotal, iconic literary work of Spanish literature.

María Josefa

Michael Gómez notes that "As we well know from Lorca's presentation of her, María Josefa is insane" (234); interestingly, however, the critic expands on this idea of madness by explaining that "María Josefa's insanity is far more than an embarrassing 'defect.' It is, over and above this, an expression of her radical individuality" (234–35). In short, the critic aptly presents a case for María Josefa as representative of the Romantic ethos. This is further emphasized by Reed Anderson who, while not explicitly naming the Romantic movement, does exposit that "[María Josefa] is the prisoner of the household, but her words evoke a world that seems ironically remote and idealized" (125).

Romanticism, the predominant cultural movement in Spain from approximately 1833 to 1850, is based upon the basic tenet of the "culto del yo"—"worship of the self." While certainly Romanticism existed in Spain prior to the death of Fernando VII,[3] this movement's apogee in the Iberian Peninsula occurs after the death of the king and the return of those exiled under his conservative absolutism. In essence, then, Spanish Romanticism corresponds historically to the beginning of the political, social, and cultural polarization between the conservative elements of the Church, the Carlists, and the landed gentry in opposition to the more liberal elements of the progressives, the emerging middle class, and the disenfranchised lower class. As such, emotions were running high; Queen Isabel's reign suffered through several military overthrows and some sixty different governments until she herself was forced from power in the Glorious Revolution of 1868. These polarizing political ideas and ethos bled over into the cultural scene, being converted into the literary trope of starkly contrasting details and descriptions, a basic characteristic of the Romantic aesthetic.[4]

Donald L. Shaw names other major characteristics of the movement such as the work displaying "ideales libertarios [...] y el héroe con su orígen misterioso, su melancolía, su tendencia a relacionar la vida misma con el amor, y su sugeción a la fatalidad hostil" (32)—"libertarian ideals [...] and the hero with his mysterious origin, his melancholy, his tendency to relate life itself to love, and his subjugation to hostile fatality." Courtney F. Tarr speaks of:

> those peculiar traits of Spanish culture and the Spanish temper which have increasingly come to be regarded (even among Spanish critics) as esentially romantic [...]: the co-existence and clash of extremes, the persistence of medieval and national themes and attitudes, the intense individualism and resistance to rules, schools, and all forms of purely human authority, the preponderance of the popular and the spontaneously creative over the aristocratic and the critical [36].

María Josefa reflects quite strongly many of these characteristics. Disregarded as a crazy old lady by both Bernarda (García Lorca 123) and Poncia (98), she is incarcerated within the confines of the Bernarda estate. Bernarda herself shows little concern for her mother's safety or well-being, ordering a servant to keep her away from the well, not out of fear of her drowning, but out of a strong sense of the Spanish "¿Qué dirán?" ("What will others say?"): "desde aquel sitio las vecinas pueden verla desde su ventana" (108)—"from that site all the neighbors can see her from their window." Bernarda orders her mother to be quiet (124), but María Josefa refuses to submit to her caretaker's demands, saying that "No quiero ver a estas mujeres solteras rabiando por la boda, haciéndose polvo el corazón [...] Yo quiero un varón para casarme y para tener alegría" (124)—"I do not want to see these single women terribly suffering for marriage, spoiling their heart [...] I want a man to marry and to be happy." As is the case with other Romantic heroes and heroines, however, love is not to be; her heart will continue pining. In fact, she will suffer further debasement of hostile handling on the part of even her own granddaughters dragging her back to her enclosure.

On the other hand, a closer examination of María Josefa reveals that she is fiercely independent, escaping from her cloister on two occasions. The maid states that "Tuve durante el duelo que taparle varias veces la boca con un costal vacía" (109)—"I had to stuff her mouth with a bag several times during the wake." María Josefa's preponderance toward the spontaneously creative is emphasized in her later escapade when she appears with a lamb, calling it her "niño mío" (171)—"my child," and singing a lullaby. As Bárbara Mujica notes, the Romantic hero "siempre persigue su destino sin preocuparse por el 'qué dirán'" (208)—"always pursues his destiny without worrying about 'What will others say?';" María Josefa exemplifies this almost perfectly, first asking Martirio when she is going to have a child, stating that she herself has had one—indicating the lamb—and then saying that she knows that Martirio thinks she is too old to have children (173). She tells Martirio, who has intercepted her while spying on Adela late at night, "Yo quiero campo. Yo quiero casas, pero casas abiertas" (173)—"I want countryside. I want houses, but open houses," offering a romanticized positive version of the rural environment and a constant yearning for love, a better life, and what can not be. She also verbalizes a destructive goyaesque premonition of Pepe el Roman's influence over her granddaughters: "Todas lo queréis. Pero él os va a devorar" (173)—"All of you want him. But he is going to devour you all." Through the course of these exchanges, it becomes abundantly clear to the reader that María Josefa is not as crazy as the others make her out to be; in fact, the clairvoyance of her thoughts amply demonstrates that she is, in fact, reminiscent of the suffering innocent prevalent both in Romantic literature and as symbolized by the animal in her arms (Cirlot 175).

Bernarda

Harriet Turner notes that "When we think of realism in fiction, we think first of mimesis — the imitation of life" (81); that is, the desire to depict a verisimilar portrayal of everyday life is paramount to this movement. The reason for such is apparent upon an analysis of this movement's genesis and philosophical underpinnings. The title "Realism" was first used in describing painting in France, but it soon expanded to the other arts in the mid-nineteenth century. Philosophically, the movement arose as a reaction to what some would call the excesses of Romanticism — in particular, the extreme emotionalism, influence of the Gothic, and prevailing subjectivism of that period. Fortuitously, around the same time, new scientific discoveries and ideas were taking hold: Charles Darwin published his *On the Origins of Species* (1859); Auguste Comte was developing his epistemology of positivism and his "religion" of Humanism, and Hippolyte Taine was developing his interdisciplinary concept of literature as a science. Soon, second-generation Realist writers — or Naturalists — began to stretch the verisimilar portrayals of the earlier Realists into more focused calls for social reform through descriptions of the baser instincts and sordid aspects of society.

Various critics have examined the Realist aspect of the drama as a whole; my focus in this study, however, is on the characters themselves. Thus, I will simply state that, as Blum notes, "The wake ceremony at the beginning of *The House of Bernarda Alba* underscores Lorca's sense of reality, as it was certainly inspired by similar ceremonies taking place in Spain at that time" (77). I offer this brief quote from Blum since my argument is that Bernarda, as the principal character at the wake, is representative of the more "extreme" form of realism; that is, naturalism. Arising from the former movement — and, thus, demonstrating in theory a desire to replicate a believable everyday realism — naturalism has, at its core, an inclusion of, if not outright belief in, the evolutionary theories of Darwin and the deterministic restraints of *race, milieu* and *moment* of Taine's sociological positivism. Three other core characteristics of naturalism related to Bernarda include an emphasis on the harshness of life, dehumanization, and an inherent social criticism. Interestingly, Gómez notes the social criticism and naturalist undertones of *La casa de Bernarda Alba* when he says that "we must conclude [...] that Lorca's ultimate view of things here is [...] one of extreme pessimism. That is, even taking into consideration the apparently *self-* and life-affirming attitudes expressed by these characters, there is ultimately no chance for the individual to break free and to live to tell the tale" (237).

Gómez more specifically addresses the naturalist aspect of the title character when he opines that "rather than being one of those self-determining individual 'free spirits' to whom Nietzsche points in works such as his *Anti-Christ*, Bernarda is profoundly *determined* by her environment" (227). Additionally, he posits that "even considering her limited exercise of power, Bernarda is at bottom a profoundly weak individual [...] Far more likely [... is that Lorca views] her merely as a socially determined product, enslaved in the most profound sense of the word" (230). Such is noted in her imposition of eight years of mourning, following the dictates of the customs in both her father's and grandfather's houses (107) and her being convinced that her family lineage will protect her from harm while La Poncia's servitude owes itself to the less than reputable past of her mother (150). Bernarda is also predestined by her own sense of the Spanish "¿Qué dirán?" which results in her abuse of her own mother and refusal to admit, at the end of the play, that Adela has died other than a virgin (180).

In addition to Bernarda being deterministically predestined, she also quite dramatically portrays the naturalist characteristic of dehumanization. From the very beginning of the play, she is described in terms that downplay the element of human compassion, the influence of love or imagination in her life, individual freedom, or any other Romantic [or motherly] quality. As Mary Rice notes, "Bernarda is equally devoid of emotion [...] the only emotion Bernarda shows is anger" (339). One of La Poncia's first comments in the drama is that Bernarda is a "Tirana de todos los que la rodean. Es capaz de sentarse encima de tu corazón y ver cómo te mueres durante un año sin que se le cierre esa sonrisa fría que lleva en su maldita cara" (98)—"Tyrant of everybody that surrounds her. She is capable of sitting on top of your heart for an entire year watching you die without losing that cold smile off her damn face." Bernarda, after only a three-sentence explanation by La Poncia concerning the uproar she hears in the street, vociferously yells in support of stoning "antes que lleguen los guardias" (156)—"before the police arrive" the unwed mother who out of shame has killed her newborn child. And at the drama's conclusion, Bernarda, pretending to kill Pepe el Romano, is the catalyst that leads to Adela's suicide, for which Magdalena accuses her mother of being "endemoniada" (179)—"demon possessed."

This dehumanization is a frequent association with Bernarda. She asserts that "Los pobres son como los animales; parece como si estuvieran hechos de otras sustancias" (103)—"Poor people are like animals; it seems that they are made out of other substances." She dehumanizes her own mother by giving her, so María Josefa alleges, only wash water to drink and dog meat to eat (109). When the women are gathered at Bernarda's house in honor of Bernarda's now-dead husband, one neighbor comments that Bernarda has a "¡Lengua de cuchillo!" (104)—"Knife tongue!" while another whispers that Bernarda is a "¡Vieja lagarta recocida!" (104)—"Old shrivelled up lizard," to which La Poncia responds that she is "¡Sarmentosa por calentura de varón!" (104)—"Sarmentous for a man's heat," further emphasizing Bernarda's animalistic instincts. And her own mother dehumanizes her in song: "Bernarda, / cara de leoparda" (171, 172, 173)—"Bernarda, / leopard face."

Bernarda's Daughters

Bernarda's daughters represent the philosophical underpinnings of early twentieth-century Spain. As a unit, their search for identity and a meaningful future, while being hemmed up in a restraining environment bound by traditions of the past, corresponds closely to what is commonly called the second wave of the Generation of 98; i.e., the Generation of 27, or the *avant-garde*, to which García Lorca himself is often tied. As was the case with Romanticism, in this period individualism becomes the focal point of the cultural ethos, but this group is tremendously impacted by the Spanish Civil War (1936–1939) and its aftermath. García Lorca was summarily executed barely a month into the war, and almost all of the others suffered either internal or external exile. García Lorca had finished writing *La casa de Bernarda Alba* only one month before the outbreak of the war, and Galerstein notes that the drama was the author's attempt to send a message regarding the importance of individualism: "I believe it was important for Lorca to reaffirm the sanctity of the individual during a time of political chaos, a period when the experiments of the Republic were collapsing. It is as though he might be sending this message to the Republican government: 'The individual has rights, and the individual must prevail'" (188).

In a similar fashion to the political climate of Spain of that day, while all the daughters are seeking change in their situation, they have little in common other than family ties. Angustias, the oldest daughter at 39, is a half-sister to the other four but clearly not accepted by the others; in part, this owes itself to her betrothal to Pepe el Romano and because she is willed the bulk of the estate in Antonio María Benavides' testament. All the daughters — to say nothing of the conflict between the daughters and their mother — reflect quite forcefully the internecine conflicts of Spain's Second Republic and the coming Civil

War. The girls are all "progressive," wanting to break away from the mold and restraints imposed by the animalistic predestination of their mother and society, but to different degrees with Martirio (24 yrs old) who is the most inclined toward traditional conservatism. Martirio believes that fate controls and that history repeats itself (115); she is in favor of killing the girl who has, out of shame, killed her own illegitimate child (156), and she awakens Bernarda in order to keep Adela from going to meet Pepe el Romano (177). Magdalena (30 yrs old) opines that "youth was a happier time" (116) and that "all women should be strong and order the man around" (131), but she is in favor of just letting Adela disappear with Pepe el Romano or go elsewhere (178). The textual descriptions/actions of Amelia (27 yrs old) are few in quantity, but what the reader does learn is that she remonstrates her mother for talking badly about the other town women who have come to her father's wake (107), believes that "nacer mujer es el mayor castigo" (139)—"being born a woman is the greatest punishment," and is scared by the white horse in the stable (164) and by shooting stars (165). Adela (20 yrs old), the most distinct and—I argue—the representative of surrealism, will be discussed below.

García Lorca's debt to surrealism—and his friendship/collaboration with surrealists such as Salvador Dalí and Luis Buñuel—is well documented. Adriana Romano and Juana Terán state that "En los primeros meses del 26 publicó 'Oda a Salvador Dalí' en la *Revista de Occidente*, donde las imágenes utilizadas por Federico denotan su adhesión al movimiento surrealista" (22)—"In the first months of 26 he published 'Ode to Salvador Dali' in the *Revista de Occidente*, where the images utilized by Federico denote his adherence to the surrealist movement." Jacqueline Cockburn affirms that "the arrival of Cubism [...] meant most to him" (124) and "in the drawings of Lorca is the reworking of traditional genres within the context of the twentieth-century *avant-garde*" (133). And Antonio F. Cao posits that "sin el auge del surrealismo, no hubiese escrito Lorca *Poeta en Nueva York* ni su teatro irrepresentable" (67)—"without the peak of surrealism, Lorca would not have written *Poet in New York* or his unstageable theater." Admittedly, the influence of surrealism on García Lorca is most frequently observed in his poetry, but some of his drama—most notably *Así que pasen cinco años* (1931)—*Once Five Years Pass*—has received substantial critical acclaim for its surrealist character as well.

In light of such, and in spite of the lack of critical attention addressing the issue, it is logical to analyze *La casa de Bernarda Alba* with the expectation that surrealism also may play a substantial role in this drama as well. Upon closer inspection of the work, it is my contention that surrealism is, in fact, a major philosophical and artistic movement personified in the work. Stephen Little mentions major terms related to the movement as "el subconsciente, lo irracional, lo onírico, automatismo, yuxtaposición, destrucción, [y] erotismo" (118)—"the subconscious, irrational, oneiric, automatism, juxtaposition, destruction [and] eroticism." The historian further explains that "los sueños parecen reales y extraños a un tiempo, pero los surrealistas buscaban estos elementos perturbadores de la vida cotidiana como parte del proceso artístico" (118)— "dreams seem real and strange at the same time, but the surrealists sought out these disturbing elements of daily life as a part of the artistic process."

While present to a certain degree among all the daughters (note all of their desires to escape the house into the "real world" not seen beyond the confines of the home), surrealism is most clearly represented in the drama by Adela. She is the most progressive and rebellious of the daughters. Ricardo Doménech observes that "la rebeldía de Adela no sólo supone el enfrentamiento a Bernarda, sino a la sociedad entera" (194)—"Adela's rebellion not only supposes confrontation with Bernardo but with the entire society." Unlike Doménech, however, I argue that this confrontation is a destructive one: Adela grabs Bernarda's cane, breaks it in two, declaring that "¡Aquí se acabaron las voces de presidio! [...] Esto hago yo con la vara de la dominadora. No dé un paso más" (178)—"This is where the voices of imprisonment have ended! [...] This is what I do with the staff of the domineering female. Don't take another step." But the destruction is much more than simply a violent confrontation with the domineering Bernarda. Adela then immediately says she belongs to Pepe and turns to Angustias, telling her to wake up, metaphorically, and, literally, to go out to the corral to tell him so because he will dominate all of them (178). It should also be remembered that immediately prior to Adela's confrontation with Bernarda she has threatened her sister Martirio, saying "a un caballo encabritado soy capaz de poner de rodillas con la fuerza de mi dedo meñique" (176)—"I am able with the strength of my pinky finger to make a riled up horse go to its knees." Admittedly, the destruction turns inward with Adela's suicide, but this certainty is destruction as well. It should be noted that this surrealist characteristic of Adela has been foretold by both Adela and La Poncia. Adela tells Martirio that she would jump over her own mother to put out the inner fire burning within her (135), while La Poncia more emphatically prognosticates to Bernarda that a lightning bold is going to stop her heart (168) and to the maid that a storm is brewing which will sweep them all away (169).

These particular instances of violence and destruction are quite dramatic for a female in 1930s Spanish culture and literature. However, it was not a goal of the surrealist movement to demonstrate tranquil settings but to express the unseen, to "get in touch" with the order contained in the subconscious. Thus, the focus is on automatism, or on automatic responses and behaviors performed without conscious thought. Adela is — stated another way — quite the impetu-ous character who vocalizes quite rashly her inner self/reality. There is no prior indication that she is planning the breaking of her mother's cane and breakup of Angustias' marriage; she indicates, in fact, in her fight with Martirio less than two pages prior that "vamos a dejar que se case con Angustias, ya no me importa, pero yo me iré a una casita sola donde él me verá cuando quiera" (176)—"let's let [Pepe] marry Angustias; it doesn't matter any more to me, but I will go to a little solitary house where he will see me whenever he wants." On the day of her father's wake, she thoughtlessly gives her mother a flowery fan (107), in direct violation of the customs of the day. She tactlessly says that Pepe likes Angustias only for the money (147), tells Angustias that the engage-ment ring should have been diamonds (160), and impulsively hugs Martirio in an attempt to console her (155), only later to blurt out thoughtlessly to the same sister that it is not her fault that Pepe loves her instead of any of the others (176). While all of these comments are unwitting expressions of Adela's subconscious, the author also includes a reference to the eyes and thereby reveals the surrealist aspect of the play even further. As Carolin Ruwe states, "The eye is the gateway to the heart [...] the eyes can also give off information about a person's inner world: the body's macrocosm can be mirrored in the microcosm of the eye and it can reflect inner truths similar to a mirror reflecting the soul" (8). In light of this, Adela's remark that "Mirando sus ojos me parece que bebo su sangre lentamente" (136)—"Looking in his eyes, I seem to slowly drink his blood"—takes on both a greater metaphorical and aesthetic meaning.

Of course, this statement should also be considered as an expression of both Adela's irrationality and eroticism, two additional characteristics of the surrealist movement. Other examples of the irrational include her comments that the eight years of mourning for her father's death have caught her at the worst possible time (121), her desire to be invisible so that Martirio will be unable to ask her where she is going (133), and her mood swings during the heated discussion with La Poncia concerning her desire for Pepe el Romano, which swing from emphatically ordering the maid to be quiet, to crying, to mocking La Poncia's concern for Angustias, to daring her to bring four thousand flares to stop her (134–36). La Poncia makes reference to this irrationality, say-ing that Adela is acting "como si tuviese una lagartija entre los pechos" (126)— "as if she had a lizard in her breast," and Angustias says that "Se le está poniendo mirar de loca" (132)—"She's starting to get the look of a mad person," blaming it on envy. But, perhaps, the strongest example of her irrationality is her suicide, a life-ending action that serves no useful purpose or protest other than relieving her immediate, temporal loss of the object of her affection.

Carl W. Cobb notes that Adela's comments and actions can be summarized as "revealing an erotic fixation amounting to a mania" (140). This eroticism — another surrealist characteristic — is observed in various ways. The first mention of Adela in the play, in fact, is in reference to her green dress (177), which she has donned and flaunts in the hen house. Vernon A. Chamberlin notes that "green has been used and still is used *primarily* as a symbol of love and libidinuous desire" (35, emphasis in original) in Hispanic literature. After noting that this is the best dress that her sister Magdalena has ever made (120), Adela informs her sisters that she refuses to be like her sisters, that "mañana me pondré mi vestido verde y me echaré a pasear por la calle" (121) — "tomorrow I'm putting on my green dress and taking a stroll down the street." Obviously, the sexual connotation is strong since the only references to the dress are the previously mentioned flaunting of herself in the hen house, where she was pricked by the many fleas there (120). Later, she emphatically affirms that she will do what she wants with her body (132) and, to La Poncia, that "Mi cuerpo será de quien yo quiera" (133) — "My body will belong to who I want." In the same argument, La Poncia casts in Adela's face the report that "te pusiste casi desnuda con la luz encendida y la ventana abierta al pasar Pepe" (134) — "you made yourself almost totally nude with the light turned on and the window open when Pepe passed." And a final instance of Adela's obsession with eroticism — laying aside her attempt at the end of the drama to escape from her sisters and run to the corral to be with Pepe — occurs in her struggle with Martirio immediately prior to her sister awakening Bernard, when Adela proclaims that "Ya no aguanto el horror de estos techos después de haber probado el sabor de su boca" (176) — "I can not stand the horror of this house after having experienced the taste of his mouth," thereby juxtaposing her own eroticism with the repressive horrors of the Bernarda estate.

While Little indicates "juxtapositioning" as a key word for the surrealist aesthetic, Robert E. Lott further clarifies such by noting "surrealism's startling juxtaposition of incongruous and distant realities" (315). Other indications of this characteristic related to Adela include the previously mentioned green dress, Adela's "Sunday best," in which she serenades the hens and gets riddled with flea bites. She notes her own physical attributes and contrasts them with Martirio: "Si quieres te daré mis ojos, que son frescos, y mis espaldas para que te compongas la joroba que tienes" (133) — "If you want, I will give you my eyes, which are fresh, and my shoulders so that you can correct the hunchback that you have." She describes the night sky as "Tiene el cielo unas estrellas como puños" (164) — "The sky has some stars [that look] like fists." In one of the last events of the play, Adela tells the others in the house that Pepe is in the corral, "respirando como si fuera un león" (178) — "breathing as if he were a lion"; Pepe/lion thus replaces the stallion — "en el centro del corral, ¡blanco! Doble de grande, llenando todo lo oscuro" (164) — "in the middle of the corral, white! Twice as large, filling all the darkness" — that has up to this point been causing such a ruckus that Bernarda fears he will tear down the house (158). And the symbolic juxtapositioning of Adela comparing herself to Jesus Christ — "me pondré la corona de espinas que tiene las que son queridas de algún hombre casado" (176) — "I will wear the crown of thorns that the lovers of a married man have" — approaches borderline heresy in the Catholic society of Spain at the time.

In conclusion, through a careful portrayal of women characters García Lorca presents a cultural overview of the predominant literary and cultural aesthetics and ethos of nineteenth and twentieth-century Spain in his 1936 *La casa de Bernarda Alba*. María Josefa, the oldest woman imprisoned by her family who yearns for the countryside and a love not to be fulfilled, aptly represents Romanticism. Bernarda demonstrates characteristics of Naturalism, such as being deterministically predestined and dehumanized. And Adela quite remarkably reflects many aspects of Surrealism through her association with the subconscious, the irrational, automatism, destruction, and eroticism. While many critics have examined the drama from the realist aspect, and others have analyzed the socio-political aspects of Bernarda and/or the Bernarda-Adela conflict, until now none have examined the drama as a critique of the literary and cultural ethos of Spain. That such a summary of the philosophical and literary trends would be personified by women makes the drama even more of a revolutionary work and firmly plants both the drama itself as well as the women portrayed in it as pivotal, iconic elements of Spanish literature.

Notes

1. All translations in the text are mine.

2. One must take care in emphasizing that the women's movement of 1930s Spain was facing major social obstacles and not yet mature. As Mercedes Montero notes, "Durante el primer tercio del siglo XX — incluso en los años republicanos — la mujer simplemente *no contaba* en el ámbito social [...] en aquellos momentos existía una densa mentalidad social, ampliamente difundida y bastante compartida por casi todos, incluso también por los que se confesaban librepensadores, y admitida además como natural por la inmensa mayoría de las mujeres: considerar que la función esencial de la mujer eran el matrimonio, la maternidad y la educación de los hijos. (153) During the first third of the twentieth century — including in the years of the Republic — women simply *did not* count in the social arena [...] in those moments a dense social mentality, wide-spread and shared by almost everyone including as well those who professed to be free-thinkers, existed, and it was accepted moreover as natural by the immense majority of women: considering the essential function of the woman to be matrimony, maternity and the rearing of the children."

See Mercedes Montero. "Los primeros pasos hacia la igualdad: Mujer y universidad en España (1910–1936)." *Historia Crítica* 40 (2010): 148–68.

3. This should be evident in that Francisco de Goya y Lucientes, often considered the greatest Romantic artist from Spain, died in 1828 (Fernarndo VII died in 1833). Carlos Franco de Espés more specifically states that "El período romántico en España está acotado

por dos fechas: 1808 y 1874" (4)—"The Romantic period in Spain is bounded by two dates: 1808 and 1874.

    4. Consider Goya's *Disasters of War*, José de Espronceda's "Canción del pirata," Gustavo Adolfo Bécquer's "Rayo de luna," as well as many others, to cite only a few examples.

Works Cited

Anderson, Reed. *Federico García Lorca*. London: Macmillan, 1984. Print.

Blum, Bilha. "'¡Silencio, he dicho!' Space, Language, and Characterization as Agents of Social Protest in Lorca's Rural Tragedies." *Modern Drama* 48.1 (2005): 71–86. Print.

Cao, Antonio F. *Federico García Lorca y las vanguardias: Hacia el teatro*. London: Tamesis Books Limited, 1984. Print.

Chamberlin, Vernon A. "Symbolic Green: A Time-Honored Characterizing Device in Spanish Literature." *Hispania* 51.1 (1968): 29–37. Print.

Cirlot, J. E. *A Dictionary of Symbols*. Trans. Jack Sage. 2nd ed. New York: Philosophical Library, 1983. Print.

Cobb, Carl W. *Federico Garcia Lorca*. New York: Twayne, 1967. Print.

Cockburn, Jacqueline. "Learning From the Master: Lorca's Homage to Picasso." In *Fire, Blood and the Alphabet: One Hundred Years of Lorca*. Eds. Segbastian Doggart and Michael Thompson. Manchester: Manchester University Press, 2010. 123–42. Print.

Corbin, John. "Lorca's *Casa*." *Modern Language Review* 95.3 (2000): 712–27. Print.

Crispin, John. "*La casa de Bernarda Alba* dentro de la visión mítica lorquiana." In *La casa de Bernarda Alba y el teatro de García Lorca*. Ed. Ricardo Doménech. Madrid: Cátedra, 1985. 171–85. Print.

Doménech, Ricardo. "Símbolo, mito y rito en *La casa de Bernarda Alba*." In *La casa de Bernarda Alba y el teatro de García Lorca*. Ed. Ricardo Doménech. Madrid: Cátedra, 1985. 187–209. Print.

Franco de Espés, Carlos. *Así vivían en la España del Romanticismo*. Madrid: Grupo Anaya, 1994. Print.

Gabriele, John P. "Of Mothers and Freedom: Adela's Struggle for Selfhood in *La casa de Bernarda Alba*." *Symposium* 47.3 (1993): 188–99. Print.

Galerstein, Carolyn. "The Political Power of Bernarda Alba." In *Drama, Sex and Politics*. Ed. James Redmond. Cambridge: Cambridge University Press, 1985. 183–90. Print.

García Lorca, Federica. *Yerma. La casa de Bernarda Alba. Doña Rosita la soltera*. Ed. Ricardo Domenech. Madrid: Editorial Magisterio Español, 1974. Print.

Gómez, Michael A. "*La casa de Bernarda Alba*: A Nietzschean Reading." *Bulletin of Hispanic Studies* 87.2 (2010): 221–39. Print.

Little, Stephen. *...Ismos: Para entender el arte*. Madrid: Turner, 2004. Print.

Lott, Robert E. "Azorín's Experimental Period and Surrealism." *PMLA* 79.3 (1964): 305–20. Print.

Mujica, Bárbara. *Milenio. Mil años de literatura española*. New York: John Wiley and Sons, 2002. Print.

Rice, Mary. "Gender and Authority in *La casa de Bernarda Alba* and *Escuadra hacia la muerte*." In *Entre actos: Diálogos sobre teatro español entre siglos*. Eds. Martha T. Halsey and Phyllis Zatlin. University Park, PA: Estreno, 1999. 337–44. Print.

Romano, Adriana, and Juana Terán. *Federico. Antología Federico García Lorca*. Buenos Aires: Ediciones Colihue, 1999. Print.

Rude, Roberta N., and Harriet S. Turner. "The Circles and Mirrors of Women's Lives in *The House of Bernarda Alba*." *Literature in Performance: A Journal of Literary and Performing Art* 3.1 (1982): 75–82. Print.

Ruwe, Carolin. *Symbols in Stanley Kubrick's Movie "Eyes Wide Shut."* Norderstedt, Germany: Druck und Bindung, 2002. Print.

Shaw, Donald L. *Historia de la literatura española. El siglo XIX.* 10th ed. Barcelona: Editorial Ariel, 1992. Print.

Tarr, F. Courtney. "Romanticism in Spain." *Hispania* 55.1 (1940): 35–46. Print.

Turner, Harriet. "The Realist Novel." In *The Cambridge Companion to the Spanish Novel: From 1600 to the Present.* Eds. Harriet Turner and Adelaida López de Martínez. Cambridge: Cambridge University Press, 2003. 81–101. Print.

III

WOMAN AS THE PERVERSE POWERS OF RACE AND SEX

8

Blackness, Otherness, Woman(ness): Sierva María de Todos los Ángeles or the Death Throes of Colonial Cartagena

LEONORA SIMONOVIS

Sometimes people hold a core belief that is very strong. When they are presented with evidence that works against that belief, the new evidence cannot be accepted. It would create a feeling that is extremely uncomfortable, called cognitive dissonance. And because it is so important to protect the core belief, they will rationalize, ignore and even deny anything that doesn't fit in with the core belief.—Frantz Fanon. *Black Skin, White Masks*

The narrative of Gabriel García Márquez (Aracataca, Colombia 1927–) has been vastly recognized around the world as one of the most representative of magical realism. His work covers a wide range of topics and a varied array of characters that dwell in all levels of society. From the impoverished colonel who waits for a pension that never comes in *El coronel no tiene quien le escriba* (1961)—*No One Writes to the Colonel,* to several generations of Aurelianos and José Arcadios Buendía in *Cien años de soledad* (1967)—*One Hundred Years of Solitude,* to the exploration of absolute power in *El otoño del patriarca* (1975)— *The Autumn of the Patriarch,* García Márquez's work delves into the intricacies of Latin American history, politics, culture, and the interaction between the diversity of its people. Even though most of his male characters have been the focus of literary critics and scholars, his female characters also represent the author's deep understanding of the power struggles that take place in Latin

American societies and that affect each one of its members, especially those who are marginalized or excluded.

Some of the author's most remarkable female characters include Eréndira and her grandmother, from the 1978 novella "La increíble y triste historia de la cándida Eréndira y su abuela desalmada"—"The Incredible and Sad Story of Innocent Eréndira and Her Heartless Grandmother," in which 14 year old Eréndira accidentally sets fire to the house where she lives with her grandmother, and the latter forces the girl to become a prostitute. Also in *Cien años de soledad*, characters such as Amaranta Úrsula, Úrsula Iguarán, and Remedios la Bella, among others, represent the counterparts of the Buendías, as well as the oppression and lack of freedom that women experience in Macondo. In *Cien años*, as in other novels, female characters often have a secondary role which reflects the gendered disequilibrium that often pervades in masculine oriented societies.

One exception to this trait is Sierva María de Todos los Ángeles, the main character in the novel *Del amor y otros demonios* (1994)—*Of Love and Other Demons*. Sierva stands out as the main character of the novel and is constructed as a compelling and multifaceted character. In this essay, I explore Sierva María's empowerment in which beliefs, customs, and use of African languages question and undermine the norms and impositions of colonial Cartagena de Indias. She is the daughter of the Marquis de Casalduero and his second wife Bernarda Cabrera. Both characters have lost their prestige and their authority, and their property remains a ruin of the past. Since the death of Dominga de Adviento, a black slave who oversaw the household and liaised between masters and slaves, the slaves do as they please. The Marquis is assailed by his fear of a slave revolt and so he surrounds himself with guard dogs. Bernarda is addicted to cacao and honey water, and suffers from a lingering disease. Her body is bloated and she spends her days confined to her room bearing her pain and bitterness.

The decadence of the plantation and the dissipation in which the Marquis and his wife live represent the situation of the colonial system at the time: "The house had been the pride of the city until the beginning of the century. Now it was a melancholy ruin..." (García Márquez 10). It is filled with empty spaces and memories of a glorious past for which the owners seem to have no regard. The story takes place in seventeenth-century Cartagena de Indias and portrays the destruction that plagues the city, as well as the tenuous presence of Spain and the lack of control of the colonizers over their slaves. Corruption affects every level of society, including the Church, and intolerance and ignorance prevail towards non-white cultures.[1]

When Sierva María was born, her mother rejected her almost immediately. She was then nursed by Dominga de Adviento and raised in the slave quarters.

Dominga teaches Sierva all that is related to African cultures. Sierva spends most of her time with her and the other slaves, to the point where she feels uncomfortable when she has to go into the house to see her parents. As she learns African languages and customs, participates in their various rituals, and helps with the house chores, she distances herself from her biological family and the world that they represent, creating a breach between them that will never be closed.

In his book *Orality and Literacy: The Technologizing of the World*, Walter Ong focuses on the impact that the introduction of writing has had in all areas of life for oral cultures. He discusses the shift from orality to literacy and explains the difference in worldviews before and after the introduction of writing. His reflections can be connected with Sierva's upbringing among slaves who are illiterate and who rely on orality for the transmission of traditions and beliefs. Following Ong's writings, we can see that the slaves in García Márquez's novel

> learn a great deal and possess and practice great wisdom, but they do not "study." They learn by apprenticeship ... by discipleship, which is a kind of apprenticeship, by listening, by repeating what they hear, by mastering proverbs and ways of combining and recombining them, by assimilating other formulary materials, by participation in a kind of corporate retrospection [23–24].

Due to her upbringing among slaves, Sierva's perception of things is related to more concrete experiences, to rituals, dances, sound, and song, rather than books or schooling. However, this perception puts her in a contradictory situation because in spite of being a white woman, Sierva María is not accepted or seen as such by other whites. Indeed, she defines herself as African and thus she challenges her society's norms by asserting her identity and preserving her beliefs. The more time she spends with the slaves, the more she distances herself from her biological family and from others like them. Curiously enough, Sierva's mother, Bernarda, is of mixed blood — indigenous and white — so Sierva's seclusion and silences also represent those of indigenous population, even though she identifies predominantly with the Africans.

Sierva's story is a tragic one. At the beginning of the novel she accompanies a female slave to the market and they cross over into a slave neighborhood where a rabid dog bites her. The bite triggers a series of events that lead to Sierva's seclusion in the convent of Santa Clara, where she will be exorcised and will eventually die. When she returns home after being bitten, the slaves treat the wound and leave it to close on its own. They do not believe anything will happen to Sierva, so they do not tell her parents, but soon the Marquis finds out when a healer offers to "cure" the girl and make some profit out of it. The Marquis, guilt-ridden for the abandonment that he has subjected Sierva to and thinking that she will soon die, has the healer and others treat her, although she is not sick. The treatments are harsh and Sierva's health declines, making the Marquis more concerned and protective. He dedicates every minute of his life to her, taking her to puppet shows and attractions in the city, where "Sierva María learned more about white people's ways that she had ever before" (49). He opens up a space for her inside the house, which she refuses to occupy for a while, and so the Marquis brings a female slave inside to be with her at all times. He has to relent and accept some of Sierva's ways, in order to be able to get close to her. The narrator describes him as a "different man" and it is implied that Sierva's presence in his life and his newfound love for her have brought this change about.

Of Love and Other Demons delves into the conflict that, according to Margaret Olsen, arises from the "infiltration" of oral African cultures and customs into colonial society. Olsen argues that the Marquis' house represents colonial society, and that his fear of an invasion or a rebellion can translate to the rest of the white population (1071). The two groups that interact in the novel — Africans and whites — communicate at different levels since what they consider valuable knowledge greatly differs from one to the other. In this regard, Laura Rendón establishes a difference between wisdom and knowledge and, although she primarily talks about this distinction in the context of pedagogy, this difference can be applied to the conflicts of interests present in the novel. Rendón compares the ways of learning of indigenous groups to that of Western culture and explains that they are not mutually exclusive but complementary: "ancient wisdom and spiritual traditions articulate a different truth, an epistemology not based on separation but on wholeness, ... not on the polarization of faith and reason but on the unitive nature of science and the divine" (67). In the novel, this polarization is evident in the way that the members of the Church, as well as plantation owners, disregard African beliefs because they consider them superstitious and primitive. Sierva María's character represents a failed attempt to integrate African culture into colonial society.

The opposition between ancient/oral traditions and modern/"lettered" societies carries within it implications about the marginalization of African culture, as well as the stereotypes associated with this ethnic group. For instance, Sierva lies to her parents because it amuses her and because she can manipulate situations to her advantage. For her, lying is part of a game, but her mother attributes this behavior to the fact that she spends more times with slaves who, according to her, lie by nature. This type of assumption is similar to the description of indigenous people in some colonial accounts, where they are portrayed as deceiving and cunning. *Of Love and Other Demons* problematizes the relationship between the two cultures by juxtaposing their beliefs and showing both sides of the equation. The novel invites the reader to reflect on the nature of the conflict and its consequences for all of the characters, since Sierva is not the only one who is affected.

For Olsen, Sierva is a free person because she does not dwell in an in-between world. She considers herself African in spite of her whiteness and even adopts the African name of María Mandinga: "La identidad racial se construye desde adentro y desde afuera y Sierva María/María Mandinga fabrica la suya como negra africana" (1073) — "Racial identity is constructed from within and from without and thus Sierva María/María Mandinga identifies her identity as African."[2]

The critic mentions how the rabid dog bit five people, four of which are slaves and then Sierva, who lives among them; that is, within the narration, Sierva is constructed as part of the African world. When the slaves are cele-brating Sierva's twelfth birthday, with drums and dances and song, the narrator explains that in "that oppressive world where no one was free, Sierva María was: she alone. And so that was where her birthday was celebrated, in her true home and with her true family" (12). Since the Marquis and Bernarda are care-less about the whereabouts of the slaves, they can celebrate their rituals, tra-ditions, and feasts without anyone interfering. The slaves are Sierva's only family and they accept her for who she is because she has grown among them and shares their customs and beliefs: "She could dance with more grace and fire than the Africans, sing in voices different from her own in the various lan-guages of Africa, agitate the birds and animals when she imitated their voices" (12).

Sierva behaves like the slaves, but her whiteness and social position allow her the freedom that slaves cannot have. Her freedom is twofold, however, in the sense that it also comes from the fact that she does not yield to white soci-ety's norms, traditions or religious beliefs. As Olsen affirms, "empieza ya en *Del amor y otros demonios* una trasferencia de poder a sectores que no son mas-culinos, ni europeos ni criollos" — "*Of Love and Other Demons* empowers char-acters who are neither masculine, nor European, or creole" (1071). This strategy counteracts the predominant ideology of colonial society and its representa-tives.

Unlike Dominga, who serves as a bridge between white and African cul-ture and who has converted to Catholicism while still maintaining her Yoruban beliefs, Sierva is not interested in serving as a translator/communicator between the slaves and her parents, neither is she curious about their world ways. In fact, when her father hires a tutor for her, she refuses to learn because reading and writing are difficult and do not hold her attention. Going out with the Marquis is a mere entertainment, but she knows that she does not belong with him. She prefers to spend time with slaves because she is heard, respected, and included; besides, she does not feel at home among the whites that try to contain her.

Like Olsen, other critics such as Eugenia Muñoz and Diógenes Fajardo speak of the racial aspect of Sierva María from different perspectives, underlining the fact that her character constitutes a challenge to the norms and regulations of colonial society. She is constructed as a signifier of the obliteration of African heritage in Colombia in particular and in Latin America in general. Sierva is a free African woman and this implies a complexity that is unique in García Márquez's work. In this sense it is important to explore Sierva's character from the intersections between gender, race, and class that her character embodies, since, as Moya Lloyd states, "racial, class, gender, sexual orientation and gender divisions traverse contemporary cultural and socio-political formations multiplying *across* and *through* one another in a host of elaborate ways in ways that affect everyone (45; author's emphasis).

Sierva's womanhood differs notably from that of white women because she does not have the same constraints. She does not have to deal with the taboos imposed by colonial society; this explains why at the end of the novel she asks Cayetano Delaura, the priest in charge of studying her case and with whom she falls in love, to run away with her and live among other slaves. Sierva has an awareness of her body and her sexuality that is related to her connection with the practical aspects of life. The notion of privacy is not one that she is familiar with, since she used to sleep in the slave quarters with other women. This particular world vision is considered objectionable, so most white people who come in contact with Sierva immediately express their prejudice by staying away from her, creating distance and preserving their own space, as if she would contaminate them just by her proximity. What Olsen refers to as the "interference" of the slaves in the Marquis' house could also apply to the way that whites perceive blacks; their communal ways destabilize the white customs that permeate their society.

Throughout the novel, the different characters related to Sierva, or who come in contact with her, speak about women's secondary role in colonial society. If they transgress the norm, they will be punished. For instance, when the Marquis decides to take care of Sierva and assume his paternity and she protests and refuses, he insists until she yields because "he had to make her understand that a masculine order governed the world" (García Márquez 25). Also, when the reader learns about the story of Dulce Olivia, the Marquis' first and only love, the narrator explains the class differences between these two characters, as well as the fact that Olivia had learned the art of saddle-making from her father because she was an only child, and the family did not want the tradition to die. However, Olivia ends up in an asylum after becoming mentally ill, and the narrator informs the reader that, "So unusual an incursion into a man's trade was the explanation given for her losing her reason" (34). Thus, by learning a masculine trade and making a living for her family and herself, Olivia goes against the norms imposed by her society and must pay a price.

Sierva María, however, is somewhat isolated from this worldview. For all purposes, as well as for herself, she is African and the same rules that apply to women such as Olivia do not apply to her. When she is born, she almost dies, but Dominga de Adviento prays to her saints and the girl is saved. Sierva is baptized both in the Christian and the Yoruba religions, and the narrator says that "she learned to dance before she could speak, learned three African languages at the same time, learned to drink rooster's blood before breakfast and to glide past Christians unseen and unheard, like an incorporeal being" (42). This "invisibility" is an integral part of her growing up with slaves who had to submit to their owners and become unseen and unheard so as to not disturb them. Sierva learns to be inconspicuous; as a result, others usually overlook her. While this behavior is advantageous for her, in the sense that she can come and go as she pleases, it turns against her in Santa Clara. When the nuns do not see her as they pass her by, rather than confessing to their own lack of attention, they claim that Sierva can become invisible, and that her invisibility derives from her connection to the devil.

Sierva belongs to another culture that is feared for various reasons (slave revolts and whites' fears of them taking over the colony, racial intermixing, religious beliefs, etc.), as well as her disregard for the scientific/written knowledge that in colonial society is reserved for men. Sierva is not used to these hierarchies since in her community everyone — including the very young — has access to learning the traditions, stories, and ways of living so that they, in turn, can teach others. Most white people fear her because she refuses to communicate with them in their own language, and instead either speaks African languages or remains completely silent. For example, the representatives of the Church perceive this as a transgression of the norm, and it translates into Sierva being seen as "otherworldly," but not in a positive way. To Bishop de Cáceres and the nuns of Santa Clara, Sierva's behavior is a result of her being possessed by demons.

Nonetheless, Sierva does not relent, even when she faces death. At first she does not understand why she has been put in a cell, isolated from everyone else and with barely any food or water. When she was brought to the convent, she was left alone for a few moments and was "unseen" by the Abbess and other nuns who passed her by. After being seated there for a long time, two slaves find her and take her to the kitchen, where she is delighted to be in a familiar environment: "She had recovered her world" (65). When the Abbess finds her, she is singing, surrounded by slaves. The Abbess confronts her with a crucifix, accusing her of becoming invisible on purpose to confound them. The nuns take Sierva away while she fights with hands and feet until finally, exhausted and scared, she relents.

In spite of her fear while in the convent of Santa Clara, Sierva still preserves some of her playfulness and creativity, attributes and skills that help her survive in the hostile environment of Santa Clara. One of the things that she loves is to manipulate situations to her advantage for her own entertainment. She understands that in order to survive and get others to leave her alone, she needs to create defense mechanisms that confuse and scare others. In this way, she can safeguard her own freedom.

Imagination, Gender, and Power

Diógenes Fajardo discusses the fact that Sierva has the ability "de imaginar, de jugar a crear verdad con las palabras" (103) — "to imagine, to play at inventing the truth with words." He states that Sierva María is not the only one who possesses this ability, since it is also common to many African cultures: "Es la manera de 'significar' el deseo por medio del lenguaje" (104) — "It is the way to signify 'desire' through language" (my translation). Sierva gives others the power to imagine the unimaginable and with this she frees them — metaphorically speaking — from their own "demons." Hence, this ability is often misunderstood because it is perceived from a Western perspective in which, as Trihn T. Mihn-Ha states in *Woman, Native, Other*: "Imagination is thus equated with falsification" (121). Because Sierva has a vivid imagination, she is accused of being a liar. However, if we consider Mihn-Ha's accounts of female storytellers and the threat they represented for civilization, we can better understand the interactions of the characters in García Márquez's novel. Mihn-Ha explains that in many parts of the world, most storytellers were women and their words carried a powerful message that would remain for many generations. However, these stories have been misrepresented and re-defined by Western culture as superstitious, untrue, or children's tales, thus diminishing their value in contrast with scientific/true/civilized discourse. But there is also a power struggle within the containment of storytellers which excludes and marginalizes women because their words and their influence represent a threat for the male establishment (129).

For Mihn-Ha, storytelling is not only a way to build "historical consciousness" in community, but also a means to awaken parts of the human

being that are dormant. It is inclusive in the sense that it requires the participation of every member of a community, and it also carries a truth that is not
necessarily factual, but that represents something valuable for the community
and for the storyteller. Mihn-Ha gives an example of a woman who, after her
grandmother dies, continues the story that the grandmother had started. In
the story, a man kills the grandmother's parents and so the granddaughter
brings closing to the story by killing the man and avenging her relatives. But
she does not kill him with her own hands, she just sets the story in motion
until everything falls in place and he dies. In the story, she goes to jail and
confesses to having poisoned this man because that is the way he is supposed
to die in the story. But the lawyer does not believe her and thinks that she is
delusional because the man fell in the ice and died. In the end the woman is
allowed to return to her people, but the lack of communication between her
and the lawyer remains as a unresolved conflict (144, 148).

This story vividly represents the clashes of two people from two different
cultures and worldviews who cannot either communicate with each other or
come to an agreement. The woman and the lawyer each have their own truth,
and the lawyer refuses to see the truth in the woman's story. In *Of Love and
Other Demons*, Sierva seems to always be lying to whites, but she is not necessarily lying. She is telling her own truth as she has been taught by the community that raised her. She also tells stories to others, especially while she is
in the convent, and triggers their imagination, fulfilling their desire of encoun-
tering demons and of experiencing first hand their pranks, even though they
will not admit it.

In one instance, Martina, another prisoner who was accused of murder
and is planning to escape, asks Sierva if she truly has experience dealing with
demons. Sierva says that she does, she names several demons and when Martina
shows interest for one of them, she promises "to inform her of his next visit
so she could meet with him." The narrator says that Sierva "took delight in
the deception" (120). In fact, while at Santa Clara, Sierva does not try to defend
herself, except when they try to take away her Yoruba necklaces, but rather
accepts the charges and constantly affirms that she has the devil inside or that
she is possessed by a demon. In this way, she becomes part of the deception
that others are playing and creates her own story. In Ong's words: "The fact
that oral peoples commonly and in all likelihood universally consider words
to have magical potency is clearly tied in, at least unconsciously, with their
sense of the word as necessarily spoken, sounded, and hence power-driven"
(47). Thus, Sierva creates her own stories using the words of others and this
empowers her, because she is able to influence their imagination so that they
also become a part of the story without realizing it.

When Martina finally escapes the confinement of Santa Clara, she leaves Sierva a note saying that she will be praying for her happiness with Cayetano. The search that the abbess and the guards conduct in the convent proves futile and so the abbess decides to interrogate Sierva María. When the abbess accuses her of having helped Martina and tries to strike her, Sierva stops her saying "I saw them leave." The abbess asked, surprised "She was not alone?" to which Sierva replies, "There were six of them" and then "They had bat's wings ... they spread them on the terrace, and then they carried her away, flying, to the other side of the ocean" (143).

Even though Sierva's story does not seem plausible — Martina has escaped through the sewers and the abbess knows it — the abbess still believes it because of her supposed contacts with demons. This scene can be connected to the epigraph at the beginning of the essay, since the "core" beliefs of the abbess and those who surround her are so deeply-rooted that they refuse to accept anything different, and so they describe Sierva's behavior in their own terms. The difference between truth and fact speaks volumes about the clashes that take place between the two cultures. While Sierva is creating an explanation for the disappearance of Martina as she has been taught to do since she was very small, the abbess and the other nuns and guards who are looking for Martina only see what they want to see. Since Sierva is speaking in their own language but conveying the truth through her worldview, they cannot understand that what she is saying is not literal and that it does not refer to the concrete facts of Martina's escape.

Sierva comes from an oral tradition that is rejected by the colonial elite because of prejudice, racism, and also because of the inner workings and power relations within the political system. However, it is that same tradition that corroborates the stories that the whites invent to condemn her, and that confirm their ignorance and lack of understanding of the "other" culture. Sierva's deceitfulness becomes a defense mechanism that helps her survive her fear of death and her loneliness, as well as the intolerance of others. Her attitude is, for the most part, one of defiance. She is usually in charge of the different situations she is in and she rebels against the oppressive system represented by her family and by the Church. When her father brings her to the house and starts to help undress her, the narrator says, "She allowed herself to be laid down on the bed, she allowed her head to be settled on the pillows, she allowed herself to be covered to the knees..." (27), and at the same time she is doing this, she does not look at her father or respond to his inquiries. The fact that the narrator uses the word "allows" is very significant, because, in spite of the fact that she is a woman child and that her father truly believes in the superiority of men, she lets him believe that he is the one in control of the situation when in reality he is not. In fact, the following day, when he comes in to check on her, he finds her gone and realizes she returned to the slave quarters. Her unmanageability has less to do with the fact that she is a twelve-year-old child than with the fact that she is a free black woman and, as such, she will neither acknowledge, nor obey the rules of the white man who wants to deny her freedom.

Sierva's silences and language games are also a way to counteract the influence of the dominant culture. Mihn-Ha notes that "language is one of the most complex forms of subjugation, being at the same time the locus of power and unconscious servility" (52). Accordingly, Sierva refuses to speak Spanish when people ask her questions. She either remains silent, gestures, or speaks the African languages she learned as a child. This causes a strong reaction on the part of the listener, who associates those languages with an/other who represents a threat to the dominant system. This system needs to maintain its hierarchical divisions because they are "a tool of self-defense and conquest" (Mihn-Ha 82). But since the rules do not apply to all in the same way, Sierva cannot be punished for speaking other languages because she is white. She can, however, be taken by the church, whose members willingly testify against her interactions with demons because, by obliterating her presence, they can return to the pre-existing order. Her threat stems from the fact that she has rattled the established hierarchies, and has both found a way to free herself from the dominant culture, and to counteract its effects.

In the same order of ideas, Mihn-Ha discusses the difference between the First and the Third World, asserting the fact that the concept of "Third World" can be conceived in a negative way — underdeveloped, or positive — as a subversive force (97). She argues that, depending on who utters the word, it can carry different connotations. For instance, when westerners refer to the "Third World" it means something different than when a member of the Third World alludes to it. This can apply to García Márquez's novel, in the sense that the colonial elite and the Church are the ones who yield economic and political power, and thus they establish social hierarchies. By identifying herself as African, even though she belongs to the "underdeveloped" part of her world — the part which has being denied freedom, a voice, and equal participation — Sierva's perspective is subversive and her actions undermine the traditions and beliefs of the colonial mindset because she represents the existing diversity in the colonial world that the whites have tried to ignore.

The confrontation between Third and First World or between the colonizer and the colonized is also what Frantz Fanon discusses in his book *Black Skin, White Masks*. In the epigraph cited at the beginning of this essay, the author reflects on the deeply rooted beliefs that lead to intolerance and oppression, as well as to miscommunications and misunderstandings among people of different races and cultures. Fanon also reflects on the importance of language for understanding black culture in the sense that "to speak is to exist absolutely for the other" (1). He refers to the fact that to adopt a language and use its syntax is to assume a certain culture and to bear "the weight of a civilization" (2). Language is used to define and express the world around us, and so by speaking the language of another, the colonized subject has to express him/herself in words that are not his own. S/he constructs his/her identities in relation to the "civilized" world, and thus has to find a space and a voice within that world. But this is not possible, because the words and even the world that those words describe do not correspond to the way of life that preceded colonization.

Fanon's reflections on language and colonization resonate with Sierva María's character, because of her (initial) refusal to speak the language of whites. For her — even though she cannot think in these terms — language is also a matter of identity; if she agreed to abandon the African languages and speak Spanish, she would assume a different identity that would come in conflict with her upbringing and beliefs. She would have to re-define herself and give up her freedom and her voice. Therefore, she only speaks in African languages or remains silent, and when she uses Spanish, she does so in her own terms, inventing the stories that she so much enjoys because of their capacity to make others react strongly and to cause fear and awe. By asserting her blackness, Sierva carves a space for those who have been forgotten, neglected, and marginalized. As a black woman, she poses a challenge to a moribund system that responds by annihilating any type of defiance. But, at the end of the novel, Sierva's long hair — which keeps growing after she dies — remains as a signifier of her resistance, as well as of the myriad of possibilities for change and legitimization of peripheral subjects.

Notes

1. Margaret M. Olsen affirms that the historical moment in which the novel takes place is essential to understand the topics of decadence, *mestizaje*, and repression that she talks about in her essay (1067). However, Diógenes Fajardo insists that the plot of the novel takes place in the seventeenth-century because of certain historical facts that took place during that time period, such as the importance of Compañía Gaditana de Negros, which was historically in charge of transporting slaves to Cartagena, and which is mentioned at the beginning of the novel. Also, Fajardo talks about the flour trade and the profits it brought for the colony. He mentions that the Marquesa de Valdehoyos was given a license to introduce slaves in the market, along with two barrels of flour per slave, so that she could sell it. Fajardo quotes Julio Ortega, who believes that the Bernarda character is a fictional representation of the Marquesa (92).
2. This and all subsequent translations from Olsen's article are mine.

Works Cited

Fajardo V., Diógenes. "El mundo africano en Del amor y otros demonios." In *XX Congreso Nacional de Literatura, Lingüística y Semiótica: Cien años de soledad treinta años después: Memorias.* Bogotá, Colombia: Instituto Caro y Cuervo; Universidad Nacional de Colombia, 1998. MLA International Bibliography. EBSCO. Web. 21 Apr. 2011. Print.

Fanon, Frantz. *Black Skin, White Masks.* Trans. Richard Philcox. New York: Grove Press, 2008. Print.

García Márquez, Gabriel. *Del amor y otros demonios.* New York: Penguin, 1994. Print.

_____. *Of Love and Other Demons.* Trans. Edith Grossman. New York: Alfred A. Knopff, 1995. Print.

Lloyd, Moya. *Beyond Identity Politics: feminism, power, and politics.* London: Sage Publications, 2005. Print.

Mihn-Ha, Trihn T. *Woman, Native, Other.* Bloomington: Indiana University Press, 1989. Print.

Muñoz, Eugenia. "La verdad en un caso de segregación e hibridación cultural en *Del amor y otros demonios* de Gabriel García Márquez." In *Apuntes sobre literatura colombiana.* Comp. Carmenza Kline. Bogotá: Ceiba Editores, 1997. 95–107. Print.

Olsen, Margaret M. "La patología de la africanía en *Del amor y otros demonios* de García Márquez." *Revista Iberoamericana* 68.201 (2002): 1067–1080. MLA International Bibliography. EBSCO. Web. 21 Apr. 2011.

Ong, Walter J. *Orality and Literacy: The Technologizing of the Word.* New York: Routledge, 1982. ebrary collections. 15 Apr. 2011. Web.

Rendón, Laura. *Sentipensante (Sensing/Thinking) Pedagogy: Educating for Wholeness, Social Justice, and Liberation.* Sterling, VA: Stylus Publishing, 2009. Print.

9

Gabriela, or
Freedom Versus Marriage

LINDA LEDFORD-MILLER

Jorge Amado (1912–2001) is Brazil's best known and most popular novelist. His works have been translated to dozens of languages and some have been made into feature films and television series.[1] Born on a cacao farm in Bahia, he moved with his family to Ilhéus when only a year old, and he published his first novel at the age of eighteen (*O País do Carnaval*, 1931; *Carnival Country*). He set his early, leftist-leaning works in the *cacao*, or chocolate, plantations of his home state of Bahia, and demonstrated an often grim realism in telling the fictionalized history of a region where the fiercest "colonel" with the most hired guns claimed the most land and controlled the most people.[2] The publication of *Gabriela, Cravo e Canela, Crônica de uma cidade do interior* in 1958, published in English as *Gabriela, Clove and Cinnamon* in 1962, signaled a shift in Amado's writing, not away from the cacao region, or from concerns for the poor of Bahia, but rather towards a more humorous, light-hearted approach to some of the same issues.

Gabriela is the first of a trio of novels placed firmly in the Afro-Brazilian culture of Bahia, and with protagonists who are women of color. Edna Carlos de A. Holanda writes that "[d]entro da problemática do romance moderno brasileiro, Gabriela toma assento no mundo ficcional ao lado de Iracema, Senhora, A Escrava Isaura, Capitu, Conceição e muitos outros mitos que a ficção brasileira criou ao longo dos tempos"—"[w]ithin the problematic of the modern Brazilian novel, Gabriela takes her place in the ficcional world besides Iracema, Senhora, the Slave Isaura, Capitu, Conceição and many other myths that Brazilian fiction created over time."[3] Amado followed *Gabriela* (1958) with

129

Dona Flor e seus dois maridos (1966) translated as *Dona Flor and Her Two Husbands: A Moral and Amorous Tale* (1969), and *Tenda dos Milagres* (1969) — *Tent of Miracles* (1971). Though different in plot and themes, the three novels argue that miscegenation, or racial mixing, is both the solution to racial tensions and eventually the key to Brazilian identity. In the process, the three novels reveal Amado's deep love of syncretic Bahian culture, including its spicy food based on a fusion of African and Portuguese influences.

This approach to an understanding of Brazilian identity as the product of miscegenation was first proposed by the sociologist Gilberto Freyre.[4] Even though at present there are many critics of this idea, it is still considered one of the best ways to understand the peculiar traits of Brazilian culture. In this context, the fact that Gabriela's name is followed by the names of two spices is significant. Clove and cinnamon suggest, immediately, that she may be the color of these spices (dark skinned). In addition, since both cloves and cinnamon are used in traditional Brazilian sweets, "clove and cinnamon" may mean that she is sweet and smells like these two spices. Gabriela thus embodies, in these two epithets, aspects that have for a long time been associated with women: a sensuous aspect related to nature.[5]

However, *Gabriela's* Portuguese title also contains a sub-title omitted in the English translation: "Chronicle of a City of the Interior."[6] As the original title suggests, the novel tells two interwoven stories: the tale of the city of Ilhéus over the period of a year, beginning in 1925, and the tale of Gabriela, an immigrant from the impoverished, drought-stricken backlands to the coastal town of Ilhéus. That is, the novel will present two possibly antagonistic realms: "nature," embodied in the woman Gabriela, and "culture," represented by the small town of Ilhéus, in the state of Bahia.

The Tale of a Changing Town

At the time of the story of *Gabriela*, Ilhéus was a just small coastal city in the northeastern state of Bahia. Bahia itself is far away from the political centers of Brazil, traditionally located in Rio de Janeiro and São Paulo. But Bahia has a very important place in the history of the country, because its soil and climate were ideal for one of the first crops of the then Portuguese colony: sugar. First established in the region in the sixteenth century, the sugar plantations were the economic engine of the region and, therefore, for the whole colony. To provide cheap labor to move the plantations, Brazil became a major importer of African slaves, receiving three to four million people. Salvador, the capital of Bahia, was the port of entry for half of these individuals.[7]

Competition from sugar plantations in the British and French Caribbean led to a marked decline in sugar exports. In 1881, planters introduced cacao to the region, where the trees flourished. With the decline of the sugar plantations, workers and former slaves rushed to the area seeking work, mostly in the fields; for men with excellent marksmanship, adequate courage, and not too much concern for human life, the available employment was as hired guns.[8] Cacao was called "white gold," and the rush to take possession of more and more land, was very like the Gold Rush or the cattle wars of the West in the United States. Lawlessness and violence were rampant; the "colonels" took what they wanted by force, intimidation, ambush, and assassination of their opposition. Colonels controlled everything and everyone in their domain, from workers to wives and children, to local townspeople and local elections. Colonels banded together to achieve mutually advantageous goals and loyalty was paramount to survival. Amado's early novels, *Cacau* and *Terras do sem fim* (1943) — *The Violent Land* (1945)[9] take place in this context and focus on "the abuses brought about by the traditional land-tenure system of the Brazilian interior [and] view society in terms of social classes" (Bobby Chamberlain, 1990: 17).

As *Gabriela* opens, even though the violent cacao wars are over, the colonel system of power and control remains intact.[10] But Ilhéus begins to feel the winds of change. A newcomer to town from Rio de Janeiro, seat of urbanity in all respects, Mundinho Falcão arrives bringing new ideas: he wants to dredge the shallow bay of Ilhéus so plantation owners can load their cacao directly onto large transport ships rather than paying fees to send it to the deeper port of the city of Bahia. As Mundinho returns home from a visit to Rio, Gabriela is also on her way to town after a long trek. These two characters will forever change many lives in Ilhéus, and each in her or his own way brings progress to the town and the people.

In terms of the history of philosophical and political ideas that were extremely important for the development of a national ideology, and especially taking in consideration the time the novel takes place, it is important to remember that the tenets of Comtean Positivism held sway in Brazil for a long time.[11] All of the intellectuals who took part in the movement to establish a Republic were one way or the other involved in philosophical and political discussions using the French philosopher's idea. As a matter of fact, the Brazilian flag, approved after the 1889 proclamation of the Republic, to this day contains the positivistic motto "Order and Progress." Order, in this case, means stamping out everything that is backward, not "pure," not intellectual. Gabriela, the woman of dark skin (mixed, "impure" race), reminding every one of the smells of nature (clove and cinnamon), coming into a town (urban environment, opposed to nature), provides the space for the discussion of these matters.

Only, this time, Jorge Amado makes the story humorous and even satirical, and it is clear where his allegiance rests.

In the course of a year, the townspeople of Ilhéus confront modernity. Colonel Ramiro Bastos has been running the town for decades, improving the city with parks and sidewalks, but resisting more modern ideas, such as the new highway and the new bus system between towns. He is even more resistant to Mundinho Falcão and his notion of dredging the harbor to create safe passage for large ships. Mundinho is not to be stopped: he not only fulfills his pledge to bring an engineer from Rio to do the work, but he also heads the first real opposition to Ramiro, gradually gaining even some of Ramiro's most loyal supporters.[12] In spite of his resistance, Ramiro and Ilhéus get an improved harbor; Mundinho, on his turn, wins the senate seat. The city seems to be facing a fine future, and it can boast the opening of its first restaurant, Mr. Nacib Saad's "Commercial Association," where Gabriela is the cook.

Gabriela, or How a Simple *Mulata* Cook Changes Everything, Except Herself

Though the title of the novel is *Gabriela*, and Gabriela is indeed an essential protagonist, the novel is divided into Part One and Part Two, with each part containing two chapters, and each chapter named for a different woman, the "four heroines of Ilhéus" (Richard Mazzara 551). Each chapter also begins with a song that serves as an epigraph, or a road map, to the content of the chapter, closely related to the name and fate of a woman: "Ofenísia," "Glória," "Malvina," and "Gabriela."[13] Each of these women represents a particular view of and role for women in the society of the time. Gabriela first enters the novel near the end of chapter one, but her position as head of the last of four chapters shows that she serves as a catalyst for change and embodies new possibilities for women. As Constância Lima Duarte notes:

> ao mesmo tempo em que endossa estereótipos—da donzela romântica e da mulata assanhada ... [Amado] aponta para um mundo em tranformação no que se refere às relações homem e mulher. No romance de Amado, temos ... uma amostra de como a mulher passa de objeto a sujeito da própria história, e também do proceso cultural da construção de gênero [167].

> At the same time that he endorses stereotypes — the romantic damsel and the promiscuous mulata ... [Amado] points toward a world in transformation regarding male-female relations. In Amado's novel we have a demonstration of how woman moves from object to subject of her own story, and also of the cultural process of the construction of gender.[14]

But the fact that the novel is built upon these four feminine pillars indicates that Amado wants to review the history of women and propose a model, which in this case is embodied in Gabriela.

The first "heroine," Ofenísia Ávila, a woman of a well-to-do Ilhean family, sees the Emperor Dom Pedro II pass by and falls in love with him. She longs to become his concubine, something that would dishonor the family and, according to custom, would give her brother the right to kill her; Ofenísia says she will "morrer de langor" (14)—die of languor (4). The legend of Ofenísia runs like a thread through the novel, tying together the "Foreword" (in which Colonel Jesuíno Mendoça finds his wife Dona Sinhàzinha in bed with her lover, Dr. Osmundo Pimentel) with the "Postscript." Following "the cruel law" of the time, Jesuíno shoots and kills his wife and her lover to avenge the infidelity and regain his honor as a man. Dona Sinhazinha is a distant relative of Ofenísia, hence perhaps has in her veins the taint of tragedy. The towns-people discuss the Dona Sinhazinha case intermittently throughout the narra-tive, and only in the postscript is the case settled.

The second "heroine" is Gloria, the concubine of the elderly Colonel Coriolano Ribeiro, who installs her in a house whose window overlooks the main square. While Ofenísia wanted to be mistress to the Emperor out of love, Gloria becomes a mistress to a wealthy plantation owner because of the money and the material comfort he provides, but she laments the lack of love and pas-sion in her life. Gloria's role is an accepted one in Ilhéus, where women from good families must be virgins in order to marry, and once married they lead very circumscribed lives dedicated to exclusively to their home and their hus-bands. Men, in contrast, lead public lives, which include frequenting bars and brothels, availing themselves of the "public utility" of their mistresses, or *rapari-gas*, if they are wealthy men. If they are men of more modest means they fre-quent the town prostitutes, while their wives and daughters lead private lives, restricted to the home and the Church (Chamberlain 1990: 42). After all, "o lar é a Fortaleza da muher virtuosa" (105)—"the home is the fortress of the vir-tuous woman" (*Gabriela* 115).

The third "heroine," Malvina, is the daughter of the powerful Colonel Melk Tavares, who wants her to follow local customs, marry the man he chooses for her (a choice made based on political advantage or economic concerns rather than love), take care of house and family, and attend mass. He tells her: "Não quero filha doutora: Vai pro colégio das freiras, aprender a costurar, contar e ler, gastar seu piano. Não precisas de mais. Mulher que se mete a doutora é mulher descarada, que quer se perder" (217)—I don't want my daugh-ter to be a scholar. You will attend the parochial school, learn to sew, to figure and read, and to play the piano. That's all you need. No decent woman would set herself up as a scholar; it's an invitation to men to take liberties (252). But Malvina has observed her mother's life of abject submission, a prisoner in her own house, a frightened servant to a tyrant husband, so she wants none of such a life. She plans an escape with the engineer who is in town to study the bay, but when Melk threatens him and the engineer runs away without saying good-bye, "Dava-se conta Malvina do erro cometido: para sair dali só vira um cam-inho, apoiada no braço de um homem, marido ou amante" (220) — "Malvina saw clearly the mistake she had made in thinking that the only way to get away was on the arm of a man" (256). When the school year ends at the Sisters of Mercy parochial school in Bahia, Malvina does not return to Ilhéus. She dis-appears and only months later her family discovers that she is living alone in São Paulo, working in an office and studying at night — a clear infraction of the Ilhean code of behavior for women. Her behavior is considered so scan-dalous that her father denies her existence. "Não tenho mais filha!" — "I have no daughter," says Melk, but her mother's reaction is different: "A mãe reviveu, mas nunca mais sairia de casa" (292) — "her mother took a new lease on life, but never left the house after that" (345).

Into this conservative, traditional environment comes Gabriela, a child of the backlands. She has traveled a long way with a group of migrants fleeing their barren homeland shriveled from lack of rain; to make things worse, her uncle died of consumption on the way, leaving her an orphan. She initiates a sexual alliance with a fellow migrant, Clemente, who falls in love with her and assumes that she will now be his. He professes his love and his desire to stay with her, but Gabriela tells him to go his own way and simply says, "Foi bom a genter ter se encontrado, a viagem encurtou" (88) — "I'm glad we met: it made the trip shorter"(95). Unlike other women, Gabriela does not seem to depend on men for her survival.

In Ilhéus, the migrants' camp is located near the "slave market," once used for the sale of slaves and now the place where workers wait to be hired by plantation owners. Nacib Saad, owner of the Vesuvius Bar, is desperate to find a worker to replace his cook Filomena, who left without notice. There are few women among the migrants, so he finds little from which to choose. Nacib observes a woman "vestida de trapos miseráveis, coberta de tamanha sujeira que era impossível ver-lhe as feições e dar-lhe idade" (119) — "dressed in rags and so covered with dirt that he could not make out her features or guess her age (131). He reluctantly hires her because there is no one else available. When he returns late that night from his bar and sees Gabriela for the second time, after she has bathed and dressed in clean clothes, her beauty astonishes him: long wavy black hair, "an expanse of cinnamon-brown thigh," and the smell of clove. "Meu Deus" (129) — "My God!" — he says (145). Gabriela awakens, "ela despertou amedrontada mas logo sorriu e toda a sala pareceu sorrir com ela" (129)—"startled; but then she smiled, and the whole room seemed to smile (145). But she is still an untried cook.

The next day Nacib enjoys "[com] olhos enternecidos" (131)—"with rapture in his eyes"—the breakfast Gabriela makes for him; later, the lunch Gabriela prepares is "maná dos céus.... Desta vez, valha Deus, estou bem servido" (136)—"manna from heaven.... Now, thank God, I've really got what I need"—he tells a customer (147, 153). A good cook is essential to Nacib's economic survival, so he is at first hesitant to approach her intimately for fear of losing her as a cook. She also "parecia uma criança ... fosse toda inocência" (146)—"seemed like a child ... as if she was all innocence," so he again hesitates (168). But Gabriela is his "empregada doméstica," or household employee, and such female servants often provide a "dupla serventia," or double service (Osana Patricio 30). Indeed, in her essay on Gabriela, commenting on this episode in the novel, Ilana Strozemberg observes that:

> A categoria de empregada, no entanto, é sempre mais ambígua uma vez que, executando serviços domésticos ela pode, também, em certas circustâncias, prestar serviços sexuais. Este últimos, no entanto, mesmo quando ocorrem, devem ocupar sempre um lugar periférico. As relações sexuais com a empregada, na escala de valores de Ilhéus, deve ser sempre secundária em relação aos prazeres obtidos fora do próprio domínio doméstico [79–80].

> The category of employee, however, is always more ambiguous given that while performing domestic service she might also, in certain circumstances, provide sexual services. The latter, meanwhile, when they do occur, should always occupy a peripheral space. Sexual relations with a maid, on the scale of values in Ilhéus, should always be secondary in relation to pleasure obtained outside the domestic domain itself.

Thus, it is not surprising that Nacib begins a relationship with Gabriela that soon moves beyond the merely culinary. Like the backlander Clemente before him, Nacib becomes obsessed with Gabriela, particularly after he realizes the extent to which he depends on her. For almost four months he sleeps only with her, abandoning the prostitutes he used to visit, and he eats only the food she cooks for him. But he is hardly the only one enchanted with her: the snacks she delivers to the bar encourage customers to eat and drink more, thus increasing Nacib's profits, but he suddenly understands that her presence in the bar, even more than her food, brings him more regular customers. But "não era uma simples cozinheira, mulata bonita, cor de canela, com quem deitava por desfastio?" (168)—"wasn't she simply a cook, a pretty cinnamon-brown mulatto girl with whom he slept for diversion?" (189).

However, Nacib's confidence on his "proprietary rights" fades when he hears that others are offering Gabriela higher wages to cook for them, or even a house of her own. Nacib is aware that he must keep Gabriela. And how can a man keep a woman, in the model proposed by this society? Simply, by marrying her. But, he asks, "como casar com Gabriela, cozinheira, mulata, sem família, sem cabaço, encontrada no 'mercado dos escravos'?" (200)—"how could he marry a cook picked up at the slave market, a mulatta, without family, without her maidenhead!" (228).[15] The law of the land is that marriage can only be celebrated with "a gifted young lady of good upbringing, respectable family background, carefully preserved virginity," and who brings with her "a fine trousseau" (229). Gabriela, on the other hand, has the same understanding of their social distance, and sees no reason for him to marry her. Nevertheless, when Nacib offers her marriage, she accepts, just to please him. Therefore, Nacib marries Gabriela out of economic necessity and jealousy. He assumes that the patriarchal paradigm under which Ilheans live will now guarantee him possession and control of his wife.

By accepting to marry Nacib, Gabriela is doing precisely what the other women of her society do: accepting a situation just because it is proposed by a man. In her innocence and ignorance, she does not think about the consequences of such act and cannot comprehend when, after the wedding, Nacib wastes no time in trying to mould her into his and society's image of what a Mrs. Saad should be. The rules are varied: she is not to go barefoot; she is to wear nice dresses and uncomfortable shoes and attend boring lectures rather than the circus she so appreciates. Now, she feels like the bird he once gave her. The difference is that she can release the bird, whereas Nacib — following the culture of Ilhéus — keeps her in the prison of the home.

Even though she marries Nacib just to please him, by marrying him Gabriela crosses several boundaries she herself is not aware of, or cannot care about. First, she is of mixed race, half white, half black. In the Bahian society of the time, marriage was contracted exclusively with white women. The relationships with black and mulata women existed, but always outside marriage. Second, Gabriela is uneducated and therefore incapable of enjoying the "fine life" Nacib wants her to lead. Gabriela prefers to run barefoot with the children of the neighborhood and laugh without constraints in the circus; instead, now she is forced to wear the clothes and display the attitudes her husband imposes on her. And, finally, Gabriela has no last name and does not know her birth date or her own age. In fact, the marriage can only be possible because Tonico, loyal customer of the Vesuvius Bar, notary, and town Don Juan, falsely creates this information in order to make the marriage possible.

These three characteristics indicate that Gabriela, more than a woman, is a symbol of the population and of the land of the Northeast of Brazil. By presenting her as a woman of mixed race, Amado points out the fact that the Portuguese colonizer (who came to Brazil alone, without his family) had sex with black women and produced mixed race children.[16] In other words, Gabriela can be equated with the land she emerged from: brown, sensual, illiterate, and adverse to the urban morality represented by Ilhéus.

Therefore, soon it becomes clear to Nacib that he has "done her a favor" for which she has no appreciation. On the contrary, for Gabriela, "era ruim ser casada, gostava não....Tudo quanto gostava, nada disso podia fazer. Era a senhora Saad. Podia não." (288)—"it was awful being married, she didn't like it at all.... Everything that Gabriela loved was forbidden to Mrs. Saad" (339–340). Nacib's efforts to keep Gabriela by marrying her only make her unhappy. As he tries to transform her into an educated woman who will be accepted by Ilhean society (that will in fact never accept her), she becomes increasingly sad and even passive in their love-making. Nacib does not understand that she is not grateful for the "boon" of marriage, but rather longs for the happy days when she was simply Gabriela, and not Mrs. Saad.

Eventually Nacib learns that Gabriela is unfaithful to him. He storms to his house to find her with his friend Tonico, both naked. But he counters local custom and does not kill them. Instead, he punches Tonico, who runs off, and then beats Gabriela mercilessly and mechanically. Local customs are so ingrained, so stable, that even Gabriela accepts them: "tinha direito até de matá-la. Mulher casada que engana o marido só merece morrer. Todo mundo dizia.... Ela merecia morrer. Ele era bom, dera-lhe apenas uma surra e a expulsara de casa" (314)—"He had the right to kill her if he wanted to. A married woman who deceives her husband deserves to die. Everyone said so.... She deserved to die. He was good; he only gave her a beating and put her out of his house" (373).

However, beating Gabriela is not enough. His action — or perceived inaction — towards the cheating wife puts Nacib in a complicated situation, because forgiving the wife and her lover goes against the custom, and Nacib now faces possible ridicule from his fellow Ilheans. Should he have killed his wife and her lover, as Colonel Jesuíno did? Or would he have to leave town in shame as another man did, and leave his business hopes behind?

Thanks to the clever intervention of a friend, Nacib manages to resolve his dilemma through an annulment of the marriage based on usurpation of identity. That is, because Gabriela did not have a surname or date of birth and Tonico invented them for her to make the marriage possible, she can be accused of claiming a false identity and thus Nacib can be released from his marriage vows. Now that Gabriela is not his wife but only his mistress, "the cruel law" does not apply. Not only is Nacib's honor safe, but his fellows regard him as civilized, as behaving "como um europeu" (320)—"like a European (379).

In the meantime, without Gabriela's fabulous Bahian food and joyful, tantalizing presence, business in his bar declines rapidly. To make things worse, Nacib and Mundinho have embarked upon a joint venture to open the first restaurant in Ilhéus, but who will do the cooking? Both the bar and the restaurant may fail. The only solution is to rehire Gabriela as his cook. But now she is no longer Mrs. Saad, only Gabriela. This is all she ever wanted to be. As their amorous liaison begins again, Nacib is no longer jealous and no longer strives to control Gabriela's actions. She is free, free to be "just Gabriela," to walk barefoot, to enjoy the attentions of other men. We read in the text: "E aqui termina a história de Nacib e Gabriela quando renasce a chama do amor de uma brasa dormida nas cinzas do peito"(357) — "And so ends the story of Nacib and Gabriela, with the flame of love born anew from its own ashes" (425).

The novel ends with the "Postscript" in which Jesuíno is convicted of murder: "Pela primeira vez, na história de Ilhéus, um coronel de cacau viu-se condenado à prisão por haver assassinado a esposa adúltera e seu amante" (358) — "For the first time in the history of Ilhéus, a cacao colonel found himself sentenced to prison for having murdered his adulterous wife and her lover" (426). In the end, the rule of law replaces the cruel law which gave the husband the right to take his wife's life. Along with the other indications — a better port, a bus line, a restaurant, a freely elected senator — this verdict indicates that, indeed, order and progress have come to this city of the interior. Ilhéus experiences surprising changes during the course of this year, but its customs and traditions have undergone the most important challenges and changes as well. Jesuíno's conviction, despite his status as colonel and plantation owner, and Nacib's annulment of his marriage (instead of killing his wife) are two examples.

Four Recipes for a Woman

It should be noted that perhaps Nacib and Gabriela are exceptions to the rule. Nacib is the "Turk" to his fellow citizens. Syrian by birth and technically a Muslim, he is an outsider and not expected to behave exactly like the locals.[17] Gabriela is an uneducated, mixed race woman of the backlands, relegated to the margins of society by her race and class.[18] Her attractiveness results from her great beauty and grace, but also principally from her marvelous cooking of local recipes.[19] Centered in the racialized brown body, capable of cooking the local ingredients in ways no man can resist, Gabriela is a feast for the senses. But she is not the only woman in *Gabriela*; therefore she is not the only feminine model.

Rosana Ribeiro Patricio describes four kinds of women and their relationship to patriarchy in *Gabriela*: 1. Family women (wives and daughters) whose lives are strictly controlled and limited to home and the church. These women themselves perpetuate patriarchal values when they raise their daughters and sons to follow the same rules; 2. Unmarried women, the "solteironas" or old maids, whose function is to maintain moral order, good customs, and the status quo, which is patriarchy. Unable to find a man and form a family, they still constitute a strong pillar of the patriarchal edifice, because they exert great control due to their knowledge of the social rules, and their ability to enforce them with the younger women and with their servants; 3. Domestic employees, who may or may not provide sexual services as well, but who are, in any event, exploited economically; and 4. Women at the margins of the family, namely "raparigas," or concubines, and prostitutes, who also function to preserve patriarchal values by providing sexual services so that women of the first group can maintain the virginity and concomitant virtue required for a proper marriage (21–33).[20]

Even though in *Gabriela* the different phases of the plot are announced under the name of one of the four women — "Ofenísia," "Glória," "Malvina," and "Gabriela" — each of the four resists the patriarchal system in her own way, and each pays the price for that resistance. Ofenísia, unable to be the paramour of the Emperor, dies of sadness rather than marry a plantation owner as she should. The concubine Gloria defies tradition by taking a young lover, the teacher Josué, and showering him with clothes and gifts paid for with Colonel Ribeiro's money. Her punishment is to be thrown out in the streets.[21] Malvina, Melk's daughter, is a surprisingly modern woman who rejects marriage in favor of independence, working and studying on her own in a large city in 1925 Brazil.[22] Malvina pays for her rebellion when her father disowns her, and she can never go home or see her mother again.

Gabriela at first acquiesces to the patriarchal system, marrying Nacib and changing much of her behavior to be consistent with the requirements of her new social position. However, this life does not suit her and she does not understand his possessiveness. Even as a married man, Nacib can have sex with other women; local customs encourage it and Gabriela is not at all jealous. On the other hand, once married Gabriela still believes she can have sex with young, beautiful men; unlike Glória, however, Gabriela never has sex for money, and never with old colonels.

Nacib also transgresses local customs: with Gabriela he tries to combine the public and private spheres of public/brothels/lovers/pleasure and private/domestic/wife/duty. Gabriela is also incapable of conforming to traditions; Nacib's expectations, based on traditional Ilhean social mores, are in direct conflict with Gabriela's nature. Her resistance costs her her marriage, her security, and most importantly, Nacib.

Is Gabriela "naturalmente 'amoral'"—naturally amoral—as Osana Ribeiro Patricio suggests? (124) Or is her sexual freedom part of a feminist statement advocating for "greater freedom of choice for women" as Bobby Chamberlain believes? (1981: 70). In the former view, Gabriela is amoral because of her race. Critics on this side of the argument believe that Amado promotes the "myth of the sexual mulata," in accordance with a popular saying: "branca para casar, preta para cozinhar, e mulata pra fazer amor"— White woman to marry, black woman to cook, and *mulata* to make love (Elian Bennett 228).[23] Amado endorses the stereotype of the promiscuous *mulata* for whom marriage is impossible. As a foreigner, it is not clear whether Nacib is white or not, but his financial position makes that matter inconsequent, and he "becomes" a white man; Gabriela, however, is clearly not white. Marriage symbolizes "the patriarchal paradigm;" Gabriela and Nacib's marriage is a transgression of the paradigm, in which a white man marries a proper, white wife, and consequently neither Nacib nor Gabriela is happy until the annulment eventually allows them to enjoy their earlier "master/mistress," no-strings-attached relationship (Jacquelyn Johnson 185–186). Gabriela has no surname, no date of birth and she is *mulata*, so she cannot be truly legitimated even through marriage.[24] On the other hand, Amado "trabalha sim con figuras esterotipadas, presentes no imaginário masculino, mas o mecanismo de relacionamento que estabelece entre elas consegue quebrar a fixidez dos estereótipos" (Duarte 173)—"Amado does work with stereotyped figures present in the masculine imaginary, but the mechanism of relationship that he establishes between them manages to break the fixity of the stereotypes."

The four heroines of *Gabriela* resist aspects of the patriarchal paradigm, and Amado portrays marriage as a kind of incarceration for women, from Malvina's conservative mother to the normally unfettered Gabriela. But it is still difficult to see this novel as a feminist text or a feminist statement. As for Gabriela herself, as Amado presents her, she remains a mystery—a beautiful woman with the soul of a child, a sexual expert with childlike innocence. Like the *sertão* she springs from, she is not to be possessed. She is a child of nature, a rare flower, one of nature's mysteries and, as such, she can only bloom if let free. But one can also say that Gabriela represents the writer's ultimate male fantasy: a woman-child who re-virginates each day after a night of love making, as fresh, innocent and ignorant as before. As a worker, it is no wonder Gabriela is found by Nacib in the former slave market: she is a little better off than a slave: she is a poorly-paid worker who does not make alliances with others in her position, and does not know about her own exploitation.

Notes

1. *Gabriela* is a 1983 film starring Sônia Braga as Gabriela and Marcello Mastroianni as Nacib. The film was directed by Bruno Barreto, who also directed the 1976 film *Dona Flor e seus dois maridos* with Sônia Braga as the protagonist. Braga played the role of Gabriela in a Brazilian telenovela in 1975. *Tent of Miracles* was also made into a film in 1977.

2. "Colonel" and "Doctor" were titles unrelated to the military or one's education, but rather meant to show respect towards powerful men. The powerful owners of large plantations were called colonel, and during the years of much of Amado's writing, such colonels did indeed command private militias of hired hands who might work the land, but were on call as assassins and general roustabouts as needed. Amado makes this clear in the novel: "The Doctor was not a doctor and the Captain was not a captain." Just as most of the colonels were not colonels: the title was merely a traditional symbol of ownership of a large plantation ... it had no military significance whatever" (*Gabriela* 22–23; all quotations from the Vintage 2006 edition).

3. The characters mentioned form a very distinguished line, and their authors are considered the greatest in Brazilian literature in the formative period of the Nineteenth century: Machado de Assis, José de Alencar, and Bernardo Guimarães.

4. Gilberto Freyre (1900–1987) was a Brazilian sociologist whose works promoted a new, anthropologically-based understanding of Brazil that saw racial mixture as a positive quality, rather than a negative one of the Comtean and social Darwinist view. His major works include *Casa grande e senzala: Formação da família brasileira sob o regime de economia patriarcal* (1933)—*The Masters and the Slaves: A Study in the Development of Brazilian Civilization* (1946), *Sobrados e mucambos: Decadência do patriarcado rural e desenvolvimento do urbano* (1936)—*The Mansions and the Shanties: The Making of Modern Brazil* (1963), and *Ordem e Progresso: Processo de desintegração das sociedades patriarcal e semipatriarcal no Brasil sob o regime de trabalho livre: Aspectos de um quase meio século de transição do trabalho escravo para o trabalho livre; e da Monarquia para a República* (1959)—*Order and Progress: Brazil from Monarchy to Republic* (1970). It is important to point out that Freyre and Amado were born and raised in the same region: Freyre was from Pernambuco, and Amado from Bahia. Quite possibly, both Amado and Freyre developed their views about miscegenation precisely because both were raised in a society where the majority of people are of mixed race.

5. Like *Gabriela*, *Dona Flor* equates woman with food, and *mulatta* with sensuality. See Elian Bennett and Bobby Chamberlain for an extensive discussion and comparison of the culinary aspects of the two novels.

6. Ilhéus is a coastal town, to be sure, but "interior" here means backwoods and by extension, backwards.

7. According to the August 2000 census, Brazil's population is "white 53.7%, mulatto (mixed white and black) 38.5%, black 6.2%, other (includes Japanese, Arab, Amerindian) 0.9%, unspecified 0.7%" (2000 census cited in the *CIA World Fact Book Brazil*, http://sites.google.com/site/brazilcountrystudy/Home/basic-facts accessed 21 July 2011). The 2010 census will for the first time allow the descendents of runaway slaves to identify themselves as such; http://www.censo2010.ibge.gov.br/sinopse/ accessed 21 July 2011). The city of Salvador still has the largest concentration of Afro-Brazilians in Brazil, though it should be noted that most individuals classify themselves simply as "Brazilian."

8. In 1826 Brazil declared that the slave trade would be illegal beginning in 1829, but in fact it did not end until 1853. Slavery was not completely abolished until 1888, even though some categories existed to create free Africans at earlier dates. As of 1871, for example, the children of slave women in Brazil were born free. Not long after abolition the government promoted a national policy of "branqueamento," or a "whitening," of the Brazilian population by facilitating the arrival of white European immigrants as farm laborers.

9. *Cacau*. São Paulo: Record, 2000; *Terras do sem fim*. São Paulo: Record, 1987.

10. Some critics see *Gabriela* as a kind of sequel to *The Violent Land*, in part because the novel takes place in the same locale just after the events of the earlier novel.

11. Auguste Comte (1798–1857) is the founder of positivism, a philosophy based on empiricism, or the data of experience and observation. An unfortunate consequence of positivism was a kind of racial profiling. For example, if a slave did not want to work, by extension Africans were deemed lazy by nature, based on supposed empirical observation of members of the race.

12. Brazilian custom is to use first names, even for the most famous or powerful. Hence Colonel Ramiro Bastos is Ramiro, Raimundo Falcão is Mundinho, Melk Tavares is Melk, and so on.

13. "The "Rondó de Ofenísia" ("Rondeau of Ofenísia"), "O langor de Ofenísia"(The Languor of Ofenísia), "O lamento de Glória" ("Gloria's Lament"), "A solidão de Glória" ("The Loneliness of Gloria") "Cantiga para ninar Malvina" ("Lullaby for Malvina"), "O segredo de Malvina" ("The Secret of Malvina"), "Cantar de amigo de Gabriela" ("Plaint on Behalf of Gabriela") and "O luar de Gabriela" ("The Moonlight of Gabriela"). All quotations from the Portuguese text are from "Gabriela, Cravo e Canela, Editora Record, 67th edition. Quotations from the English translation are from *Gabriela, Clove and Cinnamon*, Vintage edition of 2006.

14. This and other translations, unless otherwise noted, are mine.

15. The term *mulatto* comes from sixteenth-century Spanish and means a person of mixed race, with one white and one black parent. The origin is uncertain, but seems to be related to the hybrid origin of mules, in Spanish *mulo*, mule, and *mulato* a young mule. The mule is a mix of a male donkey and a female horse, and mules are sterile. Mulatto was considered a pejorative term.

16. Whether the black women consented or not was besides the point for the white colonizer. During slavery the body of the slave belonged to the owner, and, of course, there is not one official record of one complaint from a slave woman about this state of affairs. But there is a famous literary rendition of the anguish of the black woman who does not want to surrender to her owner: Isaura, the protagonist of the novel *Escrava Isaura* by Bernardo de Guimarães. However, Isaura cannot even be seen as a *mullata*: her father is Portuguese, her mother was a very light *mulatta*, therefore Isaura's skin is so completely white, and her education so perfect, that she can pass for a white woman. After a struggle to escape the lust of her white owner, she manages to secure a good marriage with a white man in the end of the story. See Bernardo Guimarães, *A escrava Isaura*. São Paulo: Editora Atica, 1990.

17. The word "turco"—"Turk"—in Brazilian Portuguese does not necessarily mean that the person was born in Turkey. Indeed, in the beginning of the twentieth century, many persons from different countries arrived in Brazil under a Turkish passport, and, from them on, any dark skinned foreigner who deals with commerce is simply called a "turco." These "Turks" were the first and most numerous traveling salesmen in Brazil from the beginning to the mid-Twentieth century. See more details about the Arab immigration to Brazil and their transformation into Turks, in "Turcos ou libaneses," published in *Liban by Lody*.

18. Backlanders or "sertanejos" are often portrayed as and considered backward yokels. The main characters in Graciliano Ramos' *Barren Lives* (*Vidas secas*) for example, are illiterate. Fabiano can hardly string two words or thoughts together and his wife Vitória does calculations by using beans to add and subtract. But *Barren Lives* is a sympathetic portrayal of drought victims, who are shown as strong and resilient as the parched land where they live. In *Vidas secas*. Rio de Janeiro: Editora Record, 2002.

19. Gabriela is similar to Tita of *Como agua para chocolate* (1989)—*Like Water for Chocolate* (1991), whose mother, Mamá Elena, confines her youngest daughter to the kitchen and denies her any possibility of love or marriage. Tita is white, not *mulatta*, and she is from a wealthy family, but she is nevertheless as marginalized by her tyrant of a mother as Gabriela is by standards of race and class. Both women are imaginative cooks confined to the home in the service of others. Consult Laura Esquivel's *Como agua para chocolate: novela de entregas*

mensuales con recetas, amores, y remedios caseros. Mexico: Editorial Planeta Mexicana, 1989. *Like Water for Chocolate: A Novel in Monthly Installments, with Recipes, Romances, and Home Remedies.* Translated by Carol Christensen and Thomas Christensen. New York: Doubleday, 1991.

20. At a time when only maternity was verifiable, a woman's virginity and her faithfulness were essential to guarantee the paternity of any children born in the marriage.

21. Eventually their affair becomes so public that the colonel puts her out on the street with her belongings. The Ilhean code of honor does not require a man to kill his unfaithful concubine — only his wife.

22. Malvina's courage is even greater when considered in context: Virginia Woolf was already a famous author when she gave a series of lectures on "Women and Fiction" at two women's colleges at *Cambridge University* in October 1928, where she was not permitted to enter the library. Her entry would require that she be accompanied by a Fellow of the College, or present a letter of introduction, while a man would be permitted free entry without question. The lectures were published as the famous *A Room of One's Own*, in 1929. See *A Room of One's Own.* New York: Harcourt Brace & Co., 1989.

23. Amado "sucumbe aos estereótipos ou até concorda com eles: suas mulatas são mulheres sensuais, a maior parte do tempo incapazes de fidelidade, inclusive Dona Flor..." [Amado succumbs to stereotypes or at least agrees with them: his mulatas are sensual women who most of the time are incapable of fidelity, including Dona Flor] (Guméry-Emery 177). Like her sister mulata, Dona Flor, of *Dona Flor e seus dois maridos* (*Dona Flor and Her Two Husbands*), Gabriela is unfaithful to her husband. In Dona Flor's case, however, she is unfaithful to her second husband by consorting with her first, ghost husband. *Dona Flor*, like *Gabriela*, is a very popular novel. Both are used as examples of Amado's shift "from politics and toward pornography" (Vincent 1156). See Jon S. Vincent. "Jorge Amado." *Latin American Writers, Vol. II.I,* Eds. Carlos A. Solé and Maria Isabel Abreu. New York: Charles Scribner's Sons, 1989. 1153–1162.

24. In "Brazil in Black and White; Discrimination and Affirmative Action in Brazil," Edward E. Telles notes: "From the 16th through the 19th century, Brazil's economy was based on agriculture and mining, which depended on a large African origin slave population. During more than 300 years of slavery, Brazil was the world's largest importer of African slaves, bringing in seven times as many African slaves to the country compared to the United States." (http://www.pbs.org/wnet/wideangle/lessons/brazil-in-black-and-white/discrimina tion-and-affirmative-action-in-brazil/4323/, 18 August 2011). Indeed, when Brazil officially ended slavery on May 13, 1888 (by a "Golden Law" signed by Princess Isabel), the country had a high contingent of black and mulatto population. Telles writes that, "[t]oday, Brazilians often pride themselves on their history of miscegenation and they continue to have rates of intermarriage that are far greater than those of the United States" (1). It is important to point out that, in Brazil, the understanding of the racial spectrum is different, perhaps much more subtle than it is in the United States: the categories of "white" and "black" there are a number of others to refer to persons of mixed racial background, such as "mulato," "moreno," "escuro," "cafuso," "mestiço," etc. This subtlety can of course have many political consequences, and among them — as seen in the latest efforts to admit a quota of black Brazilians to the universities — is that the category of "black" becomes highly arguable, and benefits to be obtained through affirmative action can be denied or obtained on the basis of appearance.

Works Cited

Amado, Jorge. *Gabriela, Cravo e Canela, Crônica de uma cidade do interior.* São Paulo: Martins, 1958.

_____. *Gabriela, Clove and Cinnamon.* Trans. James L. Taylor and William L. Grossman. New York: Knopf, 1962. New York: Vintage, 2006. Print.

_____. *Dona Flor e seus dois maridos: história moral e de amor.* São Paulo: Martins, 1966.

_____. *Dona Flor and Her Two Husbands.* Trans. by Harriet Onis. New York: Knopf, 1969. Print.

Bennett, Elian Guerreiro Ramos. "*Gabriela, Cravo e Canela*" Jorge Amado and the Myth of the Sexual Mulata in Brazilian Culture." In *The African Diaspora: African origins and New World Identities.* Eds. Isidore Okpewho, Carole Boyce Davies, and Ali A. Mazrui. Bloomington: Indiana University Press, 1999. 227–233. Print.

Chamberlain, Bobby J. "Recipes, Menus and Sensual Delights Gastronomic Interludes in Jorge Amado's *Dona Flor e seu dois maridos.*" *Tropos* 6.1 (Spring, 1977): 9–26. Print

_____. *Jorge Amado.* Boston: Twayne, 1990. Print.

_____. "Escape from the Tower: Women's Liberation in Amado's *Gabriela, Cravo e Canela.*" *Prismal/Cabral: Revista de Literatura Hispanica/Caderno Afro-Brasileiro Asiatico Lusitano* 6 (Spring, 1981): 70–86. Print.

CIA World Fact Book Brazil. 7/21/2011. Web.

Duarte, Constância Lima. "As relações sociais de gênero em *Gabriela, cravo e canela*, de Jorge Amado (Social Relations of Gender in *Gabriela, Clove and* Cinnamon by Jorge Amado)." In *Jorge Amado. Leituras e diálogos em torno de uma obra.* Eds. Rita Olivieri-Godet and Jacqueline Penjon. Salvador-Bahia: Casa de Palavras, 2004. 165–174. Print.

Guméry-Emery, Claude. "A significação das personagens mulatas nos romances de Jorge Amado," In *Jorge Amado. Leituras e diálogos em torno de uma obra.* (The Meaning of Mulata Characters in the Novels of Jorge Amado) Eds. Rita Olivieri Godet and Jacqueline Penjon. Salvador-Bahia: Casa de Palavras, 2004. 175–187. Print.

Holanda, Edna Carlos de A. "*Gabriela, Cravo e Canela.*" *Jornal da Poesia* (August 30, 2005). Accessed July 24, 2011, at http://www.revista.agulha.nom.br/ednaholandal.html. Web.

Johnson, Jacquelyn. "Jorge Amado and Gabriela: Shoring up the Patriarch Paradigm with the *Mulata* Identify." In *Pictures and Mirrors: Race and Ethnicity in Brazil and the United States.* São Paulo: FEA/USP, 2009. 171–188. Print.

Mazzara, Richard A.. "Poetry and Progress in Jorge Amado's *Gabriela, Cravo e Canela.*" *Hispania* 46.3 (Sep., 1963): 551–556. Print.

Patricio, Osana Ribeiro. *Imagens de mulher em* Gabriela *de Jorge Amado* (Images of Women in Gabriela by Jorge Amado). Salvador: FCJA, 1999. Print.

Ramos, Graciliano. *Vidas Secas.* São Paulo: Martins, 1938.

_____. *Barren Lives.* Trans. Ralph Edward Dimmick. Austin: University of Texas Press, 1965. Print.

Strozemberg, Ilana. "*Gabriela, Cravo e Canela* ou as confusões de uma cozinheira bem temperada [Gabriela, Clove and Cinnamon, or the Confusions of a well-seasoned cook]." In *Jorge Amado, km 70.* Roberto Da Matta et al. Rio de Janeiro: Tempo Brasileiro, 1983. 66–93. Print.

Telles, Edward E. *Race in Another America: The Significance of Skin Color in Brazil.* Princeton: Princeton University Press, 2004. Print.

IV

WOMAN AND THE BURDEN OF GLOBALIZATION

10

Sex and the Two Cartagenas in Óscar Collazos' *Rencor*

ALDONA POBUTSKY

In the opening pages of Óscar Collazos' 2006 novel *Rencor*, Keyla, a preteen *mulata* from a Cartagena shantytown, is trying to fight off her menacing father as he attacks her with pent-up lust and fury. Defenseless under his parental fists, the girl finally gives in, detaching herself from the pain and letting her mind float away into a series of memories that introduce us to her life. One cannot exactly follow her thoughts and what is happening in the narrative present, because this flashback to the incest trauma is just too disturbing to set aside. Towering over his hapless daughter, Keyla's father tears off her clothes, degrades her for flirting with a local hoodlum, tells her she is going to get what she so badly wanted, and proceeds to rape her. This violation scene — certainly the most lurid but not the only one in the novel — prolongs itself interminably, coming back every time it seems that the focus of the story will shift to a different topic.

The sledgehammer sexuality of the opening scene only expands to pigeonhole its female protagonist in the role of a sex commodity. The reader senses that social condemnation is at the core of the novel, and that the burden of racialized stereotype is weighed and reweighed constantly in the text. Keyla, the protagonist, is angry. Her "rancor" — anger — stems from repeated instances of oppression and continuous losses, which by the end of the book leave her defeated, orphaned, and alone in the world, locked up in a correctional institution for attacking the policeman who has just killed Fercho, her boyfriend.

In broader terms, different facets of Keyla's sexual subjugation constitute the central prism through which *Rencor* dismantles the image of Cartagena as a Caribbean Paradise, unearthing instead its legacies of racism, sexism, internal political violence and neocolonial dependency tied to the global economy of leisure. Keyla drags the reader into the "other" Cartagena, with its vast shantytowns and disenfranchised inhabitants. They shed light on the enormous contrasts between the rich elite and the dispossessed multitudes that, to a degree, have been cordoned off from the eyes of the tourists and of the world in general.[1] *Rencor* also reveals the brutal conditions behind the city's growing sex tourism industry, where the youngest victims of economic deprivation feed the growing market of wealthy thrill seekers.

The background of the novel and Keyla's neighborhood is the real-life barrio Nelson Mandela, home to over 58,000 squatters. It is inhabited by displaced people caught in the crossfire between different warring groups, decimated by rampant violence, uprooted from their rural land, and forced to relocate from one day to the next. Through this sequence of misfortunes, they are left to endure poverty, sexual exploitation, miserable childhoods, premature aging, and frequently early death. Collazos, an acclaimed writer and journalist known for his social commitment, is well aware of the living conditions in the shantytowns surrounding the city. His earlier, 2003 testimonial narrative unveils misfortunes experienced by the underage inhabitants of that very slum through a series of interviews conducted over a period of one year. [2]

Thus, even though Keyla is a fictional character, she combines the fates of a number of real-life individuals whom the author encountered during his research in Cartagena's slums. Her dreams and aspirations, curtailed by continuous losses and setbacks, provide an insight into a hopeless struggle that the poor put up with Cartagena every day. The sexual abuse she suffers, beginning with rape at home, through servicing a wealthy *patrón*, and then European tourists long before she reaches maturity, brings attention to the social problem that has branded Cartagena as the "Caribbean Sex Paradise." Lax legal enforcement regarding sex trafficking of the young,[3] combined with thriving tourism and beautiful locale, cause foreigners in search of forbidden pleasures to flock to Cartagena for their illegal rendezvous. Thus through Keyla's hardships, *Rencor* reflects on a number of real social problems that plague contemporary Cartagena, such as its vast inequalities and the sexual exploitation of women and minors in neocolonial conditions of economic dependency.

In the popular imagination Cartagena has been synonymous with architectural and geographical beauty. Known as "the Jewel of the Caribbean," it attracts multitudes from within Colombia and from abroad thanks to its beaches, its islands, and its colonial charm enclosed within the imposing stone walls that used to protect the city from pirates.[4] Presently, these same walls that envelop the old part of town circumscribe the trademark image that the city projects to the world on a symbolic level. Although small in size compared to the rest of the city, it is the historic section that defines Cartagena as the tourist hub, aside from the less charming yet popular Bocagrande beachfront section. Commanding international prices and filled with picturesque plazas and elegant boutiques, the old Cartagena appears to be free of crime and somehow devoid of poor people. Yet its nightlife tells a different story, as it brings together visitors, foreign sex tourists, and despondent child prostitutes of both genders who descend upon the seedier streets along the ancient walls, filled with hotels offering hourly rates.[5]

Thus, despite its well-earned fame of an architectural gem, Cartagena in its broader terms is plagued with crime and poverty. In 2007 it was home to more than seventy youth gangs, and it was short some 600 hospital beds, where each month an average of 24 people died as they were turned away by overcrowded hospitals. One in five of its children suffered chronic hunger, three in five lived on less than $2.00 per day, and one in ten was uprooted by Colombia's violence (Bayak). For the inhabitants of the shantytowns, touristy Cartagena is alien and inaccessible, even though its high-rise condos loom on the horizon, easily visible from where they live. A young gang member named Elkin from the northeastern slum of San Francisco — one of the barrios mentioned in Collazos' *Rencor*— reveals how persistent hunger, utter lack of opportunities and widespread unemployment lock young lives into a circle of despair: "Aquí no existe el tiempo. Por estas calles y estos barrios no existe nada. Lo único que uno ve es la rabia, el hambre y la miseria"—"Time has come to a standstill here. There is nothing in these streets and these barrios. The only thing one sees is rage, hunger and misery" (Arrázola). In a palimpsestic fashion, Elkin reinscribes the clichéd motto of Cartagena "la heróica" to reflect his quotidian Darwinian struggle; it is the wealthy who enjoy the benefits of the historical city and the poor whose heroism rests on continuous effort to survive in the grim Cartagena slums.

Needless to say, this deprivation and neglect feed rampant sexual exploitation and sex tourism. *Fundación Renacer*, a non-governmental organization whose mission is the prevention of sexual abuse of the young, estimates that between 1,500 and 3,000 children work in the sex trade in the city, with the majority being coerced by their parents and relatives. The organization's alarming findings mention girls as young as 7, and 9 year-old boys involved in the business. Other reports quote cases of underage victims offering sexual favors in exchange for food to sustain their even younger siblings. They also signal frighteningly growing numbers of up to 5,000 underage sex workers during the high tourism season.[6]

Keyla, the heroine of Collazos' novel, becomes acquainted with the celebrated city as a member of its underclass, an exploited maid for the wealthy, and their sex provider later on. She is one of the have-nots whose skin color and social status brand them as second-class citizens, outsiders, or worse, intruders in the space created for and fiercely guarded by the privileged. As a young girl Keyla quickly learns that dark-skinned people are unwelcome in the pretty parts of Cartagena, and that their presence is met with fear and resentment, if not outright hostility. Even though the girl's ancestry mirrors the Caribbean amalgam of indigenous, black and white — thereby contributing to her lighter complexion and a mixed racial composite — she remains part of the lumpen in the eyes of the rich. When Keyla's mother one day takes her to her affluent employers, hoping to impress her daughter with the view from the lavish terrace of their high-rise apartment, the girl instead learns a harsh lesson on economic inequality. For the first time she comprehends that the Cartagena she thought she inhabited was out of reach for those of her ilk:

> Era como si hubiera vivido encerrada y apenas ese día conociera la ciudad. De pronto era cierto lo que pensaba: había vivido encerrada en un rancho asqueroso, durmiendo sobre un colchón destripado, saliendo a un patio lleno de barro, a unas calles inundadas de agua sucia de donde salían las ratas [19].

> It is as if I had lived locked up and only that day I got to see the city for the first time. I guess it was true what I was thinking: I had lived locked in a filthy shack, sleeping on a threadbare mattress, going out to the patio full of mud, and to the streets flooded with dirty water, from where rats would crawl out.[7]

This painful realization is further reinforced by continuous reminders of Keyla's lower status; orders, snide remarks and prohibitions reiterated not only by her mother's light-skinned boss but also by the service sector in the city (often composed of other Afro-Colombians). Keyla can enter the apartment but must remain in the servants' quarters at all times (18), and she is forbidden to use the dishes from the house (73). Likewise, neither Keyla nor her gravely ill mother can take advantage of the elevator to reach their employer's apartment on the twelfth floor, for it is reserved for the residents of the building who refuse to share their space with the have-nots (19). The completion of this order is piloted by a black security guard whose compliant stance is perceived by Keyla as an act of disloyalty to their own race, an attitude that perpetuates discords and injustice among the poor: "Yo no sé por qué, no entiendo, negritos como son y se la velan a los negros. Les ponen un uniforme y ya se creen blancos" (75) — "I don't know why, I don't get them Blacks who pick on other Blacks. You dress them in a uniform and they think they are white."

On another occasion, when Fercho, Keyla's gangsta sweetheart, takes her to the beach in Bocagrande to cheer her up, his defying look scares privileged *señoras* in the ice-cream line. Keyla perceives women's fear as they instinctively reach for their purses to check if anything is missing. She concludes that people of color spell trouble in the white man's world (63), and it seems that the unpredictable and defiant Fercho has assumed his bad boy role just to repay society for what it made him; he steals, disobeys traffic rules and threatens everyone at will. Another time, when Keyla encourages her mother and siblings to stroll leisurely alongside the historic seawalls the way tourists and privileged members of society do, a black policeman harasses them for no reason. Their subsequent failure to find a taxi that would take them back to their home in Nelson Mandela, drives the last nail in their coffin of lowly status: "Comprendí entonces que no vivíamos en Cartagena sino en el infierno, porque el infierno es el lugar adonde nadie quiere ir cuando se muere, al infierno nadie quiere ir vivo ni muerto" (89) — "I understood then that we were not living in Cartagena but in hell, because hell is where no one wants to go when they die, no one wants to go to hell dead or alive." Even later, when Keyla visits her *patrón*, Ricardo, in his law firm located in the old part of town, she is hassled by the doorman. Her appearance makes her an outsider in her own hometown, a presence incongruent with the travel-brochure vision of Cartagena — unless, of course, she caters to the needs of the affluent. Tourism has become so engrained in the reality of the city that, in an ironic fashion, it has contributed to further polarization of the social classes: the subaltern can participate in the tourist economy in its service sector or else they are stigmatized as an undesirable if not an illegitimate presence that threatens the city's socioeconomic status quo. [8] Keyla disrupts this balance as she attempts to make historical Cartagena her own space, yet the harassment she receives is a constant reminder that racism has becomes inseparable from the global economy of leisure.

Collazos' fiction, which highlights class and race divisions within the community, mirrors the city's reality. Social exclusion in Cartagena has been intimately tied to racism, though, as Alejandra Azuero observes, neither public opinion nor the victims themselves are ready to acknowledge the existence of racial prejudice. In the country overall, both the illiteracy and mortality rate among blacks is three times higher than in the rest of the population, with 76 percent of its members living in extreme poverty, and unemployment at 43 percent (Garavito). In his assessment of Bocagrande as a space purposefully constructed to both offer protection to tourists and to better control the members of the popular classes, Joel Streicker points out the reorganization of space predicated on an implicit racism and fear of the poor. There is class segregation with isolated tourist facilities where the police can regulate "the 'natives' — that is, the poor and dark-skinned" who are

> domesticated and clearly marked as subservient to tourists' desires: the female fruit vendors from the village of Palenque, descendants of self-emancipated African slaves; the dark-skinned coachmen whipping their thin nags through Bocagrande and the colonial quarter; the hotel chambermaids [...] This sort of tourism is meant to take place *among* the "natives" as docile workers but not *with* them, that is, not as neighbors or as political actors with their own agendas distinct from tourism [1997: 111–112].

Streicker refers to a systematic domestication of the dark-skinned population who must play the role of "well-behaved" and docile members of the service sector in order to be allowed into the space of affluence. Simultaneously he notes the irony of racial control in that it is precisely the city's connection to Africanness which underwrites its unique past and its present-day touristic charm. In other words, Cartagena's appeal — aptly exploited in travel brochures circulating the world — rests on its legacy of slavery, on its racial fusion and supposed acceptance of other cultures. Yet this imagined spatial cartography takes into consideration the popular classes only insofar as they comply with the prescribed performance of the obedient "native."

This commentary echoes Frantz Fanon's earlier observations on the nuances and pitfalls of decolonialization in Latin America. In *The Wretched on the Earth,* Fanon condemns the ruling classes for perpetuating fiscal dependency to colonial powers by imitating the objectives and methodolo-gies of the Western bourgeoisie. Fanon refers to tourism as a questionable national industry which exploited agricultural workers, ignored interior areas, failed to reinvest profits, refused to take financial risks to enhance general wellbeing, and instead spent large sums on conspicuous commodities destined for the wealthy few. Thus, "the beaches of Rio, the little Brazilian and Mexican girls, the half-breed thirteen-year-olds, the ports of Acapulco and Copacabana" (Fanon 154) only testify to society's failure to integrate the popular sector into its economy, instead perpetuating the oppression of the masses. This is how they set up their countries "as the brothel of Europe" (Fanon 154), a metaphor which in the case of Collazos' *Rencor* adheres painfully to its literal meaning.

To suggest that sex is intrinsically linked to power, or that it is embedded at the very heart of racism, is not to say anything new. Nor is it to evoke cultural stereotypes in which the non-white-hence-exotic (and particularly black) female body signifies unbridled passion, danger, fertility and excess. Yet the extent to which such stereotypes are utilized in the state-sanctioned industries remains consistently underestimated. In the countries where tourism receives its greater boost, it often happens that the elite condones and even resorts to exploiting racist stereotypes of women as exotic and erotic to allure outside visitors.[9] In fact, some critics argue that global sex trade, strengthened through vast economic contrasts between the starving masses and the affluent citizens, leans principally on the bodies of women of color, whose sexual services are "drawn upon as a way to 'develop' 'underdeveloped' regions of the world."[10] Prostitution driven by extreme poverty has become so embedded in social relations that it is often seen by its victims as one of the few income-generat-ing alternatives, particularly when it is more lucrative than domestic service or any other manual labor.[11] Likewise, in Collazos' *Rencor*, the non-white female body and sexuality are subjugated, controlled and exploited by masculine interests, thereby pointing to the pervasiveness of gender-based violence. Yet there is also domestic abuse, internal armed conflict, racism, and legacies of colonialism that freeze Keyla's body in the stereotype of the "erotic-exotic woman of color" who for centuries has been positioned as a sexual servant to the white world.

It should not surprise that Keyla, whose childhood is truncated by socio-economic violence — not to mention sexual molestation suffered at home — grows to understand her reality and her self-worth through the prism of her maturing *mulata* body. In a paradoxical fashion that steers her female friends into prostitution, her budding sensuality attracts trouble, while simultaneously affording her short-term escapes from her economic predicaments. Keyla learns early on that there are plenty of lascivious men willing to pay for her services, thereby sparing her from the hardship of physical labor that has ravished her mother's body and health. As a school girl wondering in the historical part of town, Keyla resorts to begging to buy candy and as a result gets her first taste of how servicing male strangers brings immediate monetary benefit (34). On the other hand, the tragic fate of her girlfriend, Miladys, whose descent into prostitution spurred by economic necessity, her subsequent drug addiction and total ruin ending in violent death, proves equally devastating. Thus Keyla is torn between the desire to form a relationship with her beloved Fercho — a union reminiscent of her mother's failed marriage in that it could potentially subjugate the girl to an unskilled, volatile man — and the economic imperative to sell her body when it is still in high demand.

Collazos' novel is structured as a long monologue of the protagonist who recounts her life story in front of the camera for a sympathetic yet silent interviewer. From the opening pages, Keyla reveals her subjectivity through her sexualized body as she focuses on the physical attributes typically fetishized by men. Her language is crude, often bordering on vulgar:

> Eso pasó antes de cumplir los diez años [...] tenía unos botoncitos oscuros, bien apretaditas las nalgas. Me había desarrollado este año. Y cuando uno se desarrolla le empieza a crecer todo: las tetas, las nalgas, las caderas, le van saliendo pelos y uno se los muestra a las amigas [48].

This happened before I turned ten [...] I had little dark buttons, a tight little butt. I had developed that year. And when you develop, everything starts to grow: boobies, butt, hips, hair starts to grow, and you wanna show it to your girlfriends.

Elsewhere she reiterates: "[d]esde los once años tuve senos duros y grandes" (10), and 'tengo nalgas de negra aunque no sea negra" (73) — "from age eleven I had big and hard breasts" and "I have a butt of a Black woman even though I'm not Black." The reader becomes uneasy with the register of this self-discovery because its explicit and coarse eroticism is dangerously close to the stereotype of an uninhibited black female whose lack of sexual modesty was a determinant for her racial inferiority in the imperialist discourse of the past.[12]

Yet, an equally viable interpretation would suggest that Keyla's self-objectification and her crude language stem from growing up in a sexually pathological environment which distorted her self-image and shaped her opinion on gender and power in general. In other words, the fact that Keyla eroticizes her body and by extension all her relations with men, implies that her earliest encounters with the opposite sex were forcefully eroticized for her. In consequence, she anticipates men to pursue her with sexual intent, viewing her own body through the prism of the male gaze. At home, in the barrio, and later on in the tourist zone of Cartagena, Keyla grows accustomed to the reality where men treat her as an object of sexual gratification, and only mutual feelings of love for Fercho make her vacillate in fulfilling the destiny of a paid sex worker that she deems inevitable.

Keyla's sexual initiation begins with childhood "games" in her seedy slum, where promiscuity is commonplace, and child abuse goes unpunished. Local hoodlums of all ages harass and molest girls as young as six or eight, only to laugh it off when infuriated mothers rush to report them to the indifferent police (44). The barrio Nelson Mandela emerges as a prison for its children, and as a male preserve. Surrounded by violence and demoralized by the lack of opportunities in outside society, men succumb to alcoholism and to an overpowering rage, which they lash out onto those who depend on them. Aggressors who have failed to be protectors, they forge relationships predicated on domination, humiliation, and abuse.

Misery and its disastrous effects are best illustrated in Keyla's depiction of her own family. Her father fulfills the classic "man of the house" role in the girl's early memories of their forced displacement from Belén de Bajirá in Urabá, the arduous journey through a landscape ridden with violence, and the difficult transition to Cartagena's somber slums. Keyla still looks up to him when he builds an illegal shack under the cover of night, steals electricity from electrical grids, and improves their makeshift home piece by piece. This sense of protection soon crumbles, as her father descends into alcoholism and destitution, faced with persistent unemployment and the indifference of the city towards its rapidly expanding margins. Again, Collazos' fiction echoes the reality of the nation in that, when it comes to the urban labor market, the forced displacement of rural population affected the two genders differently. Men, whose primary occupation used to be agriculture, lacked qualifications to transition seamlessly to the few skilled jobs in the city. In consequence, they were relegated to migrant work, general construction, and sporadic manual labor that provided temporary economic relief.

Women, on the other hand, filled the demand for domestic servants by offering what they were used to do back home before their dislocation. Reflecting the effects of forced migrations of Colombia's rural population, national statistics from the 1990s show a fivefold increase in unemployment for male heads of household, with simultaneous rise of precarious domestic force among women from 4.1 to 20 percent. This new job reality placed the largest burden on women whose work outside of home became essential for family survival (Meertens 143). Meanwhile, excluded from the labor market, men faced their own uselessness and eventual despair, which in turn steered them to vice. In the same fashion, Keyla's household becomes her mother's full responsibility, whereas her father's unemployment and social exclusion prompt his demoralization and eventually lead to the disintegration of their family and the man's descent into drug use and vagrancy.

Things only get worse when Keyla's maturing body becomes the object of her father's sexual desire. Abysmal living conditions that force all family members to share one mattress bring promiscuity to a new level: Keyla and her younger siblings become unwilling witnesses to their parents' physical intimacy, or worse, the target of their father's sexual advances. Before Keyla turns nine, her father fondles her and forces her to touch him whenever the mother falls asleep, worn out from arduous work (42). At other moments, he insists on teaching her intimate hygiene, eagerly resorting to demonstrations that violate the girl's sense of shame. Keyla confirms this intrusive behavior as a widespread practice in her community when she finds out from her girlfriend that sexual molestation is practically unavoidable:

> Me dijo que su padrastro le hacía lo mismo, que antes de su padrastro se lo hacía un primo mayor que paraba a veces por la casa. Esas cosas pasan en todas partes, los papás, los padrastros, los tíos, los primos, los hermanos y hasta los vecinos mayores, todos se quieren comer a las peladitas, es como si eso no estuviera prohibido [48].

> She told me that her stepfather was doing the same to her, that before her stepfather an older cousin who used to stop by the house. Those kinds of things hap-

pen all over the place, dads, stepfathers, uncles, cousins, brothers and even older neighbors, they all want to do it with the little girls, as if it wasn't forbidden.

Not only does Keyla's father eventually force himself upon her but worse, he turns incest into an afternoon routine. Collazos emphasizes the girl's vulnerability from the start: locked inside a body too small and fragile to protect itself, Keyla submits inertly to his desire as she grows numb to what is being done to her. Feeling defiled both physically and emotionally, she nevertheless anticipates her father's advances — even facilitating penetration — and succumbs to it with harrowing self-abasement. Her passive acquiescence reveals that far from intentionally encouraging her father's attention, she does not know how to prevent what she believes to be unavoidable. Her father exploits Keyla's acquired tendency to be objectified as the girl re-enacts an event she dreads yet is compelled to repeat, all the while fantasizing about different ways of doing away with him: "Hablaba mentalmente con el sicario que le pegaría a mi papá tres tiros en la cabeza o lo rajaría a puñaladas hasta dejarlo sin respiración en el piso, destripado como la rata que me peló los dientes" (28)—"I was mentally talking to a killer who would pump three bullets into my dad's head or would slice him up and leave him for dead on the ground, gutted like the rat that flashed its teeth at me."

Sexual molestation does not limit itself to the confines of her home and her family, although it is incest that constitutes the story's deepest wound. As Keyla fills out prematurely, men take notice of her transformation and attempt to take advantage of her budding beauty; but by now, Keyla is well aware of the meaning such attention attracts. She describes how men ogle and fondle her in crowded buses: "se arrimaban y me ponían el huevo en las nalgas, me miraban descaradamente el escote, me tocaban las tetas con la mirada" (72–3)—"They would move closer, and they would press their cocks against my buttocks, they would shamelessly stare at my cleavage, they were touching my boobs with their eyes," while passers-by in the historic district pester her incessantly, asking about her fees (162). Soon after, when she becomes a junior servant under her mother, the white pre-adolescent son of her employer harasses her as well: "Se iba detrás de mí cuando me veía limpiando los vidrios, me subía el vestido y me tocaba las nalgas" (74)—"He would follow me around when he saw me clean glass, he would lift my dress and touch my butt." However, it is the boy's father, doctor Ricardo, who finds her so irresistible—"le temblaban los labios, hasta los ojos le temblaban con la miradera" (75)—"his lips would quiver, even his eyes quivered from so much staring"—that one night he sneaks into her room and rapes her without further ado. Afterwards, he leaves behind the equivalent of five days' salary on her nightstand, thereby teaching Keyla that sexual submission can bring her economic reward.

There are at least two issues at work here; first that as Streicker notes, sex in the working class sector of Cartagena "instantiates men's power over women" (1993: 363), as it always takes place between unequals. The masculine self-image among the popular classes applauds a man's enjoyment, privileging drinking, partying and the sexual conquest of multiple women. Keyla's father not only breaks the family bond by forcing an incestuous relationship upon his daughter; he repeatedly breaks her mother's heart by hooking up with a much younger woman in a neighboring slum, and by engendering kids he cannot and does not support economically. Likewise, Keyla's beloved Fercho sleeps around with local girls, proving to Keyla his "exclusivity" in that he never spends the night in any of these women's beds. His bad-boy reputation is so enticing that, as Keyla reasons, women throw themselves at him, begging him to impregnate them. Whether she likes it or not, Keyla has no choice but to put up with Fercho's promiscuity as part of the prevailing, non-monogamous gender model in their community. In the same vein, she learns to tolerate constant sexual harassment from men who resort to implicit and explicit advances because it is socially condoned.

Another factor that locks Keyla in the Hegelian structure of domination and servitude is related to sex and race, the two modalities central to colonial constructions of Otherness and for locating and defining inferiority. There exists a long tradition and acceptance of upper-class males satisfying their sexual desires with "other" women, a habit facilitated through slavery and colonization in that it has allowed white men an unconditional sexual access to black and brown women's bodies (Kempadoo 2001: 40). This practice ties neatly with the stereotype of women of color as highly sexual and naturally uninhibited, a trope and collective fantasy which reveal more about the white desire for "Black flesh" than about women themselves. The racist discourse that constantly teetered between sexual attraction for "the other" and a simultaneous repulsion felt by white colonizers in the face of the specter of racial hybridity has contributed to the strengthening of the custom of concubinage. At once an object of desire and derision, or in psychoanalytical terms, of phobia and fetish, women of color have been treated as potential mistresses or sexual servants, but never as wives. They have served "for the satisfaction of sexual desires and to construct colonial and imperial white male power and privilege outside the confines of marriage and citizenship."[13]

Collazos' novel replays faithfully this cliché-laden power structure: doctor Ricardo, a respectable citizen whose photographs appear frequently in Cartagena's social chronicles, counterbalances his conventional marriage to a sexually frigid white wife by having affairs with local girls of color less than half his age. Their submissiveness, no doubt spurred by economic necessity, empowers him in that he can construct his own bold sexual fantasies at will. True, he is polite, clean, and rewards his mistress with trinkets far beyond what men from Keyla's own slum can offer, but his is clearly an economic transaction where she must display sexual readiness at times and places convenient for him. Keyla becomes a kept woman, who promotes the sexual pleasure of her white lover by instinctively performing the role of an uninhibited Lolita. Her worth rests on her youth and supposed unbridled passion that she learns quickly with the blessing of her defeated mother. Keyla thus becomes the proverbial sexual stereotype of the sensuous *mulata* who, as David Brookshaw noted elsewhere, "is a symbol of sexual license. She is respected neither as a woman nor as an individual. Her function is to attract men, to be exploited by them, and to exploit in turn by obtaining her own ends through sex" (164).

Abundant graphic descriptions of Keyla's trysts with the *patrón* are disquieting on at least two levels: first, they serve as a chilling testimony of contemporary forms of slavery founded on acute economic contrasts. In his pursue of sexual satisfaction, the ever-pleasant Ricardo does away with societal norms, as if his privileged status and his lovers' lack of the same placed them outside of the law. He takes advantage of underage girls simply because he can, and Keyla exemplifies the norm rather than the exception in his lifestyle. When, at one point, the heroine inquires about his previous affairs, Ricardo's silences reveal more than words, attesting to the chilling reality of sexual exploitation of Cartagena's children, where wealth and extreme poverty converge, throwing human rights out the door: "¿Ha tenido una querida más joven que yo?, le pregunté. Se quedó callado. ¿Sabe que apenas tengo catorce años? Para mí eres toda una mujer, no me importa que tengas catorce o dieciseis, me dijo" (95)— "Have you ever had a lover younger than me? I asked him. He remained quiet. Do you know I'm barely 14 years old? For me you are a real woman, I don't care whether you are 14 or 16 years old, he replied."

The second, certainly inadvertent effect of dwelling on Keyla's numerous sexual experiences is that rather than dismantling the stereotype, the focus instead threatens to bolster the iconography of an oversexualized woman of color. Keyla's life choices are closely tied to her body — a vehicle of pleasure, of her entrapment, of abuse, and of the discord among desiring men. Next to sexual aggression experienced in her barrio and in the historic center, Keyla appreciates Ricardo's mild manners and she enjoys their rendezvous as well as the effect she has on him. In their trysts she explores her own attractiveness and sexuality, submitting to his urges with curiosity and eagerness:

> Yo ya había aprendido a respirar como si me estuviera viniendo, respiraba y susurraba cuando sentía que él se estaba viniendo. Nunca me vine con él, le decía sabroso, sabroso, respiraba como si me estuviera ahogando y cuando sentía que se

derrumbaba encima de mí yo hacía lo mismo, cerraba los ojos y le daba a entender que me estaba desmayando [92].

I had already learnt to breathe as if I were coming, I breathed and sighed when I felt that he was getting off. I never came with him, I would tell him, nice, nice, I breathed as if I were drowning and when I felt that he was about to collapse on top of me, I would close my eyes and make him think that I was fainting.

She entertains the thought of leaving her slum behind, subsidized by her lover in return for her youth and the feigned zeal with which she welcomes each and every one of their encounters.

This period of contentment and economic hope comes to a sudden halt when, bullied by the jealous Fercho, the *patrón* cuts his ties with Keyla, and the protagonist feels forced to resort to street prostitution to feed herself and her siblings. This is also her final descent into a Dantesque hell, curiously located in the heart of Cartagena's storybook old center, where Keyla stumbles into modern slavery and the human trafficking of minors. Pregnant children with glossy, soulless eyes prostitute themselves for next to nothing in rat-infested makeshift hotels in order to keep their even younger siblings alive. Keyla "scores" better deals by becoming a weekend companion to Spanish sex tourists, men thrilled with the opportunity to exploit adolescents and go unpunished. This is when Keyla finds herself trapped in a position of sexual servant for an endless string of foreigners.

Collazos' *Rencor* accentuates the distinction between the two cities — meaning the slums and the historic walled center — as it blames vast economic differences, latent racism, and the exclusionary practices embedded in Cartagena's tourist economy for the collapse and utter hopelessness of the heroine's world. The two Cartagenas represent two possible fates for Keyla, of which neither is a real way out of her predicament. Keyla can sell her body and dignity in the utterly debasing child sex trade thriving in Cartagena's picturesque streets, or else she can choose love in the shantytowns, thereby risking repeating her mother's thankless life. Thus sexuality is the key for viewing Keyla's oppression, yet ample sexual references provided throughout the novel are also reminiscent of the discourse that has historically stereotyped the Caribbean body as a site of erotic exuberance.

Again, even though *Rencor* admittedly serves as an eye-opening testimony to the corruption and degradation of society which exploits its most vulnerable members, the extent to which Collazos dwells on the graphic descriptions of Keyla's sexual knowledge might have just the opposite effect in the reader. To Collazos' defense, speaking of sex work not only as a form of victimization but as woman's agency and at times pleasure is indeed tricky ground, in that it is in constant danger of slipping back into the stereotypical sexualization of woman of color. While it is evident that Keyla's fate serves as a metaphor for social decay, a vehicle through which Collazos bemoans what Luis Fernando Restrepo called elsewhere "the defilement of the Caribbean social body under the effects of the tourist industry" (264), the reader is left with a nagging sensation that Collazos' critique is somewhat betrayed by his own discourse.[14] True, the novel articulates socio-political issues through Eros, criticizing the debasement of the Caribbean as a phenomenon reinforced by internal and external economic forces that oppress the popular sector. Yet this view is controlled by the male gaze, shaped and reshaped for a male spectator, where Keyla represents the primitive Other, affordable and available exotic female flesh. In other words, in the end there remains a constant tension in the text between Keyla's subaltern voice and the male optic implicit in the sensual imagery of the narrative. On one hand, the novel disavows the myth of the picture-perfect Caribbean city, baring instead its wounds through a marginalized voice, yet on the other, it reiterates the trope of the seductive *mulata*, whose body weighs heavier in the representation than her discourse.

Notes

1. Inés Echavarría points to significant discrepancy between the rich and the poor in Cartagena, where the minimum monthly salary is $515,000 (roughly U.S. $280), yet many restaurants charge U.S. $60,000 for a dinner. Echavarría quotes the Fiesta de Santa Teresa as the ultimate sign of extravagance, where a ticket for a dinner buffet complemented by a glass of champagne runs U.S. $800,000 per person. See Echavarría's, "Cartagena, la Riviera del tercer mundo." *Elespectador.com* 5 Jan. 2010. Web. 10 Mar. 2010. Likewise, María del Rosario Arrázola makes a distinction between the two Cartagenas, the tourist hub and, as a delegate from the United Nations commented once, an image reminiscent of Africa and its worst ailments located in the city's shantytowns. María Antonia García de la Torre quotes the city's "barrio popular" beauty contest as a fitting metaphor for Cartagena's division between masters and slaves; the city's ancient seawalls constitute a clear division between the bourgeois glamour of its privileged citizens and the non-white poor, whose titles of beauty queens serve as a passport to prostitution rather than celebrity. Consult María Antonia García de la Torre, "Cartagena: el país de las maravillas." *Semana.com* 12 Feb. 2006. Web. 10 Jan 2010.

2. Collazos, Óscar. *Desplazados del futuro.* Medellín, Colombia: Intermedio, 2003.

3. Sebastian Castaneda blames lax legal regulations against sex tourism and related corruption in Colombia for Cartagena's transformation into "the Thailand of the Americas." He quotes cases of sexual exploitation of minors that have gone cold due to the alleged lack of Spanish-English interpreters in this cosmopolitan city. Recently however, efforts have been made to combat corruption and sex trafficking. In "Developing Colombia's Sex Tourism Industry." *Colombia Reports* 25 Aug. 2009. Web. 12 Jan. 2011. The newsweekly *Semana* reported on a new law approved by Congress, which punishes the promoters of child prostitution with sentences up to twenty years and enablers/participants of sex tourism with up to eight ("Quedó lista la Ley que eleva las penas del turismo sexual." *Semana.com* 11 June 2009. Web. 10 Nov. 2010). Also, see Ibarra Socarrás, Carlos. "Buscan prisión para los clientes de pornografía y turismo sexual infantil." *Eltiempo.com* 23 June 2008. Web. 15 Dec 2010.

4. Jane Wooldridge reports that some 80 percent of the 1.2 million visitors to Colombia include Cartagena in their itinerary. In "Cartagena Sparkles with Modern Sophistication." McClatchy Newspapers *Postgazette.com* 29 July 2009. Web. 13 Jan. 2011.

5. Mayerlin Vergara, from *Fundación Renacer,* points to the alarming rise of sex trafficking in Cartagena by stating that roughly half the people on city's streets after a certain hour at night are connected to the illegal sex industry (See Castaneda).

6. "El turismo sexual en Cartagena sigue en auge." *Eltiempo.com* 21 Feb. 2008. Web. 28 Nov 2010.

7. All the translations of *Rencor* are mine.

8. Elisabeth Cunin notes how a Cartagena-based black community leader equated a chance to be a tourist in Cartagena with feeling like the city's rightful inhabitant. In other words, the inability to participate in the economy of leisure was the most exclusionary practice that has stigmatized and successfully excluded the Afro-Colombian community in the city because tourism has become the norm in Cartagena, relegating its popular classes to the position of an illegitimate presence. See Cunin's "El turismo en Cartagena: vendo, luego excluyo." *Revista Noventaynueve* 7 (2007), n.d. Web. 4 Jan. 2011.

9. See Lim quoted in Kamala Kempadoo (2001, 32).

10. Kempadoo reports that "In Cartagena, on the Caribbean coast of Colombia, and Osúa in the Dominican Republic, for example, it has been noted that the humiliations, abuse, and hunger experienced in domestic work were reasons enough for a woman to state that she preferred prostitution as a way to make a living." In *Sexing the Caribbean: Gender, Race and Sexual Labor.* New York: Routledge, 2004, 60.

11. See Kempadoo (2001, 33).

12. See Kempadoo (2004, 29–30).

13. Stoler in Kempadoo (2001, 39)

14. Jorge Ladino Gaitán Bayona, for example, addresses *Rencor*'s shortcomings as he deems Keyla's monologue unnaturally explicit and at times semi-pornographic for no apparent reason: "¿Por qué el lector siente que esas descripciones sexuales, más allá de referir la descomposición familiar generada por la violencia, no suscitan instancias textuales e ideológicas más profundas? No serían eliminables tantas de esas escenas en la novela cuando ni siquiera existe un clima de sordidez credible para que el lector pudiera justificarlo?" — "Why does the reader feel that these sexual descriptions, aside from illustrating the family's unraveling caused by violence, do not raise more profound textual and ideological questions? Wouldn't it be better to delete so many of these scenes, particularly since there is no climate of credible sordidness that would allow the reader to justify them?" (Jorge Ladino Gaitán Bayona, "Rencor: Sin morada estética para el desplazado." *Facetas: Cultura al día* 28 Jun. 2009. Web. 15 Dec. 2010).

Works Cited

Arrázola, María del Rosario. "Los heroicos somos nosotros, que sobrevivimos." *Elespectador.com* 4 Jul. 2009. Web. 15 Dec. 2010.

Azuero, Alejandra. "Cartagena ¿La heroica?" *Semana.com.* 25 Aug. 2007. Web. 20 Dec. 2010.

Bayak, Frank. "Colombian Tourist Mecca Losing Immunity from Violence, Poverty." *USA Today* 27 Mar. 2007. Web. 18 Nov. 2010.

Brookshaw, David. *Race and Color in Brazilian Literature.* Metuchen, NJ: Scarecrow, 1986. Print.

Collozos, Óscar. *Rencor.* Bogotá: Seix Barral, 2009. Print.

Fanon, Frantz. *The Wretched of the Earth.* New York: Grove Press, 1963. Print.

Garavito, César A. Rodríguez. "¿Colombia racista?" *Elespectador.com* 21 May 2008. Web. 13 Feb. 2011.

Kempadoo, Kamala. "Women of Color and the Global Sex Trade. Transnational Feminist Perspectives." *Meridians* 1.2 (2001): 28–51. Print.

Meertens, Donny. "Facing Destruction, Rebuilding Life. Gender and the Internally Displaced in Colombia." Trans. Richard Stoller. *Latin American Perspectives* 28.1 (2001): 132–148. Print.

Restrepo, Luis Fernando. "Closure and Disclosure of the Caribbean Body: Gabriel García Márquez and Derek Walcott." In *A History of Literature in the Caribbean: Cross-Cultural Studies*. Ed. A. James Arnold. Amsterdam: John Benjamins, 1997. 251–266. Print.

Streicker, Joel. "Sexuality, Power, and Social Order in Cartagena, Colombia." *Ethnology* 32.4 (1993): 359–374. Print.

_____. "Spatial Reconfigurations, Imagined Geographies, and Social Conflicts in Cartagena, Colombia." *Cultural Anthropology* 12.1 (1997): 109–128. Print.

11

Reality by the Garbage Truckload: The Case of Unica Oconitrillo

JERRY HOEG

The Costa Rican author Fernando Contreras Castro's (1963–) novel *Unica mirando al mar—Unica Gazing at the Sea* (1993) is generally considered to be an indictment of consumer society and its attendant ecological devastation in Costa Rica and, by extension, Latin America and beyond.[1] It is worth noting that the novel has enjoyed significant commercial success in Costa Rica; the Costa Rican Ministry of Education has made it obligatory reading for all ninth graders, and it is regularly taught at the two public universities, the Universidad de Costa Rica and the Universidad Nacional (Minor Calderón Salas 173). Additionally, it has been adapted for the stage, and as such enjoyed success in various venues throughout the country, including the prestigious Teatro Mélico Salazar in the nation's capital, San José (Lidia Díaz 9).[2] A new version of the novel (2010), updated to reflect the fact that Río Azul has now closed and a new dump opened, has recently been released, and there are a variety of videos on YouTube treating the novel.

The setting is an actual landfill in San José, called Río Azul (Blue River). The story line is actually pretty simple. Having lost her job as a teacher, Unica Oconitrillo finds herself living on the city dump, scavenging what she can to get by. One of the things she finds is a husband, one Monboñobo Moñagallo, former night watchman at the National Library. Fired for reporting the sale of library books to a toilet paper manufacturer, he attempts suicide by throwing himself on a passing garbage truck, a move that lands him, alive and well, on the dump. Unica also finds a child, El Bacán, abandoned on the dump, and adopts him as her own. Together, the three comprise a family until El Bacán

162

dies from endemic diseases resulting from the unsanitary landfill conditions. Following his death, Unica and Monboñobo relocate to the coastal town of Puntarenas, where they carry on as best they can, still unable to escape the sea of garbage that has inundated the country.

Though recently closed, as mentioned above, for more than twenty years the landfill received 1200 tons of the capital's garbage on a daily basis. Despite the fact that it was originally billed as a sanitary landfill, it quickly became an open air garbage dump with neither controls nor treatment facilities. Rainfall on the location caused contaminants to infiltrate into the ground water, "... inyectándose de manera intravenosa en el cuerpo de la tierra"—"... injecting themselves intravenously into the body of the earth" (Contreras 49).[3] Additionally, contaminated runoff from the site was and is improperly treated—if treated at all—and allowed to flow into the local watershed and from there, either into the local aquifers or on to the sea. This problem is especially acute in the rainy season due to the fact that the rain causes the containment walls of the landfill to collapse, releasing the garbage onto the streets of the adjoining neighborhoods (Walter Rojas Pérez 8). The odor from the landfill is so bad it makes the neighboring communities nearly uninhabitable. In his research for the book, Contreras Castro managed to visit only once, being driven off by the stench in subsequent attempts: "Pretendía ir más de una vez pero no me atreví, el olor es insoportable"—"I tried to go more than once but I couldn't bring myself to do it: the odor is unbearable" (Contreras qtd. in M. L. Carlos Villalobos 15). As in much of Latin America, this hostile environment is populated by desperate people who scratch a living from what they can find in the dump. Those who comb the beaches of this sea of refuse are called *buzos* (scuba divers). They are seen as symbols of the shortcomings of the disposable consumer society:

> [...] todo el país se estaba convirtiendo en un basurero ... todos, absolutamente todos, nos vemos obligados a bucear en las profundidades del humo de los escapes en busca de un poco de aire para respirar ... en las profundidades de las aguas contaminadas en busca de algo de beber ... a bucear entre los alimentos contaminados de agroquímicos y plaguicidas en busca de algo fresco de comer ... a bucear entre la basura que hablan los políticos en busca de una actitud sincera [...] [116].

> [...] the entire country was turning into a garbage dump ... everyone, absolutely everyone, is obliged to dive into the contaminated air in search of fresh air to breath, into the depths of our contaminated waters in search of something clean to drink, to search among the foods contaminated with agrochemicals and pesticides to find something fresh to eat, and among the garbage politicians speak to find something sincere.

Ironically, although Unica's name means "unique" in Spanish, she represents a sort of Latin American "every woman": "Unica es un personaje que refleja el carácter arquetípico de la mujer latina: ser fuerte, estar decidida a luchar para seguir viviendo" — "Unica is the archetypical Latin American woman: strong, committed to struggle in order to carry on living" (Contreras Castro, qtd. in Edin Hernández, 2). As stated, Unica was a teacher before budget cuts eliminated her position and relegated her to the category of useless, disposable item. Her job loss stems from an oversupply of unskilled — or at least uncertified by the Ministry of Education — workers in a free market economy. Unica was a "... maestra agregada, es decir, de las que ejercieron sin título" — "an adjunct teacher, that is to say, a teacher without a university degree." Addressing this issue in a letter to the President of the Republic regarding the proposed closing of Río Azul, Moñagallo, speaking on behalf of the *buzos*, writes:

> [...] el problema es que ¿qué vamos a hacer nosotros? ¿de qué vamos a vivir cuando el basurero lo cierren? ... el problema es que si existiera otra cosa que nosotros pudiéramos hacer para ganarnos el pan, pero mucha gente aquí no sabe ni leer ni escribir ni hacer otra cosa que rebuscarse una platilla con lo que se encuentran en el basurero [119–20].

> [...] the problem is, What are we going to do? ... the problem is, well, if there were something else we could do to earn a living, but, many people here don't even know how to read or write, or to do anything else except scavenge the dump.

Because the book is critical of governmental negligence and under funding in general, the question often arises as to why the Ministry of Education should make the novel mandatory reading in Costa Rican schools. The answer is provided in part by the previous citation, which indicates that the real buzos' precarious situation derives from a lack of education, this in turn occasioned by budget cuts. Therefore, it is in the best interest of the Ministry of Education of Costa Rica to promote a position which argues that the solution to the social problems outlined in the novel is to increase education through increased funding. It is important to observe how the Costa Rican Ministry of Education concentrates on one detail of the novel — the fact that Unica lost her job because she did not have a degree — to read the novel as an argument for more education as a solution to the problems the protagonist brings upon herself by trying to shortcut the educational system.

But the novel does not question the fundamental structure of the economic system. That is, in the final analysis, it supports a market ideology of economic exchange and trade. The *buzos* do not seek systemic economic change, rather simply better living conditions and opportunities within the existing system. As Costa Rican social commentator Minor Calderón Salas observes, the novel is critical of the handling of the landfill, but not of social and family order and values writ large: "... la novela es ... transgresora ... sin embargo, pienso que apoya ciertas instituciones sociales ... la familia tradicional ... ritos sociales ... no "llama" a romper el orden social, la estructura vigente, etc." (184)—"... the novel is ... transgressive ... nevertheless, I think it supports certain social institutions ... the traditional family ... social rites ... it doesn't call for a break with the social order, the current social structure, etc."

Indeed, in the novel, Unica forms a family from what is discarded onto the dump. She creates a family by adopting El Bacán, an abandoned baby she rescues/recycles from the garbage, and by marrying Moñagalo in a ceremony presided over by the self-ordained priest—also a buzo—known as El Oso Carmuco. Though living at a garbage dump, Unica does her best to maintain a connection to the middle class to which she once belonged by adhering to traditional values such as the marriage ceremony or the installation of a TV antenna on the roof of her dumpside hovel: "En el techo de la casita había una antena de televisor que no cumplía función, pero que Unica había puesto ahí para darle un toque de distinción" (31)—"On the roof of the shack was a TV antenna that wasn't hooked up to anything, but that Unica had put there to give the place a touch of class."

These consumerist touches, such as the TV antenna, reflect Unica's support for a market ideology of economic exchange and trade. The very first page of the novel makes clear the economic motor that drives the *buzos*. The landfill is characterized as an ocean, and those scavenging it as divers plunge below its surface to harvest valuable exchange goods:

Los buzos habían extraído varios cargamentos importantes de las profundidades de su mar muerto [...] se apresuraban a seleccionar sus presas para la venta en distintas recicladoras de latas, botellas y papel, o en las fundidoras de metales más pesados (11).

The divers had extracted various important cargos from the depths of their dead sea ... they hastened to pick over their catch for sale to various recyclers of cans, bottles, paper, or heavy metals.

The *buzos* represent low skill, low wage workers everywhere. The great promise of the global knowledge economy has always been that education and prosperity go hand in hand. The assumption, supported by Ministries of Education everywhere, is that through investments in education, nations could deliver prosperity, justice, and social solidarity, while individuals could secure a better future for themselves and their families. By humanizing the *buzos*, Contreras makes it easier, from a cultural relativist position, to respect their cultural identity — they are just like the rest of Costa Rican society, only poor and uneducated. To solve their social problems one need only support the allocation of public funding for those who wish to take the opportunities for vertical social mobility available to all through public education. The irony is, of course, that in the real world education may well serve not to eliminate inequality, but to perpetuate it. Although the Ministry of Education would consider it anathema to say so, within the Costa Rican educational system the odds are stacked against the *buzos* and, indeed, all those with low levels of social and cultural capital. In their influential study of education in the United States, *Academically Adrift: Limited Learning on College Campuses* (2011), Richard Arum and Josipa Roksa make the case that education reproduces social inequality because:

> Students from upper-class families acquire linguistic and cultural competence and familiarity with the dominant culture. These skills and predispositions are in turn rewarded in school, granting children from more privileged families higher grades, better course placements, and other positive educational outcomes. Since schools expect but do not teach these cultural competencies, children from less advantaged families are left to fend for themselves, and in the process they typically reproduce their class location [37].

These observations replicate the results obtained by Pierre Bourdieu in *Homo Academicus* (1984), his groundbreaking study of academic stratification in French society, in which he demonstrated the tight connection between family of origin and the jobs graduates of the French Educational system obtained:

> [...] social heredity plays such an important part in the reproduction of all those professional bodies which are implicated in the reproduction of the social order [...] what is unconditionally demanded by this kind of highly selective club is learnt less by educational apprenticeship that by previous and external experiences [...] a style of expression and thought, and all of those "indefinable somethings..." [56].

The "indefinable somethings" are those social skills, attitudes, and beliefs — what Bourdieu calls social and cultural capital — that are internalized through growing up in a given social milieu, in this case the French "dominant class." These are specific social narratives or dialects, expressed in many ways, among them dress, comportment, taste, and so on, that allow members of a given class to distinguish not only one another but also to identify outsiders and potential freeriders (Don Nettle and Robin Dunbar). We know that subjects listening to taped speakers regard those with their own dialect as having higher reliability and attractiveness (W. M. Cheyne; H. Giles).[4] Moreover, "dialects have two key properties that make them valuable as cues of origin: they are hard to learn ... and they mark you out unmistakably as having grown up in a particular community" (Louis Barrett, Robin Dunbar, and John Lycett 259). From Bourdieu's work it seems clear that social dialects follow the same patterns, and are to put to the same uses as linguistic dialects or any other communicational dialect, and so effectively constrain social mobility, marking us out unmistakably different.[5]

Recent studies confirm that universal education has produced a global competition for good jobs, driving down wages and devaluing educational credentials in the measure in which these credentials increase.[6] Furthermore, social mobility through education is blocked at every turn by social structure. Simply being talented and working hard is not enough to offset non-merit factors such as inheritance and with it access to educational opportunities, political power, and insider trading, social capital (who you know), cultural capital (how and where you fit in socially), and at times simple dumb luck (physical attractiveness, regional accents, religious affiliation, and so on) (Stephen J. McNamee and Robert K. Miller).

An important issue in terms of Unica's persona is that much of her motivation in the novel stems from her efforts to support herself and to provide for her family. A drive that mirrors much of the motivating force behind women's movements across Latin America, including the Mothers of the Plaza de Mayo in Argentina, the Empty Pots movement and the Arpilleristas movement (supported by the Catholic Church) in Chile, the grassroots Christian groups in Brazil (*comunidades eclesiais de base*), and many more less famous efforts by Latin American women to support their families. The necessity to leave the confines of the home and take up political action on the national stage has opened many doors for women, and also brought about a renewed questioning of their traditional roles. In a certain sense, Unica represents this new Latin American feminism, more an equity feminism than a gender feminism.[7]

By defining hers as an equity feminism, I mean that Unica opposes all forms of unfairness, not only to women but to all people, especially the *buzos*, who are emblematic of all the invisible and voiceless poor in the world. She is, however, by no means a cultural constructivist. That is, she does not feel the differences between men and women are solely a social construction designed by men to enslave women. She sees far too many enslaved men on the dump to believe that. Nor does she believe human interactions derive only from group interaction. Unica is neither a Marxist, nor a postcolonialist, nor a gender feminist, but rather a person very much devoted to relating with her fellow *buzos* as individuals. Indeed, Moñagallo's political campaign on behalf of the *buzo* constituency is satirized in the book because no such constituency exists. The *buzos* see themselves as individuals, not as a social class, and have no desire to overthrow the existing order, but rather seek merely to improve their lot in it. Unica is very much aware that people have a variety of desires other than power. If Río Azul is anything, it is a non–Foucauldian world, one in which people want only clean and fresh food, water, and air, a safe place to raise their children, and the love of another human being.

The Construction of Social Constructivism

As I discussed in an earlier essay on *Unica* (3–5), Moñagallo is a parody of the traditional ethnologist, while Unica is the firm but gentle realist, a pragmatic Sancho to Moñagallo's Quixotic tilting at the windmills of the establishment. Their relationship satirizes the prevailing Boasian cultural constructivism which denies the biological side of culture, and argues that anything is possible in the right social setting. In Latin America, the patron saint of this view is Gilberto de Mello Freyre (1900–1987), who was in fact a student of Franz Boas at Colombia University between 1920 and 1922.[8] Before Freyre, Brazil had gone from the Comtean Positivism of the early Republic, beginning with Luis Pereira Barreto's (1840–1923) *Três Filosofias*[9] to first a biological Darwinism beginning in the 1870's, and shortly thereafter on to a social Darwinism thanks to the work of writers such as Earnst Haeckel (1834–1919) and Herbert Spencer (1820–1903). Spencerism, in its turn, came to an abrupt halt thanks to Darwin's half-cousin, Francis Galton (1822–1911).[10]

It was Galton who first introduced the idea of eugenics, arguing that the state should intervene in human reproductive affairs, selectively mating those with the most desirable characteristics with each other, while simultaneously culling the weak and undesirable from the herd. The results of the implementation of his ideas were disastrous, especially in Germany where, in January of 1933, Adolf Hitler's government announced that it would begin a massive program to sterilize eugenic "undesirables." Within a couple of years the enormity and brutality of the Nazi eugenics program became known and was condemned. Eugenics would thereafter be associated with racist propaganda, reactionary pseudoscience, and Nazism. With biological explanations of human behavior effectively ruled off limits, a new explanation for all things human was needed. It was into this breach that stepped Franz Boas.

Boas' position was that culture is a social construction, and had nothing to do with human biology, instincts, genetics, or anything else non-cultural. At the time, Boasian cultural constructivism was supported by the hostility of psychology, then under the sway of the behavioralists such as John B. Watson (1878–1958) and Burrhus Frederic Skinner (1904–1990), to the notion of instincts.[11] In addition, Boas' contemporary, Emile Durkheim (1858–1917), a founding father of the new science of sociology, argued that all social phenomena could be explained by social facts alone: *Omnia cultura ex cultura*.[12] Yet another contemporary, Sigmund Freud, argued that an unveiling of repressed life history events — a "talking cure" — was the key to uncovering the causes of patient's psychological problems. For the Freudians as well, biological explanations of mental illness were heresy. To look for them was simply more proof of how sick you really were.[13]

Boas' students spread out over the globe to successfully advocate for the elimination of biology from cultural studies. As we have mentioned, Freyre set the tone for all subsequent social science and humanities investigations in Latin America with his hugely influential *The Masters and the Slaves* (Casa-Grande e Senzala [1933]). This work, which has appeared in over forty print editions, one television mini-series, and been translated into nine languages, redefined Brazilian identity by valorizing African and Amer-Indian contributions to a hybrid society and demonstrating the fatal flaws inherent in previous Spencerist and eugenicist accounts of Brazilian society and culture.

Another of Boas' students was Margaret Mead, whose book *Coming of Age in Samoa* (1973) was enormously influential in disseminating the Boasian idea that "... our every thought and movement was a product not of race, not of instinct, but derived from the society within which an individual was reared" (preface iv). One more was Ruth Benedict, who wrote of American Indians, "... not one item of his tribal social organization, of his language, of his local religion, is carried in his germ cells" (12). Yet another was Ruth Landes, who reported a ruling "cult matriarchate" in Brazilian Candomblé, religion in which women ruled in all crucial affairs of the Bahian black community, an arrangement which offered a model for the social construction of universal women's equality that was the antithesis of the sexism she found in her U.S. homeland.

It is worth noting that the work of all three women has subsequently been proven erroneous: "Unfortunately, it was learned years later that both Benedict and Mead had presented disturbingly selective and limited data, thus skewing their conclusions" (Gillette 111). In spite of the fact that these and similar cultural constructivist interpretations are based on demonstrably false data, a Boasian-inspired cultural and social constructivism continues to be the leading paradigm in the social sciences and in the humanities in Latin America. In this regard the case of Rigoberta Menchú and David Stoll comes to mind, as does the preservation of the myth of Candomblé as a bastion of black women's power, this latter thanks to popularizing accounts from the international feminist movement such as Simone de Beauvoir's *Force of Circumstance* (1968), Sally Cole's reedition of *City of Women* (1994), Kim D. Butler's *Freedoms Given, Freedoms Won* (1998), and Rachael Harding's *Refuge in Thunder* (2000).[14]

To see how cultural constructivism in Latin America arrived at this level of political correctness, in spite of demonstrably gross errors in data collection, let us follow the intellectual trail from another of Boas' students, Edward Sapir (1884–1939), up to the present day. It was Sapir who postulated the idea that language was prior to, and so determined, thinking. Sapir and his student Benjamin Whorf (1897–1941) had investigated the Hopi language, and erroneously believed that it contained no vocabulary, syntax, or other grammatical form to describe time in the sense of past, present, and future.[15] This hypothesis, called linguistic determinism, holds that language determines thought and that linguistic categories, such as time, limit and determine cognitive categories. Hence the Hopi were incapable of conceiving of time in the way English speakers do, as past, present, future, and so on.

On this view, therefore, language limits and controls thinking, which then controls and constrains social action. The current example of this vision is typically referred to as political correctness, a standpoint which argues that by controlling what people say, their pattern of thought can be controlled, and with thought under control, action cannot but follow. As Friedrich Nietzsche (1844–1900) famously observed, "We have to cease to think if we refuse to do it in the prisonhouse of language" (45). Ludwig Wittgenstein (1889–1851) concurred, stating "The limits of my language are the limits of my world" (39). Eventually, Sapir-Whorf was proven wrong, initially through experiments on categories of color, first by Roger Brown and Eric Lenneberg, and later by Brent Berlin and Paul Kay, but the idea that language was the stuff of thought came to underlie literary and critical theory in the last third of the twentieth century and the beginning of the twenty-first, and has yet to be invalidated in the field of cultural studies.

This movement toward linguistic determinism can be traced through the works of first structuralist, then deconstructionist, and finally postmodern theoreticians. Claude Levi-Strauss argued that human relationships were coded like a linguistic system, and everyone acquired meaning through their relations to everyone else within the system. Thus human relations became a self-enclosed, textual, system.[16] Later French thinkers such as Jacques Derrida would take this a step further, and insist "No escape from language is possible" (317), "Text is self referential" (44) and "There is nothing outside the text" (30). That is, they would argue both language and culture are self-contained systems, either semiotic or ideological or both, constructed by their own internal principals, and even human agency, the intent of the author for example, can be ignored, hence "the death of the author." Both language and culture do not refer to the world but rather construct it from their internal rules and relations. Society and culture become semiotic constructions free of real world "foundations," a postmodern term for objective truths.

The net effect of decoupling language from reality, and society from nature, has been a decades-long process of denaturalization. According to Jonathan Gottschall, "... almost everything that people considered to be "natural"—gender roles, sexual orientations, suites of attitudes, ideologies, and norms—were actually the local, contingent, and endlessly malleable outgrowths of specific historical and social forces" (4). What is more, critical theory in the humanities and social sciences has attempted to demonstrate that not only is the social a discursive construct, a series of myths, but that these myths have been propagated by privileged white males in order to maintain their positions of oppressive dominance. The discourses of these men are "situated" in their privileged positions, and the supposedly objective foundations of their knowledge turn out to be simply subjective desires camouflaged as universal truths. By denaturalizing the myths of power, postmodern theory has sought to liberate the victims of these oppressive discourses, and create a new, carefully, and justly constructed world.

Unica as an Icon for Latin America

It is against this background that *Unica* has been written and interpreted, and it is in its break with this Boasian worldview that *Unica* becomes a landmark in Latin American literature. For Unica, and the rest of the *buzos*, the real world really exists, and keeps arriving daily by the truckload. There is an "outside the text" and, indeed, everything in Río Azul has been renaturalized, having lost all its value—semiotic and ideological—in the act of being consigned to the dump, the resting place of meaningless junk, including the *buzos*. All they have left is what is universal and natural in humans. They are, effectively, Stone Age hunter gatherers reliving the evolutionary path of *Homo sapiens*. And like all *Homo sapiens*, in all cultures, they have language, religion, patterns of socialization, sexual modesty, decorative art, they distinguish right from wrong, and some 350 other attributes that have been found to be universal in all human cultures (Donald E. Brown 1 and *passim*). As we now know, thanks to molecular biology, many of these attributes, such as language, religion, narration, and economic exchange, are hardwired into the human genome.[17] Unica is a character who has been returned to a primordial situation, with primordial values, and in this sense the book is utopian, in that she is clearly morally and ethically superior to the society that discarded her. She bears no grudges against bourgeoisie Costa Rican society, or against the government, or against any of the other buzos. She has no desire for excess accumulation, seeking only enough to provide the basics for her family, and is selfless in her dealings with them, seeking only to save them while asking nothing in return.

In this sense, she is a Romantic figure, a classic version of Marianismo, a Latin American term which refers to the piety, morality, and selfless sacrifice of Mary, the Virgin Mother of God. Many would argue that this is the same stereotype promulgated by the Latin American patriarchy so as to maintain its position of power and privilege. However, at the end of the novel this stereotype breaks down as well when El Bacán dies and Unica and Moñagallo leave the sea of garbage at Río Azul, the *mar* Unica has been gazing throughout the novel, and go to the real sea at the coastal town of Puntarenas. Yet, they cannot escape Río Azul, either figuratively (they are still trapped within the disposable society) or literally (toxins from Río Azul have contaminated the aquifer at Puntarenas). At the end of the novel Unica tosses the petals of a red rose, one by one, onto the sea at Puntarenas. The rose, the one thing of beauty in the novel, disappears without a trace into the immensity of the sea, along with any hopes for a new, or different, world.

Through the character Unica, the novel questions the ultimate value of altruism, self-sacrifice, and restraint in a society dedicated to solving Garrett Hardin's famous "tragedy of the commons" through self indulgence on the largest scale possible. It is important to keep in mind that the continual flood of discarded items into Rio Azul is a function of unrequited desire. It is not a function of advertising, but rather of marketing. The difference is critical, and takes us back to the issue of cultural constructivism. As Geoffrey Miller explains in *Spent* (2009):

> Most writing about consumerism assumes that culture shapes human nature, so that our desires conform to the dictates of advertising, through socialization and learning. This is the heart of postmodernist cultural theory [...] I argue we have inherited a rich human nature [and] ... our internal status-seeking instincts get refracted through consumerist culture to produce the products, markets, and lifestyles that constitute our modern environment (21).

What he is referring to, at least in the immediate sense, is the revolution in advertising that began in the 1960's, and is now known as the Marketing Revolution.[18] The idea was simple: rather than try to convince people to buy whatever it was a company was making, the company would make whatever it was that people desired. Since that time, the Age of Marketing has evolved, and today "products are systematically conceived, designed, tested, produced, and distributed based on the preferences of consumers rather than on the convenience of producers" (Miller 41). Market research uses empirical data gathered from social networks, focus groups, surveys, questionnaires, and a host of other tools to find out precisely what it is we want, and then to give it to us (yes, often in more ways than one). What we want, it turns out, is social status, pleasure, romance, and the satisfaction of our innate desires. What we ultimately want is not the Izod shirt, the Ferrari, or the Evian, but the status and prestige associated with their brands; not consumption, but conspicuous consumption.[19] What we want is to send a message, to brand ourselves. When Unica tries to opt out of this system by leaving Río Azul, she finds human nature comes with her. While she languishes, depressed at the death of El Bacán and so unable to forage, Moñagallo redoubles his efforts, adding city streets and markets to his beach route, and even opening a small stall from which to sell his finds, in order to accumulate ever more possessions with which to impress and arouse Unica. His solution to the humiliations, tribulations, and tragedies of Río Azul is to reassert himself in another place, becoming the dominant *buzo* of this new territory in the process. Social status, gender roles, and a propensity for economic activity are not altered by leaving *buzo* culture behind, as they were not by leaving middle class Costa Rican culture behind prior to that, but are rather strengthened in more propitious circumstances.

This faithful portrayal of human nature has made Unica a wildly popular novel and character in Costa Rica. By reinforcing traditional familial and social values in spite of adverse situations, the novel and its heroine, Unica, inspire Costa Rican readers to believe in their own values. A system of values that they not only see reflected in Unica, but that they believe are at the core of their true culture before it was perverted by consumerism.

What they do not see is that this desire to see themselves in a favorable light is yet another innate human desire fulfilled through the magic of marketing, in this case through books, theater, YouTube, etc. The universal, inherited, human nature of all Costa Ricans allows them to see themselves in the novel, and in the characters, and to take heart from the fact that no matter how bad things get, no matter where culture and society place them, they have a fundamental way of being that is prior to, supersedes, and will outlive whatever cultural form is extant at a given period in time. Unica is a character who does not seek to change her culture, but rather one who insists on living out the drives of her own human nature in spite of her dire living conditions. She represents the fundamental values of a society temporarily adrift on a sea of consumerism, a safe harbor from which to watch the sea that Río Azul represents, the rising tide of consumer waste which must, at some point, recede, leaving behind the solid rock of fundamental values. Ironically, it was these fundamental values that gave rise to consumerism in the first place. The desire to accumulate did not come from culture, but rather from our own status-seeking human nature, and this reversal of postmodern cultural analysis is what is unique to *Unica*. Culture does not construct us, we construct culture.

Notes

1. Critics agree that the novel is an indictment of consumerism from a "green" perspective. While several authors such as Lidia Díaz[0] in *"Unica mirando al mar:* una proliferación del sentido." *Káñina* 19.2 (1995): 9–14; Marjorie Gamboa in "A propósito de *Unica mirando al mar." Imágenes* 6 (1999): 111–14, and Ruth Budd in "Basura y tesoros en el relleno sanitario de Río Azul: una nueva mirada a la 'Suiza de América Central.'" *Letras* 31 (1999): 121–30, have treated a variety of facets of Contreras Castro's critique of consumerism, they have all taken its ecological concerns as their point of departure.

2. See also Edin Hernández, *"Unica:* La forteleza de la desesperación." *Signos: Semanario cultural* 36 (1994): 1–2, and Carolyn Bell and Patricia Fumero, *Drama contemporáneo costarricense: 1980–2000.* San José: Editorial Universidad de Costa Rica, 2000. 398.

3. All translations are mine unless stated otherwise.

4. Consult W.M Cheyne, "Stereotyped Reactions to Speakers with Scottish and English Regional Accents." *British Journal of Social and Clinical Psychology* 9 (1970): 77–9. Also see H. Giles, "Patterns of Evaluation in Relation to Patterns of RP, South Welsh, and Somerset Accented Speech." *British Journal of Social and Clinical Psychology* 10 (1971): 280–81.

5. For more on social mobility, and how it affects different sectors of society, see Jerry Hoeg. "The Discourse of Science in Fernando Contreras Castro's *Unica mirando al mar." Revista Canadiense de Estudios Hispánicos* 20.3 (1996): 491–504.

6. For a study of the rise of the multinational corporations' ability to hire the best educated from around the world, and the effects of these practices, see Phillip Brown, Hugh Laudner, and David Ashton, *The Global Auction: The Broken Promise of Education, Jobs, and Incomes.* Oxford: Oxford University Press, 2011 133–46.

7. Equity feminism is a moral position that opposes sex discrimination and other forms of unfairness to women. Gender feminism is, according to Steven Pinker, "an empirical doctrine committed to three claims about human nature. The first is that differences between men and women have nothing to do with biology but are socially constructed in their entirety. The second is that humans possess a single social motive — power — and that social life can be understood only in terms of how it is exercised. The third is that human interactions arise not from the motives of people dealing with each other as individuals but from the motives of groups dealing with other groups — in this case the male gender dominating the female gender" (341).

8. Although Freyre advocated variations on this theme throughout his long career, the two defining works are Gilberto Freyre, *The Masters and the Slaves: A Study in the Development of Brazilian Civilization [Casa-Grande & Senzala].* Trans. Samuel Putnam. New York: Alfred A. Knopf, 1966, and Gilberto Freyre, *The Mansions and the Shanties: The Making of Modern Brazil* Sobrados e Mucambos. Trans. Harriet de Onís. New York: Alfred A. Knopf, 1968.

9. In *Pensamiento positivista latinoamericano.* Ed. Leopoldo Zea, Madrid: Ayacucho, 1980, 297–323.

10. For further information consult Spencer's *Principles of Psychology.* London: Longman, 1855; for Haeckel see *The Riddle of the Universe at the Close of the Nineteenth Century.* Cambridge: Cambridge University Press, 2009, and for Galton see *Hereditary Genius: An Inquiry into its Laws and Consequences.* London: Macmillan, 1869.

11. Watson's classic work is *Behaviourism* (New York: Norton, 1930), while Skinner's is *Verbal Behaviour* (New York: Appleton-Century-Crofts, 1957).

12. Durkheim propounds this view in *The Rules of the Sociological Method* (Glenco, IL: Free Press, 1962 [1895]).

13. For an overview of Freud's position on these issues see his *Introductory Lectures on Psychoanalysis.* Trans. James Strachey. New York: Norton, 1966.

14. Consult Simone de Beauvoir, *Force of Circumstance.* New York: Putnam, 1968; Kim

D. Butler, *Freedoms Given, Freedoms Won*. New Brunswick, NJ: Rutgers University Press, 1998; Sally Cole, "Introduction." Albuquerque, NM: University of New Mexico Press, 1994; Ruth Landes, *City of Women*. New York: MacMillan, 1947 and Albuquerque, NM: University of New Mexico Press, 1994; Rachel Harding, *A Refuge in Thunder*. Bloomington: Indiana University Press, 2000.

15. An excellent introduction to Whorf's work is John B Carroll's, *Language, Thought, and Reality: Selected Writings of Benjamin Lee Whorf*. Cambridge, MA: MIT Press, 1964. For an overview of Sapir's approach, see his Sapir, *Language: An introduction to the study of speech* New York: Harcourt, Brace and Co., 1921.

16. See, for example, his *Structural Anthropology*. Trans. Monique Layton. New York: Basic Books, 1963.

17. See William R Clark, and Michael Grunstein. *Are We Hardwired?: The Role of Genes in Human Behavior*. Oxford: Oxford University Press, 2000, 72–81.

18. See Gad Saad, *The Evolutionary Basis of Consumption*. Mahwah, NJ: Lawerence Erlbaum, 2007, 23.

19. Thorstein Veblen in *Theory of the Leisure Class: An Economic Study of Institutions*, Boston: Houghton Mifflin, 1973 (1899) 1–25, is generally acknowledged as the first to distinguish between consumption and conspicuous consumption. Geoffrey Miller, in *Spent: Sex, Evolution, and Consumer Behavior*, New York: Viking, 2009, 1–15, and Gad Saad in *The Evolutionary Basis of Consumption*, Mahwah, NJ: Lawerence Erlbaum, 2007, 1–18, take Veblen's ideas a step further by demonstrating that conspicuous consumption is not simply a cultural construct, but an innate part of human nature.

Works Cited

Arum, Richard, and Josipa Roksa. *Academically Adrift: Limited Learning on College Campuses*. Chicago: University of Chicago Press, 2011. Print

Barrett, Louis, Robin Dunbar, and John Lycett. *Human Evolutionary Psychology*. Princeton: Princeton University Press, 2002. Print.

Benedict, Ruth. *Patterns of Culture*. New York: Houghton Mifflin, 1934. Print.

Brown, Donald E. *Human Universals*. Philadelphia: Temple University Press, 1991. Print.

Bourdieu, Pierre. *Homo Academicus*. Trans. Peter Collier. Stanford: Stanford University Press, 1984. Print.

Calderón Salas, Minor. "*Unica mirando al mar*: entre la transgresión y la norma." *Letras* 35 (2003): 173–84. Print.

Cole, Sally. "Introduction." In Landes, Ruth. *City of Women* (1947). Albuquerque, NM: University of New Mexico Press, 1994. Print.

Contreras Castro, Fernando. *Unica mirando al mar*. 2nd ed. San José, Costa Rica: Farben, 1994. Print.

Derrida, Jacques. *Of Grammatology*, Trans. Gayatri Chakravorty Spivak. Baltimore: Johns Hopkins University Press, 1976. Print.

Díaz, Lidia. "*Unica mirando al mar*: una proliferación del sentido." *Káñina* 19.2 (1995): 9–14. Print.

Freeman, Derek. *Margaret Mead and Samoa: The Making and Unmaking of an Anthropological Myth*. Cambridge: Harvard University Press, 1983. Print.

Gillette, Aaron. *Eugenics and the Nature–Nurture Debate in the Twentieth Century*. New York: Palgrave Macmillan, 2007. Print.

Gottschall, Jonathan. *Literature, Science, and a New Humanities*. New York: Palgrave Macmillan, 2008. Print.

Hardin, Garrett. "The Tragedy of the Commons." *Science* 162 (1968): 1243–48. Print.

Hernández, Edin. "*Unica*: La forteleza de la desesperación." *Signos: Semanario cultural* 36 (1994): 1–2. Print.

Landes, Ruth. *The City of Women.* New York: Macmillan, 1947. Print.

Matory, James Lorand. *Black Atlantic Religion: Tradition, Transnationalism, and Matriarchy in the Afro-Brazilian Candomblé.* Princeton: Princeton University Press, 2005. Print.

McNamee, Stephen J., and Robert K. Miller Jr. *The Meritocracy Myth.* Lanham, MD: Brown and Littlefield, 2004. Print.

Mead, Margaret. *Coming of Age in Samoa: A Psychological Study of Primitive Youth for Western Civilization.* New York: William Morrow, 1973. Print.

Miller, Geoffrey. *Spent: Sex, Evolution, and Consumer Behavior.* New York: Viking, 2009. Print.

Nettle, Don, and Robin Dunbar, "Social Markers and the Evolution of Reciprocal Exchange." *Current Anthropology* 8 (1997): 93–8. Print.

Nietzsche, Friedrich. "On Truth and Lies in a Nonmoral Sense." In *On Truth and Untruth: Selected Writings.* New York: Harper Perenial, 2010. 15–50. Print.

Pinker, Steven. *The Blank Slate: The Modern Denial of Human Nature.* New York: Penguin, 2002. Print.

Rojas Pérez, Walter. *Flujo y reflujo en Río Azul: Análisis ecocrítico de* Unica mirando al mar. San José, Costa Rica: Porvenir, 2006. Print.

Villalobos, M.L. Carlos. "*Unica mirando al mar* de Fernando Contreras." *Tertulia: Taller de literatura de San Ramón, Costa Rica* 2.3 (1994): 15–16. Print.

Wittgenstein, Ludwig. *Tractatus Logico-Philosophicus.* New York: Cosimo, 2007 (1922). Print.

V

WOMAN AS THE UNKNOWABLE OTHER

12

Women in Borges:
Teodelina Villar in "El Zahir"

MARÍA FERNÁNDEZ-LAMARQUE

Women in Borges' fiction are greatly outnumbered by the male protagonists and characters. In fact, women appear in only thirteen of Borges' sixty
short stories, and they are either completely absent or they mainly appear as
minor characters.[1] Some of Borges' female characters are not even given a proper
name; they are called only by a nickname, such as la Lujanera in "El hombre
de la esquina rosada" ["Street corner Man"] (1935), "La mujer de pelo colorado"
["Redheaded Woman"] in "El muerto" ["The Dead Man"] (1949), "La india
inglesa" ["Story of the Warrior and the Captive"] (1949), "La viuda" ["The
Widow"] in "Juan Muraña" (1970), "La señora mayor" ["The Elderly Lady"]
(1970), or "La viuda Ching, pirata" ["The Widow Ching, Lady Pirate"] (1935).
Borges' female characters are often nameless as in "El duelo" ["The Duel"]
(1970), and the maid in "El Sur" ["The South"] (1944). Nonetheless, there are
some exceptions where women's roles in Borges' fiction are substantial. They
hold a proper name and have an important presence, as in "Ulrica" (1975), "La
intrusa" ["The Intruder"] (1941), and "Emma Zunz" (1949).[2] "Ulrica," for
instance, is a woman who has a romantic encounter with the narrator but, in
the end, it is revealed that it was only part of an image in the narrator's dream.
Juliana's character in, "La intrusa" is a woman murdered by two brothers for
the sake of their mutual filial love; Emma Zunz (1949) is a woman who avenges
her father's death and sacrifices her honor to imprison the man who caused his
death. Some critics, such as Manuel Ferrer and others, have argued that Borges'
unsuccessful and scarce love life is represented by his abused, neglected and
objectified female character as depicted in these short stories.[3] Therefore, there

178

are only two female characters in Borges' fiction that are not only central to the story but who also serve as the conditional source to the story's existence in the structural, thematical and physical level: Beatriz Viterbo in "El Aleph" ["The Aleph"] (1949) and Teodelina Villar in "El Zahir" ["The Zahir"] (1949).[4]

Alicia Jurado, Alejandro Vaccaro, Donna Fitzgerald, and many others have examined Borges' life, finding autobiographical themes and parallelisms to his work and its representation of women.[5] Some have affirmed that his short stories are the representation of a Freudian Oedipus complex related to his close relationship with his mother, and distance from his father (María Esther Vásquez 254–5). Further analysis is based on Borges' long time relationship with Estela Canto, an old friend and acquaintance with whom the Argentinean author had an amorous relationship, and on his truncated relationship with Norah Lange.[6] However, Borges himself has affirmed that the absence of women in his work reinforces their essence and importance (Edwin Williamson 72).

All these studies have been based on Borges' life and/or vital experiences, or what Umberto Eco calls "empirical reading." In other words, these analyses study Borges' work, not within its own textual voice and intrinsic logic of signifiers, but within the reader's "own expectations of the text" (Eco 1992: 68). This kind of reading, Eco argues, is a complex exchange between the proficiency of the reader (the reader's world comprehension) and the kind of proficiency that produces any text, when it is read in a practical manner. The present study, on the other hand, will examine Borges within a deconstructive scope in which the reader plays a crucial role in decoding the text. This interpretation of "El Zahir" is not founded on Jorge Luis Borges' life, but on what the text and its internal coherence conveys in his portrayal of a female character that is central to the story.

Identify as a Shifting Signifier

"El Zahir" tells the story of a man named Borges using himself as narrator. Borges' infatuation for Teodelina Villar and her death are closely connected to the protagonist's accidental encounter with a coin named Zahir which has the power of becoming an obsession for anyone who comes in contact with it. All metaphors in "El Zahir" are connected as a chain of signifiers between two protagonists: Teodelina Villar and El Zahir. Thematically and structurally, "El Zahir" the work, El Zahir the coin, Teodelina the protagonist, and Borges the author and narrator mirror human nature and recreate its inner duality: as creator and destructor and as a source of good and evil.[7] For clarity, I refer to Borges' work as "El Zahir" and the coin as El Zahir, without quotation marks.

This same story, or the myth of El Zahir, exists within a number of other stories mentioned by the narrator: "Pensé que no hay moneda que no sea símbolo de las monedas que sin fin resplandecen en la historia y la fábula" (108) — "It occurred to me that every coin in the world is the symbol of all the coins that forever glitter in history and in fable" (130). The figures mentioned, Caronte, Belisario, Judas, Laís, Isaac Laquedem, Firdusi, Ahab, Bloom, and Louis XVI, all have a common link related to a coin. The historical characters are mentioned commonly in reference to those who are unthankful to their benefactors, and, not coincidentally, the ninth, last, and narrower circle in Dante Alighieri's inferno is destined to those who have been ungrateful and who have returned evil when they received goodwill. In fact, two of these names are also in Dante's opera prima: Caronte and Judas.

In "The Pharmakon," Jacques Derrida explains how writing repeats itself through history and within the eyes of the reader; in other words, according to Derrida, every reader will recreate the text, designing his/her own meaning and interpretation. Writing, in this sense, acquires a mythical condition of existence that repeats itself endlessly and mimics the core of some occult ambiguous themes (*Dissemination*, 74). In "El Zahir," this esthetic is perceived throughout the short story. The main character, Teodelina Villar, constitutes the axis of the story that is recounted by the narrator Borges. Early on, in the first paragraph, the polysemic nature and ambiguity of "El Zahir" is suggested. The narrator's explanation of El Zahir's diverse quantity of locations, meanings, names, and its ubiquitous nature, open the question of El Zahir the object and "El Zahir" the *oeuvre,* and its textual and thematic inaccessibility:

> En Guzerat, a fines del siglo XVIII, un tigre fue Zahir; en Java, un ciego de la mesquite de Surakata, a quien lapidaron los fieles; en Persia, un astrolabio que Nadir Shah hizo arrojar al fondo del mar [...] una veta en el mármol de uno de los mil doscientos pilares; en la judería de Tetuán, el fondo de un pozo [105].

> In Guzerat, toward the end of the eighteenth century, a tiger was Zahir; in Java, it was a blind man in the Surakarta mosque, a man whom the Faithful stoned; in Persia, an astrolabe which Nadir Shah ordered sunk to the bottom of the sea [...] a vein running through the marble in one of the twelve-hundred columns; in the Jewish quarter of Tetuán, it was the bottom of the well [128].

The narrator informs the reader about El Zahir: "En Buenos Aires El Zahir es una moneda común de veinte centavos" (105) — "In Buenos Aires, the Zahir is a common, ordinary coin worth twenty centavos (sic)" (128). This presentation clarifies which one of the multiple Zahirs is the protagonist in this specific place where the story unfolds. El Zahir has had multiple forms throughout history, and also the power to direct the lives of whoever encountered it. The different shapes and incarnations of El Zahir are related to the Arab, Muslim and/or Jewish culture, which trailed Christianity's popularity, and are the four predominant religions of the world. El Zahir has different names and it is personified in different subjects and objects; therefore, it can be related to the fact that historically, deities have had diverse names. Identity, therefore, is one of the themes of this short story, questioning it on a number of levels. As Blas Matamoro comments about Borges' thematic of identity: "[...] el múltiple Borges que se desdobla entre joven y ciego, entre público y secreto, entre vivo y muerto, entre olvidado y eterno. Y suma y sigue hasta componer una de las típicas enumeraciones caóticas del escritor..." (221) — "[...] Borges, the multiple, which duplicates himself between young and blind, public and the private, death and alive, forgotten and eternal. He continues adding this feature in his fiction until composing one of the writer's most typical and chaotic characteristics of his work."[8]

Thematically, both the coin and Teodelina as the two main characters constitute two faces of the same being. El Zahir and Teodelina are indissolubly, mimetically, and metaphorically linked. The narrator begins the story on November 13th, and he obtains El Zahir at dawn on June 7th, the day after Teodelina Villar's death. The direct relationship between El Zahir and Teodelina is obvious. The coin and the name of the woman have the letters N and T; the V of Villar as two Vs inverted and connected, and the N and T as the first letter of her name, Teodelina. Significantly, they coexist as the textual condition of survival within the work as the center of this *histos* or text, and at a different level, within the narrator's own story.[9] At the same time the question of identity is immersed in the idea of Teodelina and El Zahir. Both seem to be two faces of the same condition: life and death; good and evil are also ingrained in both characters. The Alpha and the Omega, the beginning and the end, are intertwined in both El Zahir and Teodelina.

The name of Teodelina is also emblematic of a creator, because it carries the name of God as the idea of the Supreme Being, appearing in two different languages in "Teodelina." On the one hand, as Patrick Dove has observed, "Teo" is Greek for "God." He also adds that "Delina" — "dēlō" in Greek — means to make visible (175). On the other hand, "dei" is also the Latin meaning of "God." The suffix "ina" means "related with." In chemical jargon it means "substance related with," whereas the suffix "ina" also expresses "insistence or intensity." Therefore, the idea of "God/Teodelina" as the creator, the beginning of the story/history, the pretext and the end of it, is vital in "El Zahir." Psiche Hughes has also noted that Borges' women, in general, incarnate the first step to a revelation, a destiny; more than an object of desire, they are a pretext for the story (35).

Structurally and physically, the short story also poses two axes/facets and faces related to the female protagonist. The first paragraph corresponds to a description of the coin: "En Buenos Aires El Zahir es una moneda común de veinte centavos" (105)—"In Buenos Aires, the Zahir is a common ordinary coin worth twenty centavos (sic)" (128). Immediately, in the second paragraph, the name and importance of Teodelina is stated: "El seis de junio murió Teodelina Villar" (105)—"Teodelina Villar died on the sixth of June" (128). Teodelina is the pretext for the story and the foundation of the protagonist's actions. At the same time, Teodelina's last name is formed by the letters V-i-l-l-a-r, which can also be an anagram for rival. The lexical term "rival" in noun form is "rivalry." Rivalry implies a person, group or organization that competes against another person or group or thing; for instance, the friend and the fiend, the medicine that cures and aids and also the poison that destroys and kills. Teodelina Villar embodies these two opposing forces represented metaphorically through numerous signs and symbols throughout the story.

Another level of dual identity and opposing forces is represented by the narrator/author. Both Borges as narrator and author is/are connected by a single thread in the text, the same name. Nonetheless, Borges and the author are not the same; although they share a namesake, they are not the same entity. In *Pharmakon,* Derrida argues that this type of recourse echoes the textual relationship between the father and the logos. Both father and logos are together but opposed at the same time; in other words, just as a/the coin has two faces, the text/the world/the logos has two faces as well. The idea of God/the creator and the demon/the destructor are two forces that are separate and together at the same time.[10] The reader's task is that of discoverer of the mystery. Silvia Kurlat also studies "El Zahir" as an intriguing puzzle: "Justamente, el sentido literal del texto de "El Zahir" oculta múltiples niveles de lectura cuyas claves aparecen dispersas a lo largo del relato" (11)—"In fact, the literal meaning of 'El Zahir' hides multiple reading levels and its hidden clues are dispersed throughout the story."

The notion of an opponent with whom it is necessary to fight and whom one must defeat is evident within the story. This notion, or "veil"— in Derrida's formulation — is only discovered while disentangling the web of the text. The opponent is not only the idea of the coin that Borges intends to overpower, but on a different level, it is also the text as the reader's opponent which the reader defeats by recreating it.[11]

Religious Meaning in El Zahir

In *The Puppet and the Dwarf* (2003), Bulgarian theorist Slavoj Žižek analyzes the conceptualization and influence of religion historically. It is a fact that Christianity has been the universal and most popular religion throughout history. According to Žižek, the basic premises of Christianity and its mores have been the domain of "life." The "Holy Spirit," as one of the most intriguing metaphysical aspects of Christianity, has permeated the actions and thoughts of millions of people, making it the largest religion in the world. According to Jacques Lacan, however, the "Holy Spirit" represents the symbolic order, which suspends all flux of emotions, free-thoughts and individual freedom. For Lacan, religion has permeated the minds and actions of the individual restraining his/her free will, producing nothing but living zombies.[12]

For the purposes of this discussion, it is useful to keep in mind that the term "El Zahir" comes from the Islamic religion, which uses it to mean "the apparent meaning of things." It is believed that El Zahir has an influence on whoever encounters it, thus becoming part of their actions, will, and decisions. As we see in the story, El Zahir in fact internalizes its power in Borges, the protagonist, turning him into a puppet the same way as Žižek says that religion does with human beings. Moreover, the force of El Zahir and its influence mark the actions of Borges, the narrator, turning his life into a living inferno. The end of the story implies this idea of possession and God: "Quizá yo acabe por gastar El Zahir a fuerza de pensarlo y repensarlo, quizá detrás de la moneda esté Dios" (116)—"Perhaps I will manage to wear away the Zahir by force of thinking about it. Perhaps behind the Zahir I shall find God" (137). Jaime Alazraki describes the world created by Borges' fiction as a metaphysical search in which "una identidad absorbe a la otra, la contiene y la representa" (296)— "one identity absorbs the other; it contains it and represents it." In this sense, El Zahir has also captivated the narrator's mind, controlling and embodying it. Human beings are constituted by feelings, logic, ideas, and experience, and these characteristics make possible our actions and thoughts. By annulling them, El Zahir forbids all possibility of knowledge or free will. In this sense, El Zahir/religion objectifies and destroys us.

In "El Zahir," Teo-de-lina is the center of the creation of the written text. This is why her death unfolds the story and the narrator Borges initiates his metaphysical and mystical journey. Teo-de-lina is the reverse of El Zahir the coin. Teodelina is her own rival, the same way that Borges (the writer) is against Borges, (the author-voice) rival. The father, the author Borges, is erased by the logos/son/narrator/text Borges. He, as narrator, appropriates the text, dissolving as the text disappears. Borges loses control of himself just like Julia, Teodelina's sister, who suffers from the same obsessive symptoms, and whose illness presents itself to the narrator as something he cannot evade when he says, "Antes de 1948, el destino de Julia me habrá alcanzado" (116)—"Julia's fate will have overtaken me before 1948" (137).

As the author loses control of the work — which is overtaken by the reader — the "meaning" of the short story becomes loose; the thread of the *histos* is dispersed as Borges' mind. As El Zahir is understood in Islamic religion, its hermeneutic power interprets their sacred book, the Koran. This interpretation is related to what the holy text hides and should be deciphered. The short story also parallels its need to be deciphered as a text or as a microcosmos that should be disentangled to be understood. This aspect has also been noted by Shlomy Mualem, who says that "[...] El Zahir is the only content of the microcosmic Zahir [...] in the case of El Zahir the microcosm *becomes* the macrocosm" (134).

In "Plato's Pharmacy," Derrida explains the idea of the *Pharmakon* and of the logos related to the interpretation of a text. According to Derrida, Plato's *Phaedrus* is a good example of what a text is: "[It] is not a text unless it hides from the first-comer, from the first glance, the law of its composition and the rules of its game" (63). That is, a text can only be interpreted and deciphered when the silent signifier can have a voice or multiple voices. The term *Pharmakon*, Derrida points out, evokes the idea of the etymological meaning of the word: the drug, the medicine, and at the same time the poison, and it appears in the body of the discourse in *Phaedrus* with its multiple meanings. In Borges' story, El Zahir as the object (the coin) given to Borges (the narrator) the day after Teo-de-lina's death has the same function within the text, simultaneously as a poison and a medicine.

The narrator finds himself enmeshed with the recurrent idea of the coin that lures him. He tries to hide it, bury it, lose it, destroy it, compose a tale, think about other coins and visit an analyst, but none of these remedies helps. He is not able to forget El Zahir: the coin eternally returns to his memory as an obsession. In his search to abandon El Zahir and its fixation, he finds the study of Barlach about El Zahir's superstition, and finally understands the origin of his illness. Indeed, according to the study, El Zahir is ubiquitous, powerful, intrudes into the minds of which it is exposed, and also is one of the 99 names of God (116). Once again, as in the first page of the story, the narrator repeats one of the multiple forms of El Zahir; "a tiger, a magical tiger" (113). Anyone who sees the tiger is never able to forget it. Moreover, the mysterious tiger is drawn in his cell by a prisoner multiple times obsessed with it in a horrific representation of God: "Verdaderamente ha visto al tigre" (113) — "He has really seen the Tiger" (134). Just as the divinity has different names and shapes in different cultures,[13] in the same way El Zahir has different faces and enters the individual's mind, thus becoming the axis of their lives. Seeing and possessing El Zahir is similar to seeing God.[14] The idea of a supreme power is intertwined within the text, El Zahir, Teodelina, and the narrator. Thus, El

Zahir as Pharmakon acts as a poison and medicine that introduces itself into the body of the discourse, the body of the text, and the body of the narrator, while also emblematizing Teodelina as its alter-ego. Derrida affirms the Pharmakon as a text: "This charm, this spellbinding virtue, this power of fascination, can be — alternately or simultaneously — beneficent or maleficent" (70). In this sense the story, on diverse levels, has hidden virtues written in cryptic depths and rejects to be scrutinized or analyzed, thus creating its own system of references and representations.

Literary Reflections

The narrator recalls the personality of Teo-de-lina Villar and her yearning for perfection and correction. In her life, Teo-de-lina was in a constant mutation and personal physical and emotional transformation: "Buscaba lo absoluto, como Flaubert, pero lo absoluto en lo momentáneo" (106) — "She sought the Absolute, like Flaubert, but the Absolute in the momentary" (129). Just as it happens to Pío Baroja's protagonist in *Camino a la perfección* (1911), Teodelina's search for perfection is not the ultimate representation of this characteristic as it is in Christian morality. Teodelina, just as Felipe Ossorio in Baroja's novel, looks for perfection in her desire of inner discovery. Teodelina's constant metamorphoses and changes are born from an interior yearning: "Su vida era ejemplar y, sin embargo, la roía sin tregua una desesperación interior" (106) — "Her life was exemplary, and yet an inner despair unremittingly gnawed her" (129). In "El Zahir," Teodelina's identity is the specular image of the mysterious object that Borges is given after her death.

As a professional model, Teodelina also represents different versions of herself. Her constant changes of physiognomy echo the obsession that Borges encounters with the idea of the coin. The circular shape of "El Zahir" also brings an eternal path of recurrence without an exit. Borges' persistent, limitless thought also parallels the repetitive thoughts and activities that are determined as punishments in *The Divine Comedy* (1308). When Borges, the narrator, receives the coin after Teodelina's wake, he walks aimlessly in alleys and streets only to return to the place where he had left: "Había errado en círculo: ahora estaba a una cuadra del almacén donde me dieron El Zahir" (108) — "I had wandered about in a random circle. I now found myself a block from the wine shop where I had been given the Zahir" (131). The narrator walks in circles carrying a circular object — a coin — in his hand. This action makes reference to the coin as a metaphor for the entrance to the inferno, as described in Dante's *Divine Comedy*, when, in the first part of his *opera prima*, Virgilio accompanies the poet to visit the inferno. The inferno has an alley entrance and its shape is that of an inverted cone, and its base has a circular shape and no exit. Borges/the narrator also enters an alley and walks the same path in circles paralleling Dante's entrance to the inferno.[15] With Teodelina's death, the narrator also enters his individual infernal living death emblematized in the coin called El Zahir, which he will never be able to forget.

The numbers at the beginning of the story —1, 2, and 9 — hold Dantescan undertones as well. The number 2 and the date 1929 are encrypted on the coin. The number 2 on the coin indicates the two axes: El Zahir and Teodelina Villar. The year 1929 encrypted on the coin shows the number nine twice. According to Dante, there are nine circles in the inferno. Numbers 1 and 2 added result in 3. The entrance to the inferno is narrated on Canto III (3). Teodelina's death occurs on June the 6th (6/6), the narrator receives El Zahir on June the 7th (6/7). The period of time between the death of Teodelina and Borges' encounter with El Zahir is 24 hours: "El día siete de junio, a la madrugada llegó a mis manos El Zahir [...] el seis de junio murió Teodelina Villar" (110) — "On the seventh of June, at dawn, the Zahir fell into my hands [...] Teodelina Villar died on the sixth of June" (128). Dante stays in the inferno exactly 24 hours. The connection between the elapsed times, the encryption on the coin, and the choice of numbers opens the angle of vision and interpretation to the idea of the dystopian infernal state that the narrator enters when he finds the coin, and which is expressed in the first paragraph: "No soy el que era entonces pero aún me es dado recordar; y acaso referir, lo ocurrido. Aún, siquiera parcialmente, soy Borges" (105) — "I am not now the person I was on that day, but still I am able to remember, and perhaps even to relate, what happened. I am still, however partially, Borges" (128).[16] That is, the narrator has also changed and has become another person after his encounter with El Zahir, but he is still able to remember.

Indeed, having memories is part of the punishment in Dante's inferno, since only those who are allowed to forget may gain forgiveness and peace, and the Leteo, the river that has the properties to make people forget, is located in Purgatory (Alghieri 61). As we read in verse 128 of the *Divine Comedy*, the waters of the Leteo possess a particular quality: whoever drinks from them will inevitably forget all the past, all sins. This condition allows the individual to have the opportunity to live a second time in their afterlife, with no memories of the past. Nevertheless, the narrator of "El Zahir's" is still able to remember. This sole condition situates him in the other part of the afterlife, the worst of all — the inferno, where, as the inscription at the entrance states: "Oh you all that enter here, lose all hope" (Alighieri 25).

Teodelina Villar *and* her death also hold Dantescan undertones. She is the daughter of a doctor, works as a model, and is described by the narrator as a superfluous and banal woman whose pleasures are those of an arrogant, upper class, spoiled young woman. Her yearning for correctness is indicated by her sophisticated taste and manners. And yet, Teodelina's beliefs are not metaphysical, but rather mundane, and "carpe diem" is her philosophy. [17] During the war, for instance, she is concerned with fashion: "La guerra le dio mucho que pensar. Ocupado París por los alemanes ¿cómo seguir la moda?" (107)—"How to follow fashion when Paris was occupied by the Germans?" (129). Teodelina's physical metamorphoses in her wake and her physical changes of style in her life are symbolic of her intimate search for endless masks. Metaphorically these changes are also emotional as a way to escape from her inner self. Teodelina's changes echo the Christian belief about God's and the Devil's power to transform physically.

There are two crucial episodes that precede Teodelina's death: the mention of the cylindrical hat that she buys from a foreigner, and the move to the "sinister" apartment on Aráoz Street.[18] These two episodes are connected to the idea of death and evil. The cylinder is shaped like a prism with parallel congruent circular bases, that is, the bases are circles. This hat, Teodelina later finds, is not part of the Parisian fashion: "... y por consiguiente no eran sombreros sino arbitrarios y desautorizados *caprichos*" (107)—... "and therefore hats were not at all but arbitrary and unauthorized aberrations" (129). The word "capricho" etymologically comes from the Italian word *capriccio*. Gérard Genétte's research finds this word in the thirteenth century as "caporiccio" meaning "horripilation" and "escalofríos" formed by the contraction of *capo* (head) and *riccio* (curled) (92). According to the narrator Borges, the hat is a "capricho." The narrator counts this as the first disgrace of a sequence which ends with Teodelina's death: "Las desgracias no vienen solas; el doctor Villar tuvo que mudarse a la calle Aráoz" (107)—"Disasters never occur singly: Doctor Villar was forced to move to Calle Aráoz" (129), a street whose name—not coincidentally—has infernal resonances. Aráoz is a Castilianized form of Basque *Araotz*, a town name in Basque country. It is also a topographical name from Basque *ara(n)* which means "valley" + an unidentified suffix, or alternatively a reduced form of Aranotz, from *aran* "valley" + *otz* "cold." Aráoz, is then the "Cold Valley." Returning once again to Dante's text, we see that the first circle in the inferno is described as follows: "Vero é che 'n su la proda mi trovai de la valle d'abisso dolorosa' che 'ntrono accoglie d'infiniti guai'" (26)—"Peering to find where I was—in truth, the lip, above the chasm of pain, which holds the din of infinite grief, a valley so dark and deep" (27). Therefore, following these associations, we can say Teodelina and her death are closely related to "El Zahir" and its obscure powers.

Because the woman and the object share the same relevance in the narrator's life and within the theme of the story, the effect of both in the narrator's
mind are crucial and similar. The narrator comments: "Teodelina Villar cometió
el solecismo de morir en pleno Barrio Sur" (107)—"Teodelina Villar committed
the solecism of dying in the southern suburbs" (129). In prescriptive grammar,
"solecism" means a grammatical mistake, an absurdity, or a non-standard usage.
It is perceived as an error. Teodelina's death was, therefore, an "error of order."

Margarita Saona writes that Teodelina's death highlights the narrator's
loss of his object of love; after her death, El Zahir becomes this object. In fact,
immediately after Teodelina's death the narrator "errs"—wanders—aimlessly:
"Había errado en círculo..." (108). The replacement of Teodelina for the Zahir
creates an error, or an unsolved problem, such as those one can find in Math.
Solving equations by substitution requires substituting a known variable from
one equation for the unknown variable of a different equation. In this case
both variables are unknown, which results in an unsolved problem, an error:
"an impossible equation."

During Teodelina's wake, the narrator remarks that after death she has
rejuvenated by twenty years. Her different faces or masks are seen within the
hours of her wake, and these several "versions" of Teodelina appear one after
the other: "Mas o menos pensé: ninguna versión de esa cara que tanto me
inquietó será la última, ya que pudo ser la primera" (108)—"I thought, more
or less, thus: no version of this face, which has so unsettled me, will be as
memorable as the one I saw; better than it be the last, especially since it could
have been the first" (130).[19] We can read these changes as the impact of the
coin in different times in history. Indeed, as the narrator states, the coin has
created different versions of lives of the people that it has touched, and this
reminds us that a coin—any coin—necessarily has two faces, therefore, anything that is related to the coin, will suffer transformations and end up with
more than "one face."

In addition, the coin symbolizes the future and the non-future. The infernal future in which he will remember the coin eternally represents also the end
of a life or the non-future, because life will end with this condemnation to
remember the coin forever. The condemnation is represented by the circular
shape of the story, the shape of the coin, and even the transformation of the
narrator *into a coin*, in his dreams: "Dormí tras tenaces cavilaciones, pero soñé
que yo era las monedas que custodiaba un grifo" (110)—"I fell asleep after tenacious caviling, but dreamt I was a heap of gold coin guarded by a griffin" (132).

The narrator leaves Teodelina's wake at 2:00 A.M. to wander the streets
and on a corner he enters a bar where he finds two men playing "el truco"
(110).[20] The card game called "el truco," "the trick," has rules to specifically trick

or fool the opponent using a number of gestures. The maximum numbers to win this card game are 6 and 7, or 6 and 6. Those two sets of numbers coincide with the days since Teodelina's death and the day she dies, as we recall: "El día siete de junio, a la madrugada llegó a mis manos El Zahir [...] el seis de junio murió Teodelina Villar" (110)—"... on the seventh of June, at dawn, the Zahir fell into my hands [...] Teodelina Villar died on the sixth of June" (128). The narrator is "tricked" or fooled by the acquisition of the coin on the day of Teodelina's death: he receives the Zahir on 6/7. It is not a coincidence that while he is receiving the Zahir, there are two men playing "the trick." Tricking, in this game, is the only way to win; or, in the case of "El Zahir," the only way to get rid of the Zahir is by tricking somebody, by passing the obsession on to somebody else, which is exactly what happens to the narrator. Players will try to deceit the other players in order to score points or pass The Zahir.[21] That is, El Zahir's elusive meaning holds the same rules of this game.

The idea of the text as a "trick" with "slippery signifiers" permeates the story. Not only does the meaning of El Zahir escape us, but it also becomes an obsession for the narrator and the reader in the form of an inescapable curse. One of the multiple metaphors and clues of El Zahir is given at the bar, where the narrator receives — or is the recipient of— the coin that will bewitch him for the rest of his life. At this bar, the narrator orders a "caña de naranja"— orange liquor — and receives El Zahir as the change.

Woman as Good and Evil

Teodelina's character incarnates the ineffable and inexorable repetition of the world and its representations of good and evil such as El Zahir. The text says, "El Zahir es la sombra de la Rosa y la rasgadura del Velo" (115)—"The Zahir is the shadow of the Rose and the rending of the Veil" (137). This phrase, mentioned towards the end of the story, entails decoding the idea of the occult meaning of El Zahir. The mention of a Rose — in initial capital letter — is also crucial. The word "rose" has several meanings as we can see, for instance, in Eco's novel *The Name of the Rose* (1980). In the beginning of the novel, we read that "signs and the signs of the signs are used only when we are lacking things" (*The name*, 8). This lack of a real, steady, and single, unique, and final signifier leads the reader to get involved in the hermeneutic of the novel. In "El Zahir," the "slipping signifier" reveals the hidden and multiple meanings of the coin as the central idea in the story. In fact, El Zahir is not only one of the many representations of the "universe" (116) as the narrator affirms, but also of the eternal duality of the human condition. It represents the two faces of the same entity — Teodelina and her Rival (Villar), two opponents battling in different levels and arenas. Within the structure of the text there is an opposition between Borges the narrator and Borges as the author of the short story; inter-textually, we can also say that the story dialogues with Derrida's idea of the *Pharmakon* and the debate between writing and speaking. In an ontologically level, El Zahir represents the divinity and its antithesis, the creator and the destructor. It also represents life and death, good and evil, and lastly it shows the duality of the reader as the creator and destructor (creator of a new work and destructor of the superficial, empirical reading).[22] The ending of the story intertwines all of these opposing ideas: "Para perderse en Dios, los sufíes repiten su propio nombre o los noventa y nueve nombres divinos hasta que éstos ya nada quieren decir. Yo anhelo recorrer esa senda" (116) — "I associate that judgment with the report that the Sufis, attempting to lose themselves in God, repeat their own name or the 99 names of the divinity until they lose all meaning. I long to tread the same path" (137). The naming of God and its 99 holy names constitute the many forms of good linked with evil, echoing the nine circles of the inferno along with the number nine repeated twice. The conjunction of these two forces will inevitably repeat itself throughout history as El Zahir, with no end or hope of escaping its human destiny.

Even though, as several critics have pointed out, women in Borges are more an absence than a presence, in "El Zahir" the female protagonist is not only the pretext for the story, but she is the core and the center of its universe. Teodelina Villar embodies the physical and the structural foundation for the existence of "El Zahir" as a text and as a reflection, both physical and mental, of our fragile and vulnerable human condition.

Notes

1. Sharon Magnarelli and Dale Carter, Jr. consider only nine of the total of thirteen of Borges' women characters. I agree with Alicia Jurado who, in her article "La mujer en la literatura de Borges" (1999), includes all Borges' female characters, even those that appear briefly in his short stories. See Dale Carter's *Women in the Short Stories of Jorge Luis Borges. Pacific Coast Philology* 14 (1979): 13.

2. Herbert Brant affirms that "El muerto" y "La intrusa" are examples of the "common triangular relationship among the characters," while Edna Aizenberg argues that "Emma Zunz" is exceptional because it shows a powerful female character. Aizenberg writes that this feature is related to Zunz's Jewish origin: "Borges creates a protagonist whose assertive femaleness cannot be understood without recourse to her Jewish mysticism" (11). In Herbert Brant "The Queer Use of Communal Women in Borges' 'El muerto' and 'La intrusa.'" *Hispanófila* 125 (1999) 38–50, and Edna Aizenberg, "Feminism and Kabbalism: Borges' (sic) 'Emma Zunz.'" *Crítica Hispánica* 15.2 (1993): 11–19.

3. Bella Brodzki comments on the relationship between the metaphors of the feminine in Borges that are used literarily in mystical and metaphysical themes, whereas Patrick Dove analyzes "El Zahir" within the "literary treatment of the image," which, he contends, does

not have an equivalent but only a form or a manner to appear (169). Consult Bella Brodzki, "Borges and the Idea of Woman." *Modern Fiction Studies* 36–2 (1990): 149–66, and Patrick Dove, "Metaphor and Image in Borges' 'El Zahir.'" *The Romanic Review* 98.2–3 (2007): 169–87.

4. Bella Brodszki observes that Beatriz Viterbo is central to the structural and thematical axis in "The Aleph" (154).

5. Consult Alicia Jurado's "La mujer en la literatura de Borges." *Boletín de la Academia Argentina de Letras* 64: 253–4 (1999): 409–423; Alejandro Vaccaro's "Borges' Women" *A Universal Argentine; Jorge Luis Borges, English Literature and Other Inquisitions.* Ed. Estela Valverde, 127–131; and Donna Fitzgerald, "Borges, Woman and Postcolonial History." *Romance Studies* 24.3 (2006): 227–239. Other authors who have written on women characters in Borges' work include: Genaro Bell-Villada, *Borges and His Fiction: A Guide to His Mind and Art.* Austin. Austin: University of Texas Press, 1999. Humberto Núñez Faraco, "The theme of lovesickness in 'El Zahir.'" *Variaciones Borges* 14 (2002): 115–55. Daniel Balderston, "'Beatriz Viterbo c'est moi': Angular Vision in Estela Canto's Borges a contraluz." *Variaciones Borges* 1 (1996): 133–39. Alberto Moreiras, "Borges y Estela Canto: La sombra de una dedicatoria." JILS 5.1 (1993): 131–46.

6. In *Borges a contraluz* (1989), Estela Canto states that Borges' mother disapproved of their relationship. Estela Canto, *Borges a contraluz.* Mexico: Espasa Calpe, 1989.

7. The reader cannot assume that the narrator, Borges, is Jorge Luis Borges, the writer.

8. Unless otherwise specified, this an all subsequent translations are mine.

9. Derrida uses the word "*histos*" to mean the text (story) as tissue: "We will keep within the limb of this tissue: between the metaphor of the *histos* and the question of the *histos* of metaphor" (*Dissemination*, 65).

10. The idea of the connectedness between good and evil is represented, for instance, in José Saramago's last novel, *Cain* (1999). In my review of the novel in *Hispania*, I contend that in that narrative God and Satan are presented as two sides of the same entity. God in Saramago portrays God as a creation of man's own fears and weaknesses, which, in turn produce man's own "imperfect Gods." María Fernández-Babineaux, *"Caín." Hispania* 94.3 (2011): 557–58.

11. In "The Death of the Author," Roland Barthes proposes to analyze the work as a neutral entity without identity, but specially without an author. According to Barthes, the author dies and loses all authority when the reader recreates the text. Symbols, metaphors and figures within the work produce this rupture inside the text, thus losing the voice of the empirical author and entering its authorial death. See Roland Barthes, "The Death of the Author" *A Barthes Reader.* Ed. Susan Sontag. New York: Hill and Wang, 1967.

12. Nietzsche also refers to religion in his work *The Genealogy of Morals* (1887), where he discusses the idea of Christian values, and describes how, according to Christian ideology, strength and wisdom are negative attributes, while submissiveness and humbleness are positive values. This moral, according to Nietzsche, interferes with human capacity to think freely, and ends up creating "slaves." In *The Genealogy of Morals.* Trans. Horace B. Samuel. New York: Penguin Books, 1887.

13. For instance, Allah, Brahma, Buda are different names of God. In Judaism God also has several names: Tetragrammaton, Yaweh, Adonai.

14. Andrés Forero establishes a comparison of the idea of God as a possession in Borges' stories "El Zahir," in "Deutsches Requiem," and in "Tigres azules." Forero writes: "... Dios, la locura y la ceguera, que son-en sí mismos-tres efectos de ver o poseer El Zahir en cualquiera de sus manifestaciones" (163)—"... God, madness, blindness which are—in themselves—three effects of seeing and possessing The Zahir in any of its manifestations. Consult Forero's, "'El Zahir' en los relatos de Jorge Luis Borges." *Variaciones Borges* 24 (2007): 153–166.

15. Sharon Magnarelli remarks on the relationship between Borges' women and death: "rather than a life-giving principle, women are depicted in Borges' work in relation to death,

violence, and often sacrifice" (142). In "Literature and Desire: Women in the Fiction of Jorge Luis Borges." *Revista Interamericana* 13.1–4 (1983): 138–49.

16. For Margarita Saona, the year 1929 corresponds to Norah Lange's definite rejection of Borges; therefore, it is a representation of his depressed state ("Melancolía y epifanía en Borges," 162). For Jean Franco, this date represents Borges' "political death" (127). In "The Utopia of a Tired Man." *Critical Passions. Selected Essays.* Eds. Mary Louise Pratt and Kathleen Newman. Durham: Duke University Press, 1999. 327–65.

17. According to René De Costa, Teodelina's banal personality represents the mediocrity of a middle class Argentinean woman. Holly Cadena, on the other hand, believes that Teodelina's superficiality is a good example of the ironic component in this short story. See René De Costa, *Humor in Borges*. Detroit: Wayne State University Press: 2000 and Holly Cadena, "Lo absurdo somos nosotros: el humor en los personajes de Borges." *Bulletin of Hispanic Studies* 82 (2005): 481–89.

18. Patrick Dove states that Borges, as a peripheral writer, does not adhere to the conventionality of a sign: "... we could say that the peripheral writer is the one who calls our attention to the finitude of the sign, or to the fact that a "hat" is not a hat, and that certain sacred philosophemes of the Western tradition — such as sign and the proper–are in fact based on the forgetting of convention..." (183).

19. In Christian tradition it is believed that the devil also appears with several masks and faces, as stated in the Bible. There are also a number of works that have represented evil with different faces. Two of the most famous literary representations are Dorian Gray and Dr. Jekyll and Mr. Hyde. See Oscar Wilde, *Dorian Gray's Portrait*. Canada: Random House, 1890 and Robert Louis Stevenson, *The Strange Case of Dr. Jekyll and Mr. Hyde*. New York: Scholastic, 1886.

20. *Truco* is a card game originating in Spain, but highly popular in Argentina. The game requires speed and the ability to trick/distract the opponents through the use of distractions.

21. This move is called "Deutreada" and in general is not a very effective way to win the game.

22. Patrick Dove comments how El Zahir represents two forces: "with El Zahir, the absolute is the simultaneous presentation of what we ordinarily perceive as opposing sides or faces" (178).

Works Cited

Alazraki Jaime. "El texto como palimpsesto: lectura intertextual de Borges." *Hispanic Review* 53.3 (1984): 281–302. Print.

Alighieri, Dante. *The Inferno of Dante*. Trans. Robert Pinsky. New York: Farrar, Strauss and Giroux, 1994. Print.

Baroja, Pío. *Camino a la perfección*. Madrid: Espasa Calpe, 1902. Print.

Borges, Jorge Luis. *A Personal Anthology*. Ed. and Trans. Anthony Kerrigan. New York: Grove Press, 1967. Print.

_____. *Obras completas*. Barcelona: Emecé Editores, 2004. Print.

Derrida, Jacques. *Dissemination*. Chicago: University of Chicago Press, 1981. Print.

Dove, Patrick. "Metaphor and Image in Borges' 'El Zahir.'" *The Romanic Review* 98.2–3 (2007): 169–87. Print.

Eco, Umberto. *The Name of the Rose* Trans. William Weaver. New York: Harcourt Brace Jovanovich Publishers, 1980. Print.

_____. "Between the Text and the Reader." In *Interpretation and Overinterpretation*. Ed. Stefan Collini. Cambridge: Cambridge University Press, 1992. Print.

Ferrer, Manuel. *Borges y la nada*. London: Tamesis Books, 1971.

Genétte, Gerard. *Fiction and Diction*. Cornell: Cornell University Press, 1993. Print.

Hughes, Psiche. "Love in the Abstract: The Role of Women in Borges' Literary World." *Chasqui* 8.3 (1979): 34–43. Print.

Kurlat, Silvia. "Sobre 'El Aleph' y 'El Zahir' la búsqueda de la escritura de Dios." *Variaciones Borges: Journal of the Jorge Luis Borges Center for Studies and Documentation* 19 (2005): 5–22.

Lacan, Jacques. *Le séminaire, livre IV: La relation d'objet.* Paris: Editions du Seuil, 1994. Print.

Matamoro, Blas. "Yo y el otro, Eros y Tánatos, masculino y femenino." *Variaciones Borges: Journal of the Jorge Luis Borges Center for Studies and Documentation* 9 (2000): 222–226. Print.

Mualem, Shlomy. "Borges and Schopenhauer: Aesthetical Observation and the Enigma of 'El Zahir.'" *Variaciones Borges: Journal of the Jorge Luis Borges Center for Studies and Documentation* 21 (2006): 107–37. Print.

Saona, Margarita. "Melancolía y epifanía en Borges." *Variaciones Borges* 25 (2008): 155–173. Print.

Vásquez, María Esther. *Borges: Esplendor y derrota.* Barcelona: Tusquets, 1996. Print.

Williamson, Edwin. *Borges a Life.* New York: Viking, 2004. Print.

Žižek, Slavoj. *The Puppet and the Dwarf.* Massachusetts: MIT Press, 2003. Print.

13

Life Amidst the Ashes:
Irene's Search for
Meaning and Connection
in María Flora Yáñez's *Las cenizas*

LISA MERSCHEL

A whole history remains to be written on *spaces* which at the same time would be the history of *powers* (both of these terms in the plural) — from the great strategies of geopolitics to the little tactics of the habitat. —*Michel Foucault*

Despite the existence today of a considerable body of literature discussing the work of Latin American women writers, Chilean writer María Flora Yáñez (1901–1981) — author of eight novels, two collections of short stories, and two memoirs — is still little known and read outside the Spanish-speaking world.[1] This essay not only seeks to address this lack of attention, but also intends to provide a space for the presentation and discussion of this original novelist, while emphasizing one of her female protagonists, Irene, from *Las cenizas* (*The Ashes*), hereafter *Cenizas* (1949).

Like other writers of her generation, Yáñez made her literary debut in a *criollista* spirit, depicting the environment and events in her native Chile. Her early works *El abrazo de la tierra* (*The Embrace of the Land*, 1933), *Mundo en sombra* (*World in Shadows*, 1935), and *Espejo sin imagen* (*Mirror Without an Image*, 1936), clearly portray the beginnings of the psychological complexity that later characterized her narrative: a profound connection between protagonists and the natural world, and the constant search for meaning in life and in human relationships. *Cenizas* marks the first of Yáñez's novels to center on the internal struggles brought on by the modern condition — an interest that will define all of her subsequent work.

This preoccupation with the inner life, however, was not the same for all Chilean writers of the time. A review of the literature from the 1940's reveals that whereas men's writings in Chile largely reflected issues of national identity and social injustice, women writers directed their attention inward, focusing on their alienation from the world around them. Such focus on the emotional and psychological aspects of the self resulted in the criticism that women's literary production in early to mid-twentieth-century Chile is largely "feminine" in nature [Lucía Guerra-Cunningham, 1987: 135]. "Enteramente femenina"— "entirely feminine" was in fact how a contemporary reviewer received *Cenizas* (Emilio González López 145).[2] The absence of obvious political and economic concerns in women's writing from this period, however, merely demonstrated that women were largely excluded from political, economic, and cultural production. Education and cultural debate in the public sphere were the privilege of few women, and it is important to stress that only in 1949 did Chilean women win the right to vote (Guerra Cunningham 1987: 136).

Marginalized from economic and intellectual production and from political participation, women were relegated to the space of "non-culture," and as such, their discourse was either discarded or received as inferior and insignificant (Patricia Rubio 14). Finding themselves excluded from the dominant discourse, women took up unusual strategies to write and to voice their needs and concerns. Yáñez, for example, wrote under the pseudonym Mari Yan, perhaps to avoid disappointing her parents, who wanted her to be a "niña *bien*" ("proper lady") and worried about public reaction to her writings (*Historia* 105).[3] Rubio writes that such women "han debido asumir la paradoja de ser sujeto de la escritura — productora de cultura — en un entorno que afirma su 'no-ser,' que devalúa y excluye su producción" (15)—"have had to take on the paradox of being the subject of their writing — a producer of culture — in an environment that affirmed their 'non-being,' that devalued and excluded their production."

Against this backdrop and through "writing what one knows," women writers from this period depicted female protagonists who, although they had fulfilled their "duty" as wives and mothers, still felt alienated and restless. Such a depiction does not, however, translate into moving these female protagonists out into the world to live lives parallel to their husbands'. Barred from the exterior world of their male counterparts, female protagonists develop instead a nuanced inner world, one that takes on a richness, expansiveness, and ultimately a connectedness that rivals the economic, political, and intellectual adventures of their husbands and lovers.

In a 1967 interview, Yáñez noted that Virginia Woolf was her favorite author. Indeed, in terms of narrative structure (the prominence of the interior monologue), action (of secondary importance to the psychological development of the characters), and style (highly lyrical), one can observe that Yáñez's narrative has much in common with that of the English modernist. The overarching idea of Woolf's "A Room of One's Own" (1929) — a keen awareness of boundaries and the cultural, psychological, and political significance of their traversal — is illustrated in Woolf's famous essay in these terms:

> It was thus that I found myself walking with extreme rapidity across a grass plot. Instantly a man's figure rose to intercept me. Nor did I at first understand that the gesticulations of a curious-looking object, in a cut-away coat and evening shirt, were aimed at me. His face expressed horror and indignation. Instinct rather than reason came to my help; he was a Beadle; I was a woman. This was the turf; there was the path. Only the Fellows and Scholars are allowed here; the gravel is the place for me. Such thoughts were the work of a moment. As I regained the path the arms of the Beadle sank, his face assumed its usual repose, and though turf is better walking than gravel, no very great harm was done. (4)

Under threat of being discovered for "audaciously trespassing" on the wrong turf, Woolf and others of her generation advocated for and carved out spaces of their own, and in doing so, articulated a critique of the hegemonic and rationalist discourse that dominated modernist thought and writing.

This passage also has extreme resonance when we study other women writers in Yáñez's native Chile, who were excluded from the "male turf" and had to "walk on the gravel," and carve out "spaces" for their literature and art. It is with these reflections in mind that this essay sets out to analyze the novel *Cenizas* and to examine the ways the protagonist, Irene Olmedo, similarly carves out "spaces" of her own since the "real" or public spaces of the polity were forbidden to women. These spaces imply a travel of sorts — into memory, into nature, and into the arms of lovers outside of marriage. Ultimately the travel serves the purpose of forging a profound, although fleeting, bond to the world around her.[4]

Narrative Structure

An analysis of the novel's narrative structure reveals how Irene's experiences are organized primarily around childhood memories, observation of nature, interactions with her husband, Agustín, and, later, her lover, Andrés. Temporal markers such as "al día siguiente" ("the following day"), "aquella noche" ("that night"), "un día" ("one day") and spatial ones such as "desde su cama" ("from her bed") and "Agustín va y viene" ("Agustín comes and goes") organize the narrative and frame Irene's thoughts, memories, emotions, actions, and reactions. Although a few instances stand out in which the omniscient narrator offers the reader a window into the thoughts of characters around Irene, these moments are rare. Such discursive markers ultimately serve to delineate spatial and temporal boundaries between Irene and her husband, a man who views Irene from a cool, skeptical distance. Recalling Woolf, Irene is unable (or unwilling) to "trespass" on her husband's positivist domain, and thus recurs to alternative spaces — ones in which "ensueño" ("daydreams") and quiet contemplation prevail.

Cenizas opens at a predawn hour as Irene gazes out the window on a silent rain. Irene notes that everything is sleeping in the old house, including her husband, whom she hears breathing calmly in the next room. Moving forward from this contemplative night watch to the events of the next morning, the reader is introduced to their relationship in this way:

> A través del follaje tupido, ella ve, en el patio de carretas, la alta silueta de Agustín que se dispone a subir al automóvil.
> –¡Agustín! ... llama.
> El vuelve la cabeza y con desgano se dirige hacia ella, inmovilizada entre los pilares del largo corredor.
> –Estoy atrasadísimo–murmura–. Buenos días, Irene. ¿Qué pasa? ¿Un encargo?
> Irene lo mira cual si lo viera por primera vez. No sabe por qué siente la impresión de estarlo observando como a través de un vidrio de aumento, pero de un vidrio mágico, cuyo poder consiste en borrar las cualidades y dejar al desnudo los defectos. "Llévame contigo–habría querido decir–. Me aburro, ahora, en Las Cenizas."
> Pero calla. No. Prefiere quedarse en el fundo [13–14].

> Through the dense foliage Irene sees the tall silhouette of her husband on the driveway, as he is getting ready to get in his car.
> Agustín! ... she calls out.
> He turns his head reluctantly and looks toward her, immobile between the pillars of the long corridor.
> –"I'm so late," he murmurs. "Good morning, Irene. What's going on? You need something?"
> Irene looks at him as if for the first time. She doesn't know why but she feels that she's looking at him through a microscope, a magical one, whose power consists of erasing the good features and leaving exposed the defects. "Take me with you," she wanted to say. "I'm bored, now, here in Cenizas." But she doesn't say anything. No, she prefers to stay here in on the ranch.

This opening scene reveals key features about Irene — her boredom, silence, and sense of alienation from her husband, a man she perceives as a stranger — and about Agustín — whose mild annoyance and reluctance to engage with her is disguised behind a courteous greeting. The scene reveals Irene's pensiveness in the face of Agustín's query if she would like anything from Santiago, as well as Agustín's impatience as he waits for an answer. While Agustín drives every morning to Santiago to work at the Stock Exchange, Irene stays home at Las Cenizas (the ashes) to care for their young son, Pablo. Of symbolic importance is Irene's "immobility" among the pillars of the corridor when she speaks to Agustín, as if she were an architectural feature of the house. For Agustín, women are secondary creatures: "la mujer había sido en su vida un elemento secundario [...] un ser fascinante y sibilino, capaz de anular la voluntad, el genio creador" (26) — "Since adolescence, women had been a secondary element in his life [...] a mysterious and fascinating being, capable of destroying one's will, one's creative genius." Despite this, he was captivated by Irene's beauty and, at first, he is intrigued at the possibility of molding her: "El era un forjador. ¡Qué voluptuosidad la de modelar a su antojo esa juventud, del mismo modo que modelaba su propia existencia! Pero Irene no era arcilla blanda" (26) — "He was a forger. What voluptuousness that of molding to his own liking that youth, in the same way that he molded his own existence! But Irene was not soft clay" (27).[5] Nonetheless, soon after their marriage, Agustín loses interest in Irene:

> Tenía demasiado que hacer para detenerse a descifrar el continuado enigma de una mente femenina [...] y, poco a poco, empezó a mirar a Irene sin verla y a intercalar en su vida de trabajo, rápidas y violentas aventuras amorosas en las que el corazón y el cerebro no tomaban parte alguna [27].

> He had too much to do to stop and decipher the constant enigma of the female mind [...] and, little by little, he began to look at Irene without seeing her and to weave into his work life quick and violent love affairs in which his heart and mind didn't take any part.

Agustín's freedom to move from the realm of the domestic to the public clearly portrays traditional binary oppositions — inside/outside, stillness/activity, womanhood/ manhood — which serve as a recurrent theme throughout the novel. Such parameters aim to delineate a private and a public space and recall Michel Foucault's observation that discourse is "not simply that which manifests (or hides) desire — it is also the object of desire" (110). Discourse in every society, Foucault reminds us, is "at once controlled, selected, organized and redistributed by a certain numbers of procedures whose role is to ward off its powers and dangers, to gain mastery over its chance events, to evade its ponderous, formidable materiality" (109). The ultimate end of this mastery is both the determination of who can speak, who can produce discourse, as well as who cannot speak, and is therefore outside discourse. The possessor of the power of discourse does not need to use physical force or coercion, but his speech and actions, Foucault asserts, "exert a sort of pressure and something like a power of constraint ... on other discourses" (113). Because she is a woman, Irene is inherently excluded from the rational, masculine, positivist world of her husband. Yet, her husband's lack of acknowledgement does not necessarily mean she cannot speak, cannot produce her own dissenting, counter hegemonic discourse, one that may exist in its own terms.

Interior Travels, Non-Linear Time, and Irrationality

As soon as Agustín departs for work that morning, memories of Irene's childhood are awoken by perfumes that emanate from the gardens around the ranch: "el perfume de los aromos trae siempre a la mente en Irene una ráfaga intensa de su niñez" (15)—"the perfume of the acacia always bring to mind in Irene an intense flashback to her childhood." The travel and movement of Agustín, who hurries to work in his car, is drawn in sharp relief to the image of Irene, standing pillar-like as she embarks on a "travel" of her own. Her imaginary journey transports her back to her family's country house, located on a street "sin historia" (16)—"without history." There, the reader is introduced to Irene's doting father, who predicts his daughter will be a queen (18). Irene, however, ignores him, listening with bemused indifference to these predictions: "Está ocupada de un universo propio"—"She is occupied with her own universe" (18). Irene's analeptic journey, or flashback, into childhood memories reveals a complex and layered narrative. This narrative framing device, which allows the female protagonist to live out a rich interior world in the face of an unfulfilling relationship, is a common trope in women's writings from this period and has been criticized as resulting in a literature of limited interest and scope. Guerra-Cunningham counters that such criticism misses the point:

> El tema de la búsqueda del amor [...] conlleva un planteamiento filosófico con respecto a la existencia femenina. En *El segundo sexo* [...] Simone de Beauvoir ha establecido que en nuestra sociedad la mujer se diferencia y define a sí misma tomando al hombre como núcleo de referencia. El hombre, por el contrario, define su existencia a partir de una variedad de elementos del mundo exterior. En una posición de superioridad producida por el sistema económico, él se ha convertido en el Sujeto, en lo Absoluto, mientras que la mujer ha constituido lo incidental, lo inesencial, el Otro. Por lo tanto, la plena realización de la existencia femenina ha dependido de sus relaciones amorosas con el sexo masculino que se ha convertido en su único destino [1987: 137].

> The pursuit of love as a theme [...] entails a philosophical approach regarding feminine existence. In *The Second Sex* [...] Simone de Beauvoir has established

that in our society women differentiate and define themselves taking men as their reference point. Men, on the contrary, define their existence based on a variety of elements from the outer world. In a superior position produced by the economic system, he has become the Subject, the Absolute, while woman has come to constitute the incidental, the unessential, the Other. Therefore, the full realization of female existence has depended on their love relationships with the male sex, which has become her only destiny.

When this pursuit of love is frustrated, the female protagonist searches for alternative ways to engage the world and ultimately comes to reject linear, logical, and rational norms. Yáñez is not the only Chilean woman writer of the time to use the same strategy for the female protagonists. In María Luisa Bombal's works, for example, the female protagonists shun "todo acercamiento lógico y científico a la realidad"—"all logical and scientific approaches to reality" (Guerra-Cunningham, 1999: 229). The protagonist of Bombal's *La última niebla* (1934), for instance, engages an imaginary lover to compensate for the lack of connection she feels with her husband, and in *La amortajada* (1938) the deceased Ana María, lying in her coffin surrounded by loved ones, finally discovers her voice.[6]

The notion of nonlinear time is seen in the opening scene of *Cenizas* when Irene dwells on the "milagro perpetuo" ("perpetual miracle"), "horas de estupor" ("hours of stupor") and "vagancia deliciosa" ("delicious idleness") that she experienced with her young friends (19–20). Later in the novel Irene ponders:

> ¿Qué importa el tiempo, en verdad? El tiempo no existe. Son los seres y su intensidad los que van marcando el pasado, el presente, el porvenir. Fuera de los acontecimientos, el tiempo no tiene realidad [202].

> What does time matter, really? Time doesn't exist—it lacks in itself existence. Living things and their intensity are what go marking the past, the present and the future. Outside of events, time has no reality.

Whereas Irene's imagined worlds (plural) are psychologically complex and fulfilling, Agustín's world (singular) is painted in quite a different, and ironic, manner:

> Limitar su vida al marco alucinante de los papeles y de las acciones. Hacer caber el universo en esa rueda de metal. Y mirar adelante y ver siempre el mismo horizonte, sin grandeza. Su existencia, desde hace un cuarto de siglo, desde los quince años, es línea vertical, en la que no tienen cabida ni el amor, ni el ensueño, ni el reposo [56].

> Limiting his life to the exciting frame of stocks and bonds. Making the universe fit within that metal wheel. And looking ahead and always seeing the same hori-

zon, without greatness. His existence, since a quarter of a century ago, since she was fifteen years old, is a vertical line in which there is room for neither love, nor daydream, nor rest.

Irene clearly rejects her husband's "exciting" world and observes that he has no room for the most valued aspects of life: love, daydreams, and rest. These are men's and women's "mundos distintos" ("different worlds"), to which Rubio refers in her observations of the major trends of this period (19).

Irene's rejection of Agustín's worldview is further revealed through her interactions with their son, Pablo, who (to Agustín's disappointment) seeks to manage their ranch at Las Cenizas instead of following in his footsteps in the financial industry: "Tanto mejor, pensaba Irene. Que no se convierta como él en un sistema. Que sea vibrante, humano" (234)—"All the better, thought Irene. May he not turn into a system. May he be vibrant, human." This desire for her son to pursue a path different from that of her husband is echoed throughout the narrative as Irene observes Agustín's work, which the narrator describes as a "fría prisión de su raciocinio, de su sequedad positivista" (178)— "a cold prison of his reason, of his dry positivism."

Another manifestation of Irene's rejection of a "rational" or positivist worldview can be seen through the theme of silence, in particular when her quiet meditation is interrupted by someone who vocalizes or intellectualizes events around her. During a Brahms performance, Irene's curiosity is piqued by a man who offers an opinion that mirrors her own. An audience member begins to comment on the ballad, but the man interrupts, saying that to comment on the performance is to break the spell. Irene notes that she has always felt this way: "hay sentimientos que al ser definidos o simplemente mencionados, se alteran, se materializan y pierden algo de su misteriosa intensidad" (222)—"there are feelings that on being defined or simply mentioned become altered, materialized and lose something of their mysterious intensity." It is thus the utterance or vocalization of what had been for Irene a meditative experience listening to Brahms that threatens her relationship to the music.

J.G.A. Pocock, writing about the influence of speech acts, has observed that verbalizations (such as the one proffered by the audience member in the novel) "act upon people—and so constitute acts of power—in at least two ways: either by informing them and so modifying their perceptions or by defining them and so modifying the ways in which they are perceived by others" (30). Irene's reaction to the analysis of Brahms is a clear rejection of this act of power and serves as further evidence of her desire to undermine and ultimately spurn such attempts to invade her own discursive space. Turning on its head Woolf's observation of a male passerby who gesticulated at her in horror because she walked on turf reserved for the university's fellows, Irene scorns the intrusion of rational analysis, found trespassing on her domain, where quiet, meditative interpretation prevails.

These "male" and "female" worlds are reflected not only in different notions of time and values, but also in the way spaces are described. If Agustín's world is positivistic, a "cold prison," Irene's is impressionistic and oneiric. Her memories of childhood are imbued with sensorial and synesthetic images that effectively upend the "orden lógico del discurso"—"logical order of the discourse" (Vera Orozco 314). The words "cuadro" ("painting") and "marco" ("frame") emerge again and again in *Cenizas* for good reason, for Irene's experiences are "framed" impressionistically, not located in linear time. If lyrical fiction is characterized by "the paradoxical submersion of narrative in imagery and portraiture," *Cenizas* is exemplary of the genre (Ralph Freedman vii).

Irene's concept of travel is additional evidence of the differences between her and her husband. Whereas Agustín engages in linear travel — to and from work — Irene prefers to wander. As a child she remembers wanting to be an artist, or better yet, a "vagabunda" ("wanderer") (41). Daydreaming (ensueño) and somnambulism not only occupy a major part of Yañez's novel, but are also a common motif of women's writings of the time.[7]

Love and Nature; Love as Nature

If turning to memory illustrates one way in which Irene seeks out more profound connections in her life, others include escaping into the arms of a lover (Andrés) and into the natural world, the latter occupying a highly symbolic place in the novel. Since the home has come to represent unhappy domesticity (the houses of the Cenizas are described as "la mole parda, taciturna"—"the brown, gloomy mass") it is not surprising that, like the protagonist of Bombal's *La última niebla* (*The Last Mist*), Irene meets a lover out in nature and his presence is intimately tied to the landscape (152). Irene sees Andrés for the first time at a beach close to Las Cenizas: "Irene mira sin verlo, cual si formara parte del paisaje" (126) — "Irene looks without seeing him, as if he formed part of the landscape." Their courtship begins, and when she goes to meet him the landscape takes on "virile" characteristics: "la ruda virilidad del paisaje" (134) — "the coarse virility of the landscape." As their relationship develops, Irene comes to associate her love for Andrés with an intimate relationship to nature: "Andrés es su paisaje [...] el agua clara en que se mira. Es sol, es viento, es llanura y follaje" (151) — "Andrés is her scenery [...] the clear water in which she gazes. He is sun, wind, prairie and foliage." One night Irene waits in anticipation to leave Agustín behind at home to meet Andrés. Symbolically, she submerges into the "corazón de la noche" — "the heart of the night," and their encounter is one that falls outside of time, space, and language:

> Nunca supo qué palabras dijeron durante esa larga entrevista en la hojarasca del parque, ni por qué aquel calor animal que traía a sus huesos el contacto de los brazos de Andrés, la hizo perder la noción del tiempo [...] No supo, lo olvidó todo cual si su entrevista hubiera transcurrido más allá de los límites del espacio y del tiempo [167].

> She never knew what words were said during that long encounter among the fallen leaves in the park, or why that animal heat that she felt in her bones at the touch of Andrés' arms made her lose any notion of time [...] She never knew, and forgot everything as if the meeting had transpired beyond the limits of space and time.

If their relationship seems to flourish outside of time, space, and language, it suffers when these notions intrude their world. When Irene writes a letter to Andrés expressing anxiety that their love affair will be discovered, he complains that the letter is "llena de sentido práctico de lógica [...] y justamente lo lindo que tenía esto entre nosotros era que ninguno de los dos pensaba, que nos dejábamos llevar" (171) — "full of logical common sense [...] and the beautiful thing that exists between us is precisely that neither one of us was thinking, that we just let ourselves be carried away." Although their relationship is initially depicted with such promise, the love affair is brief, and Irene comes to the realization that no matter how much she tries to find companionship, she will always be alone.

In fact, the most prevailing theme in Yáñez's fiction is precisely the impermanence of human relationships and the realization that one can never really know another person. She has never been able to reach the depth of those she loved: just when she begins to believe that they are secure, these relationships escape from her hands like "mariposas enloquecidas" (153) — "crazed butterflies." These fleeting relationships are not unique to Irene and the men in her life. Her world is not one in which easy or predictable alliances are forged, and the inability to bridge the distances can be seen even among the women around her, who are shown as treacherous and alienating as the men. Alienation even permeates family relations: it is not until Irene's sister Inés is on her deathbed that both sisters come to "traspasar por primera vez la invisible valla de mal entendidos que las separó siempre" (230) — "cross over for the first time the invisible hurdle of misunderstandings that always separated them."

Despite the abundant evidence that everyone is destined to a life of solitude, Yáñez's characters enjoy a certain sense of serenity and tranquility as they age, even though, to the reader, they may seem to be more alienated than ever.[8] At the end of the novel, Irene is utterly alone with her thoughts, but for once she feels completely at ease and able to live in the moment. In a financial mis-step, Agustín loses all of his money, and the family faces ruin. As a result, Las Cenizas and most of their belongings will have to be sold. Irene is still reeling from her breakup with Andrés, who has left her for another woman. Despite these tragedies, she serenely concludes that true happiness means not yearning for anything, but instead appreciating life if only for its spontaneous and ephemeral moments, such as wandering outside in the gardens: "Ah, la vida vale la pena de vivirse aunque sólo sea por estos vagabundeos alados y por el olor a miel de la primavera que despierta!" (264)—"Ah, life is worth living even if it's only for these winged wanderings and for the fragrance of honey when spring awakens." This moment at the very end of the novel is transformative for Irene. Whereas in other situations she has yearned to venture outdoors or run to her lover for comfort, here peace and tranquility come to her. The land-scape is now within her, no longer an external object of desire. However, this contemplation and reflection is short-lived, for just as she enters this meditative state, a "rama rebelde" ("rebellious branch") whips her in the face. Irene "exhala un ligero grito y vuelve de su éxtasis" (265)—"lets out a slight scream and returns from her extasis." In other words, in spite of her desire to stay in her own world, reality is always ready to interrupt her internal wanderings.

In one of Yáñez's best-known works, the autobiographical sketches from her childhood, *Visiones de infancia* (1947) (*Childhood Visions*), the author recalls a moment as a child when she was gazing upon her maternal grandmother:

> mi madre y yo miramos la ventana y la vimos con la frente pensativa apoyada en un cristal, contemplando la acera humedecida de lluvia, la larga calle triste, sin nostalgia ni pesar en sus ojos azules, con esa impasible y lejana frialdad habitual [76].

> my mother and I looked at the window and we saw her with her head leaning against the window, contemplating the sidewalk, steaming from rain, the long melancholy street, without nostalgia or sadness in her blue eyes, with her usual impassive and cold distance.

This description recalls the opening scene of *Cenizas* when Irene stares out the window to contemplate the morning rain. One could argue that the novel is the author's way of penetrating this impassiveness: imagining and recreating the world through the eyes of her grandmother — and perhaps of other women of her day — and by extension, through the character of Irene. In the words of one critic from 1950, this world is one in which people suffer the "dura ley de la incomunicabilidad"—"tough law of incommunicability" (González López 145). One wonders what Yáñez would have thought of such an assessment. Incommunicability, after all, penetrates the novel and is a lingering presence at its conclusion. Furthermore, Irene appears to embrace at the end the very stillness and passivity that served as such a source of boredom at the beginning of the novel. Nevertheless, it is clear that Irene's serenity can only be achieved by forging of discursive spaces in which she can move, act, and react, and by the silencing (as with the Brahms piece mentioned in the novel) of those voices that would break the spell has finally made life worth living among the ashes.

Notes

1. Yáñez led a prolific literary life that spanned several decades, during which she interacted with some of the most prominent writers of the time, including María Luisa Bombal, Federico García Lorca, Juana de Ibarbourou, Pablo Neruda, Victoria Ocampo, and Alfonsina Storni.

2. Unless otherwise marked, all translations are mine.

3. Yáñez noted in an interview in 1967, "Desde siempre quise escribir, pero mi padre se oponía tenazmente porque él había sufrido a causa de esto, y recuerdo una frase de él 'No te pongas en la línea del fuego' pero mi vocación fue más fuerte"—"I have always wanted to write, which my father tenaciously opposed because he had himself suffered pursuing this path, and I remember a phrase of his: 'Don't put yourself in the line of fire' but my vocation was stronger." "María Flora Yáñez: Pionera de nuestras letras." *La Nación*, Oct. 18, 1967. Santiago, Chile, n. p. Print.

4. See Bonnie Kime Scott for a discussion of Woolf as a precursor to ecofeminist criticism. This kind of critical approach to Woolf articulates an attractive framework for thinking about Yáñez's fiction, which has yet to be explored. In "Virginia Woolf, Ecofeminism, and Breaking Boundaries in Nature." *Woolfian Boundaries: Selected Papers from the Sixteenth Annual International Conference on Virginia Woolf.* 108–115. 5 July 2011. Web.

5. Agustín's desire to mold Irene recalls Enrique's intent to create the perfect married woman out of Ana María in *El abrazo de la tierra*, a novel published under the pseudonym Mari Yan. Irene likewise had the same desire to mold Agustín. Irene remembers: "Lo importante, ahora, es conquistarlo, se decía. Ya tendré tiempo luego de irle dando mis gustos, de irlo amoldando a mi modo de ser" (25)—"The important thing is to win him over, she used to say. I will have time later to let him know my wants, to mold him to my way of being." *El abrazo de la tierra.* Santiago: Universitaria, 1933.

6. See Bombal's *La última niebla* and *La Amortajada* in *María Luisa Bombal: Obras completas.* Ed. Lucía Guerra. (Santiago: Andrés Bello, 1996): 55–95 and 96–176

7. In Chela Reyes' *Puertas verdes y caminos blancos–Green Doors and White Paths* (1939), for instance, the protagonist María Milagros is transported when observing her green plants, which serve as doors to deeper thought and contemplation. In María Luisa Bombal's *La última niebla*, the protagonist's daydream-like wanderings serve as a way to escape the domestic sphere. See Carreras Guzmám's dissertation for a description of "nomadism," a common feature of women's writings of the 1930s and 1940s: "El nomadismo que prevalece en *La última niebla* no constituye del todo un movimiento físico sino un fluir de la conciencia, es decir, estamos frente a un viaje psíquico, onírico y ficcional" (128)—"The nomadism that prevails in *La última niebla* does not at all constitute a physical movement, but an interior monologue; in other words, we are facing a psychic, dream-like and fictional travel." In "La travesía femenina en *La última niebla* de María Luisa Bombal, *Salir: (La balsa), Cita capital, El contagio* y *Los conversos* de Guadalupe Santa Cruz." Diss. Universidad de Puerto Rico, 2008. ProQuest. Web. 10 Mar. 2011.

8. These feelings of peace and tranquility dominate the last few pages of the novel: "Desde hace días nota en ella una transformación, una plenitud desconocida y sin causa. Es, ahora, como una planta que hubiera encontrado al fin su clima. Y todo se le aparece tan fácil, tan simple. A tal punto que no necesita de nadie y que cada cosa, cada gesto, mirar,

respirar, es un goce" (250) — "For a few days now she has noted in herself a transformation, an unfamiliar fullness with no known cause. She is, now, like a plant that has finally found its climate. And everything seems to her so easy, so simple. To such an extent that she does not need anyone and that every thing, every gesture, look, breath, is a pleasure."

Works Cited

Bombal, María Luisa. *La última niebla; La amortajada.* Santiago de Chile: Editorial Universitaria, Editorial Andrés Bello, 1992. Print.

Foucault, Michel. "The Order of Discourse." In *Language and Politics.* Ed. Michael Shapiro. New York: New York University Press, 1984. Print.

Freedman, Ralph. *The Lyrical Novel.* Princeton: Princeton University Press, 1963. Print.

González López, Emilio. "Rev. of *Las cenizas,* by María Flora Yáñez." *Revista Hispánica Moderna* 16 (1950): 145. *Periodicals Archive Online.* 8 Mar. 2011. Web.

Guerra-Cunningham, Lucía. "Pasividad, ensoñación y existencia enajenada: Hacía una caracterización de la novela femenina chilena." In *Texto e ideología en la narrativa chilena.* Minneapolis: Prisma Institute, 1987. 133–49. Print.

_____. "María Luisa Bombal (1910–1980)." In *Escritoras chilenas.* Eds. Patricia Ruhio. vol. 3. Santiago: Cuarto Propio, 1999. Print.

"María Flora Yánez: Pionera de Nuestras Letras." *La Nación.* 18 Oct. 1967. Santiago, Chile. n. pag. Print.

Orozco Vera, María Jesús. "La Narrativa Femenina Chilena (1923–1980): Discurso subjetivo y novela lírica." *Cauce: Revista de filología y su didáctica* 16 (1993): 295–320. 10 Mar. 2011. Web.

Ortega, Eliana. "María Flora Yáñez." In *Escritoras chilenas.* vol. 3. Ed. Patricia Rubio. Santiago: Cuarto Propio, 1999. Print.

Pocock, J.G.A. "Verbalizing a Political Act: Toward a Politics of Speech." *Political Theory* 1:1 (Feb., 1973): 27–45. 14 June 2011. Web.

Reyes, Chela. *Puertas verdes y caminos blancos.* Santiago: Nascimento, 1939. Print. Rubio, Patricia. "Introducción." In *Escritoras chilenas.* vol. 3. Ed. Patricia Rubio. Santiago: Cuarto Propio, 1999. 11–26. Print.

Woolf, Virginia. *A Room of One's Own.* Orlando: Harcourt Brace, 1929. Print.

Yáñez, María Flora. *El abrazo de la tierra.* Santiago de Chile: Imprenta Universitaria, 1933. Print.

_____. *Mundo en sombra* (published as Mari Yan). Santiago de Chile: Imprenta Universo, 1935. Print.

_____. *Espejo sin imagen.* Santiago de Chile: Editorial Nascimento, 1936. Print.

_____. *Las cenizas.* 2nd ed. Santiago: Tegualda, 1949. Print.

_____. *Visiones de infancia.* Santiago: Del Pacífico, 1960. *Google Books.* Web. 26 April 2011.

_____. *Historia de mi vida: Fragmentos.* Santiago de Chile: Editorial Nascimento, 1980.

14

Can the Feminine Speak?
Narrating Madalena and Macabéa

MARCUS V.C. BRASILEIRO

Não me venha falar /Na malícia de toda mulher.
Cada um sabe a dor e a delícia / De ser o que é.
Don't come telling me / About every woman's malice.
Each one knows the pain and delight
Of being what one is.
—"Dom de iludir," Caetano Veloso

In 2010, for the first time in Brazilian history, a woman was elected president of the country. Dilma Houssef's election might suggest that gender relations in Brazil have reached a stage of equality in the last few years. It is important to keep in mind, however, that the road to this historical moment has been paved with a great deal of still visible abuse and oppression of women who, even though always present throughout all phases of the national history, have not always been respected as full-fledged citizens or obtained the deserved recognition for their participation. This essay studies the forms of construction and domination of the female body as they are represented in the narration of the lives of two significant female characters in Brazilian literature, Madalena, from the novel *São Bernardo* (1934) by Graciliano Ramos (1892–1953), and Macabéa, from *A hora da estrela* (*The Hour of the Star* 1977), by Clarice Lispector (1920–1977).[9] The essay focuses on the aspects of narration, silencing, and resistance, an orientation that help us evaluate not only the physical and psychological repercussions of Madalena's and Macabéa's subaltern condition, but also the ways in which these two novels raise questions

about the validity of the patriarchal discourse as well as the authoritarian roots
of this model.

Despite the adverse conditions both texts dramatize, the female voice in
each is still able to come through and be heard. But theirs is not a voice shouted
out on the street corners, or touted over the media. Rather, the voice of women
like Madalena and Macabéa may only be recognized and heard if we understand
the act of resistance against authoritarianism quietly embedded in their everyday
lives. The most important legacy of these two novels, as I see it, is that they
present ways in which women not only can use a different language and can
speak about different strategies of resistance, but these texts also highlight the
challenges implicated in the process of becoming a speaking subject.

We cannot, however, evoke this process without heeding Gayatri Spivak's
warning of the dangers for anyone seeking to construct an image of the Other;
after all, the two writers of these novels, Graciliano Ramos (who created a
female character), and Clarice Lispector (who created a woman of a social class
different from her own) can be seen as representatives of a gender and a class
different from their protagonists'. Speaking about cultural critics, instead of
advocating the impossibility of the subaltern to speak, Spivak emphasizes the
limits and implications of the interpretive practices (295). In this sense, the subaltern constitutes itself as an untranslatable text. To accept this argument, I would
add, the cultural critic must embrace the fact she/he is also implicated in the
process of representation; consequentially, she/he needs to become aware of the
linguistic, cultural, and political implications of gender and class constructs.

Speaking from the position of a subject who inhabits several non-norma-
tive cartographies, I too feel implicated in the process of reading the performance of Madalena and Macabéa in this manner. Such implication positions my
gaze on those characters that not only challenge, but are also victims of the
patriarchal rule. In fact, in the context of Brazilian society, the oppression
extends not just to women, but to any form of male subjectivity that does not
comply with the traditional canons of masculinity. *São Bernardo* and *A hora
da estrela* portray women characters struggling to constitute themselves outside — or despite of— a patriarchal order that limits both their body and their
mind. In the process, both novels help us understand the weapons of an authoritarian chauvinistic discourse that condemns other forms desire to nonexistence,
and ex-centric subjectivities to an abject position.

Critical Responses

Ramos' second novel, *São Bernardo* (translated into English by Robert
Scott-Buccleuch in 1975 under its original title), is considered one of the most

important modernist novels in Brazilian literature. From a social perspective, its main themes are the rural environment and the social conflicts in the Northeast region of Brazil. As Alfredo Bosi writes (1991), Ramos' characters can be considered expressions of the social mechanisms of oppression and their impact over the constitution of subjectivity. His novels articulate forms of indignation, opposition to conservative social structures, and the problems of inequality and authoritarianism in Brazil (453).

Despite the fact that Ramos' novels are set in the *sertão*, Brazil's backlands — small villages, little towns, the prison, the house filled with farmers, cowboys, public employees, vagabonds, etc.— readers will not find in his texts the description of the picturesque and the exotic for its own sake. In *Ficção and confissão* (1992), Antonio Cândido looks at *São Bernardo* in search of the ways this novel articulates aspects of regionalism, but at the same time transcends them, thus composing a scenario that takes the reader into the most profound dimensions of human subjectivity (29). In this sense, we can agree with Flora Sussekind, who writes that in *São Bernardo* one can see the dramatic dimension of the language through the difficulty of writing according to Brazil's regionalist aesthetic of the 1930's (170). Indeed, although Ramos published the novel during the high period of Regionalism in Brazil, he tried to keep from embodying such an aesthetic project fully and naively. In the interview published under the title "Resolving Doubts with Robert Schwarz," Marcos Falleiros says that, in *São Bernardo*, "the harshness of [Ramos'] style — rhetorical, judicial, extremely adjectival despite what is said and what Graciliano himself thought — was probably also a Northeastern consequence, homologous to the economy of hunger and the mold of the rent earth" (sic) (165). It is with this "harsh style" that Ramos dramatizes a highly complex narrative using the introductory chapters to establish the figure of the "narrator" (Paulo Honório), who confesses to be using a pseudonym while advancing information about his world. Bel Brunacci sees these initial chapters as a way Ramos "coloca no centro da questão a obra literária enquanto produção social" (2) — "puts the literary work as a social production right in the center of the center of the discussion."

In the case of *A hora da estrela,* for some critics the most important aspect of the novel is the use of language describing the Other, and this use is one of the most significant contributions of Lispector to the narrative form in Brazilian literature. One of the first commentaries about the novel appeared in 1977, in the *Suplemento Literário Minas Gerais*, in which Samuel Rawet states that "Devemos falar de uma nova Clarice Lispector, exterior e explícita, o coração selvagem comprometido nordestinamente com o progresso brasileiro" — "We ought to speak about a new Clarice Lispector, exterior and explicit, the savage heart Northesternly aligned with Brazilian progress."[10] *A hora da estrela* was the last novel Lispector wrote and published during her life. How did she develop throughout her career to arrive to the point of speaking "Northeasternly?" In "*No raiar de Clarice Lispector*" — "In the Dawn of Clarice Lispector,"[11] Antonio Cândido was the first major literary critic to praise the arrival of Lispector on the literary scene with her book *Perto do coração selvagem* [*Near to the Wild Heart*] (1943). In his article, Cândido sets the tone of the critical emphasis that would dominate the subsequent reception of Lispector's work: the relationship between literary practice and subjectivity. In fact, Cândido saw the appearance of Lispector in the Brazilian letters as a catalyst to improve literary expression in Brazil.

After the initial reception of Lispector's work, the criticism to her work looked at different angles. In "Clarice Lispector e a crítica," Cristina Ferreira-Pinto Bailey systematizes the main contribution of relevant literary critics and the diversity of theoretical approaches in relation to Lispector's body of work. Specifically regarding the representation of the women's experience, Bailey points out that this was not the concern of her early critics. Studies focusing on the condition of women in Lispector's fictional work came into being as a result of the emergence of feminist criticism in the United States and France during the 1970s. According to Bailey, critics noted the transgressive nature of Lispector's work in relation to language and traditional gender conventions (11). This process of transgression is constructed through irony as well as through the destabilization of narrative patterns centered in the patriarchal mode of perception. Bailey, commenting on the findings of Lúcia Helena (2006), points out that Lispector's narrative techniques in *Perto do coração selvagem* function as a deconstructive gesture of the phalocentric discourse and the realistic mode of representation (Bailey 12). In other words, Lispector's last novel represents a continuation of a work she developed from the first novel, and throughout her career. Therefore, with *A hora da estrela*, she is not a "new Clarice" at all, but the same writer who now opens the lens of her creative camera to include more of the Brazilian landscape, naming places and historical markers.[12]

Resistance in Different Times

A hora da estrela tells the story of Macabéa, a woman from Paraíba, in the Northeast of Brazil, one of the poorest regions of the country. She migrates to Rio de Janeiro in search of a better life, and finds a job as a typist. The setting of the narrative is the urban center of the second biggest city in Brazil, home of many migrants from the same Northeastern region. It is in the streets of Rio de Janeiro that the narrator, Rodrigo S.M., encounters Macabéa, and becomes intrigued by the lack of attributes that he perceives in the *nordestina* (North-easterner). The narrative becomes, then, an attempt to describe the experience of the Other, who is economically and socially the opposite of the male, middle class Brazilian narrator.

São Bernardo is narrated by Paulo Honório, a man of simple origins who, through authoritarian and violent strategies, achieves his lifelong goal: to buy the ranch called São Bernardo and to become rich. Once his principal objective is achieved, Paulo Honório feels compelled to find a wife to provide him with an heir who will carry on his legacy. He is able to persuade Madalena, a public school teacher, to marry him; however, the marriage soon begins to unravel due to political and philosophical differences between them. Life with Paulo Honório becomes unbearable for Madalena, because he does not allow her to express her opinions and her views, much less to contradict his orders. In a gesture of despair and rebellion, she commits suicide, prompting Paulo Honório to reflect on his past and on the events that led Madalena to put an end to her life. *São Bernardo* is a text that presents itself as the biography of the narrator, Paulo Honório. Madalena herself never speaks, except through her last, desperate act.

The characters of Madalena and of Macabéa are the protagonists of two novels published in two separate historical moments in Brazil, and the action takes place in two very different settings. But political reality of the two periods have something extremely important in common: at the time of the publication of both novels Brazil was living under dictatorships. *São Bernardo* was published in 1934, only four years after the populist revolution of 1930 that led to the implementation of the Estado Novo, the first period of civilian dictatorship in Brazilian history.[13] *A hora da estrela* was published in 1977, during the military dictatorship in Brazil which lasted from 1964 to 1985.[14] I believe that it is not a coincidence that these two novels show the consolidation of authority done through intimidation, force, and violence, since the daily life for most Brazilians at the time was permeated by the repressive political atmosphere. Furthermore, the lives of the two protagonists illustrate the conditions of female oppression at the time, as well as the means through which power was obtained and maintained.

Narrating the Female Body

In both novels the female body is narrated from a male perspective, and women are the mechanism that triggers what can be called "anguished writing" in their male narrators.[15] Because Macabéa and Madalena are the reasons the narrators reflect on their own past experiences and seek to reconstruct them in their respective writing, "anguished writing" becomes a modality of textualization that represents the male narrators in a self-reflective process. For different reasons, these narrators have reached a point in their lives in which their patriarchal values are challenged. The impact of this confrontation with the female Other raises doubts and uncertainties that open a lacuna between their language and the reality they are trying to capture in their narrative. In the case of Madalena, it is the disrupting of the traditional what-does-it-mean-to-be-a-good-wife narrative that inflicts anxiety and linguistic uncertainties. In the case of Macabéa, the anguish of the narrator is centered on his despair at trying to portray someone who is so different, so insignificant, and yet, so meaningful to him.

The very anguish of the writing process, along with the painful dilemma of putting into words repressed memories and emotions, constitutes different narrative modalities in these novels. In *São Bernardo*, writing becomes a therapeutic act in which the narrator, reflecting on his experiences and memories, seeks to ease the pain and guilt of the past that keep projecting upon his present. In *A hora da estrela*, by contrast, the performance of the male narrator, Rodrigo S. M., is transversed by gestures which characterize what Hélène Cixous has termed *écriture feminine*.[16] Here, the male narrator, inspired by a simple-minded and unattractive woman, ends up embodying in his writing — in his expressed incapacity to represent Macabéa's subjectivity — the situation of women who are, in Cixous' words: the "repressed of culture, [their] lovely mouths gagged with pollen, [their] wind knocked out of them" (1976: 878)

Objective distance itself is put into question by Macabéa's lack of transparency. The *nordestina*, with her delicate and vague existence, becomes a mystery to the narrator, who is accustomed to describing his object without drama or emotional attachment, characteristics that he considers attributes to the female mode of narration:

> [...] Bem, é verdade que também eu não tenho piedade do meu personagem principal, a nordestina: é um relato que desejo frio [...] descubro agora—também eu não faço a menor falta, e até o que escrevo outro escreveria. Um outro escritor, sim, mas teria que ser homem porque escritora mulher pode lacrimejar piegas [13–14].

> Well, it is true that I don't feel pity for my main character either, the *nordestina,* the northeasterner: I want this narrative to be cold [...] I've just realized now that I am not important either, and even what I write anyone could write. Another writer, yes, but it would have to be a man because woman writer might shed sappy tears.

Despite this willingness to narrate "like a man," Rodrigo S. M. is incapable of maintaining himself in the realm of objective and cold description once he is forced to confront the subjective implication in the process of describing the reality of the Other. The alterity implicated in the existence of Macabéa is defined by the many forms of difference articulated by her body. Her gender, social class, geographical origin, and non conformity to the traditional model of female beauty create the lack of knowledge and experience that transforms the task of narrating Macabéa in an epistemological exercise. Therefore, the textual structure of *A hora da estrela* constantly oscillates between a factual prose that recounts the events, and a poetic lyricism that touches subjective dimensions:

> [...] Como eu irei dizer agora, esta história será o resultado de uma visão gradual—há dois anos e meio venho aos poucos descobrindo os porquês. É visão da iminência de. De quê? Quem sabe se mais tarde saberei. Como que estou escrevendo na hora mesma em que sou lido. Só não inicio pelo fim que justificaria o começo—como a morte parece dizer sobre a vida—porque preciso registrar os fatos antecedentes [12].

> As I am about to say, this story will develop from a gradual vision — in the last two and a half years, I have been slowly learning the whys. It is a vision of the imminence of ... of what? Maybe I'll learn more later. As if I am being read at the same time I am writing. I won't start with the ending to justify the beginning — as death seems to indicate about life — only because I need to account for previous facts.

According to Olga de Sá (1979), the narrator reveals himself at the same time he allows the readers to know Macabéa. That is, in the beginning of *A hora da estrela,* the narrator is more concerned about himself and his process of writing than about making the narrative progress. In the first few pages, the narrator puts forward an approach to his project's rationale, choices, and structure: he determines when the narrative should start, how many characters it will include, and — in effect — the unproblematic "masculine" language it should employ in the story (Sá 273). For example, regarding Macabéa, he informs the reader that "[...] Pareço conhecer nos menores detalhes essa nordestina, pois se vivo com ela. E como adivinhei a seu respeito, ela se me grudou na pele qual melado pegajoso ou lama negra" (21)—"[...] I seem to know this *nordestina* in her most intimate details because I live with her. And as I had anticipated, she has clung to my skin like sticky molasses or dirty mud."

The fact that the narrator states that he "lives" with Macabéa indicates that from the first time he saw her he was stricken by a human being who lacks everything — money, looks, skills — that he thought a person should have.[17] Such a portrayal of Macabéa is what some have called "poetic engagement," a kind of writing that marks the different approaches to the relationship between art and society.[18]

When comparing *São Bernardo* and *A hora da estrela*, one can say that each writer uses different literary strategies because, on the surface, the language Ramos uses (through Paulo Honório) to describe Madalena is very dry, descriptive, and straightforward, whereas in Lispector, Macabéa is constructed with considerable self-consciousness and circumlocution. In the case of *São Bernardo*, it is important to point out that in the initial chapters Ramos uses what Bel Brunacci refers to as a "double mask": "a do narrador pelo escritor e a do pseudônimo pelo narrador" (2)—"the narrator's [mask] by the writer, and a pseudonym by the narrator." That is to say, the narrator of each novel tells the story of the Other using seemingly different techniques, but the effect is the same: the problematization of the representation of the Other. Evidently, Rodrigo S. M., the narrator in *A hora da estrela*, and Paulo Honório, the narrator of *São Bernardo*, are finally two different kinds of men: the first one is well-educated, middle class, and urbanized, whereas the second was raised in much poorer conditions, and has only an elementary education. His lack of formal education, however, does not prevent Paulo Honório from self-reflection and from experiencing a sense of regret that he expresses at the end of the narrative:

> [...] Cinquenta anos! Quantas horas inúteis! Consumir-se uma pessoa a vida inteira sem saber para quê! Comer e dormir como um porco! Como um porco! Levantar-se cedo todas as manhãs e sair correndo, procurando comida! E depois guardar comida para os filhos, para os netos, para muitas gerações. Que estupidez! Que porcaria! Não é bom vir o diabo e levar tudo? [184].

> [...] Fifty years! So many useless hours! Living your entire life without knowing what for! Eating and sleeping like a pig! Like a pig! Waking up early every morning and scouring for food! And then saving food for the children, the grandchildren, for many generations. How stupid! Wouldn't it be better if the Devil came and took everything?

The reader is confronted with a Paulo Honório who realizes the possibility of an alternative way of living and thinking different from the strict and narrow construct of the patriarchal paradigms of gender identity. While Madalena was not able to implement the material changes she wanted in the life of São Bernardo's workers, she was able to leave a memorable imprint on Paulo Honório's own awareness as a man:

> [...] Penso em Madalena com insistência. Se fosse possível recomeçarmos [...] Para que enganar-me? Se fosse possível recomeçarmos, aconteceria exatamente o que aconteceu. Não consigo modificar-me, é o que mais me aflige [188].

> I think about Madalena incessantly. If it were possible to start over [...] Why fool myself ? If it were possible to start over, the same exact thing would happen. I cannot change, and this is what torments me the most.

This passage reveals that the character/narrator cannot see in himself any possibility of change, even in the face of the tragedy of his wife's suicide and his doubts about the value of his material progress. In *A hora da estrela*, on the other hand, the narrator, whose job is to represent Macabéa, confesses the limits of his capacity to represent her accurately. According to Helena (2006), Lispector's text overcomes the limits of mimetic representation, reconfiguring and challenging the reader's notion of what constitutes a "legible" text. For Helena, Macabéa is an allegory of the "feminine" and functions as a way to handle the gender difference in the text and in the writing process itself. In this sense, *A hora da estrela* is considered a fundamental reflection on the Western philosophical tradition because it questions categories such as subject, writing process, and history (103). Lispector, according to Helena, is able to dramatize — not just with Macabéa, but also with her other female characters — the repression of the female subject in history, paying particular attention to the patriarchal tradition of the Brazilian culture. Lispector's writing reflects about the patriarchal tradition that constitutes the gender relations, and that informs Macabéa's life. In this sense, *A hora da estrela* performs a very important critique of the patriarchal system and "the mythologies of bourgeois humanism" (Helena, 108). In fact, Macabéa represents a female character incapable of deconstructing the internalized symbols that constitute her as a woman, and yet, at the same time, she is an object of disdain for not fitting the stereotype of the female object of male desire. Thus, she also becomes a mechanism through which Lispector destabilizes the stereotype of female beauty, dismantling the essentialist views about what constitutes a woman, or, for that matter, a man.

The depictions of Madalena, in *São Bernardo*, and of Macabéa, in *A hora da estrela*, show a different, but complementary perspective of the role of women in society. Madalena's performance throughout the narrative might be interpreted as an attempt to break free from the objectified position in which she is, and to gain agency over her own values and actions. Macabéa, on the other hand, is completely unaware of her "objectification" and her oppression. All the objects of her desire that constitute her subjection — the physical beauty embodied in Marilyn Monroe, the knowledge represented by the bits of information she hears on the radio, the aria "Una furtiva lacrima," that speaks about crying in silence — come from a model of assimilation that defines what it is to be a woman: physically beautiful, capable of repeating little bits of worthless information, and easily moved by romantic notions.

Macabéa is both unaware of how she is subjected by these desires and unable to deconstruct the authoritarian forces behind them. From the standpoint of the development of a feminist consciousness, such lack of awareness becomes an obstacle in the advancement of women's liberation, since these images continue to seduce women into models of femininity that solely satisfy the masculine desire. Olímpico, ascribing to the precepts of patriarchal discourse, is the one who violently alerts Macabéa about the impossibility of her desire, calling her attention to her racial, "dirty"— not white — body: "Marilyn era cor-de-rosa [...] E você tem cor suja. Nem tem rosto nem corpo para ser artista de cinema" (56)—"Marilyn Monroe was pink [...] And you are the color of mud. You don't have the face or the body to be a movie star."

Even though Macabéa's dreams and aspirations are a product of commercialized images of popular culture, these provide the only discursive basis which she can articulate in order to constitute a meaningful, although perhaps temporary, sense of identity. Olímpico's abrupt and violent intervention becomes one more act of silencing for Macabéa, thus denying her possibility to speak — even though what she has to say is clearly incongruent with her status and her physical appearance. In other words: he denies her even the space to dream. Indeed, his reaction over Macabéa's identification with movie stars does not represent a positive affirmation of the singularity of her body; it is simply a reaction of his own repressed frustration over the fact that the only woman with whom he is able relate is herself incapable of becoming the highly sexualized, traditional object of male desire: she is thin, ugly, poor, and does not have the local charm displayed by her plump and easy-talking office-mate Glória, for instance. Therefore, his words and his contempt become another form of symbolic punishment upon Macabéa's body, as she is forced to silence her words and to face her perceived inadequacies.

Silencing the Female Body

Death is a fundamental aspect in both *São Bernardo* and *A hora da estrela*; however, it has slightly different functions in each novel. Madalena's death induces Paulo Honório to write his autobiography, thus eventually making him aware of the dimensions of his repressive nature. Through writing, he realizes that he does not have control over everything and everyone. In fact, he understands that violence — as a means of imposing his will — did not work with Madalena, who, by committing suicide, escapes that which Gayatri Spivak defines as the "subaltern condition" (283).[19] In contrast, in *A hora da estrela*, Macabéa's death cannot be read as a form of political gesture. Macabéa, in her unawareness of the surrounding social condition, becomes the unconscious victim of a social system that oppresses women and the poor. Her death can be read as an "accident" of the sort that befalls the desperately poor, whom nobody sees and whose destiny does not matter to anyone. But her death by the roadside can also be read as religious sacrifice, because at this point that Rodrigo S. M. compares her to the resilient weeds, indicating that she — or others like her — will continue existing.[20]

Madalena and Macabéa can be read as representations of two different forms of patriarchal violence against the female body; however, only Macabéa is the one that can be perceived as a subaltern subject in Spivak's terms. Madalena, although living in an oppressive patriarchal system, has the means, to some extent, to articulate a vocabulary that seeks to provide its own version of history. The letter she writes to Paulo Honório at the end of her life is a testimony of this attempt. Her class position, as an educated and middle class woman, provides her with the skills and the voice to express a form of agency, albeit limited. Along these lines, one could say that *A hora da estrela* is a more adequate literary representation of the drama of the subaltern that Spivak writes about. More than an attempt to portray Macabéa's subaltern condition, the novel is a testimony of the impossibility of speaking for and constructing the Other — a tradition that the Western intellectual took as her mission. Michel Foucault has also warns us in "The Order of Things" (1971) to be skeptical of any attempt of transparency in the usage of language. He draws attention to the fact that representation has its own materiality and can reveal not a reality in itself, but a subject position, or simply a perspective about a discursive formation (327). Indeed, from *A hora da estrela* readers can see two distinct images: a blurred image of the life of a poor immigrant, Macabéa, alongside the dilemma of how to represent of her life.

In *São Bernardo,* on the other hand, the female protagonist does speak; however, she can only do so after death, through a suicide letter. Her death becomes the very text that represents the silencing process imposed on women. Hers is a "conscious" gesture of rebellion against the patriarchal system; that is, in *São Bernardo* 's highly patriarchal society, the subaltern can only speak through the tragedy that her death epitomizes. Macabéa lacks Madalena's level of education or political awareness and is doubly subjected to the "objectifying process" of the narrator because it is through Rodrigo S. M.'s gaze and imagination that the reader comes into contact with her. She does not speak for herself in the first person.

Women Speaking Women

In her 1986 essay "Women's Time," Julia Kristeva writes that there have been three important stages in Western feminism. Most germane to my discussion, the first one — structured around the masculine logic of reasoning and designation — would consider women's struggle as a fight for equal rights. This first wave — which took place the socio-political conditions before 1968 — sought to challenge the patriarchal structure in order to subvert it. The objective was to gain the same social and political rights that men had enjoyed by claiming that "women are just like men." In this sense, Kristeva argues, the first generation of activist women desired to inhabit the linear time of history, that is, they wanted to be part of the production of culture.

Being included in the production process of culture and values — instead of just keeping, protecting, and implementing patriarchal values — would mean that women could fully participate in the world of politics and power. Madalena represents a female subject who seeks to appropriate the masculine logic and political knowledge in order to establish a dialogue about different political and gender practices. In *São Bernardo*, the reader often witnesses a Madalena who discusses the region's political situation with the other male characters. She is knowledgeable, argumentative, and can position herself in an authoritative way inside the "men's club." Paulo Honório perceives this ability and consciousness as a threat to his male dominated political order. Madalena's knowledge of the political circumstances of her time, her willingness to be politically involved not just in conversation, but in the administration of São Bernardo, transform her as a figure of the abject Other who disrupts his own masculinity. Madalena, by virtue of the attempted activism in which she performs, symbolizes the first generation of feminist mentality that sought to be politically involved and to function as pioneers for the political gains that women enjoy today. Her suicidal gesture represents those women who strongly and radically refused to relegate their bodies to the roles of housewives and mothers.

One of the main differences between the first and the second waves of feminists is the recognition that the struggle for inclusion in the masculine order, through the identification with its values of logic and rationality, has its limits (Kristeva 356). The second generation is associated with the aesthetic and psychoanalytical experiences of women after 1968. Such phase is also characterized by a "quasi-universal rejection of linear temporality and by a highly pronounced mistrust of political life" (Kristeva 357). At the time, the intellectual debate focused on the specificity of a female psychology and its symbolic manifestations. Therefore, according to Kristeva, the intellectual and artistic productions aligned with this phase of feminist thought were interested in the kind of language capable of representing those female physical and intersubjective experiences silenced by the masculine voice (357). The novel *A hora da estrela* has functioned, in many critical accounts, as a modality of feminist thought and concern that embodies this second wave of feminism. Macabéa can be interpreted as a symbol of lack of political consciousness, which is, in fact, the opposite of what we see in Madalena. This lack of political knowledge and engagement that characterizes Macabéa functions, at the level of the enunciation of the novel, as a form of displacement from the linear narrative forms that characterize patriarchal discourse.

From a sociological standpoint, Macabéa also represents a very complex picture about the place of women in society. Looking only at her position as a woman in the social context as constructed in the narrative, the reader can see her lack of autonomy as a poor, immigrant woman. This is highly relevant in the novel, and cannot be underestimated since it provides a significant insight on the general subaltern condition of women in society. Having said that, however, as many critics have pointed out before, it is on the dimension of language, the mode of representation of Macabéa, that we can read the feminist gesture of Clarice Lispector's writing. Beyond the call for women's political recognition, the political gesture in *A hora da estrela* seeks also the affirmation of the singularity of the female voice. Such singularity is characterized by the representation of a female subjectivity that is multifaceted, fluid, and non-identifiable with the female models constructed by patriarchal mentality. The feminine in Lispector communicates using a singular tone, constructing a different enunciation of what it means to be a woman. This is a feminine that expresses itself by the demands of the most particular and individual aspects regarding feminine desire.[21]

A third mode of feminist thought envisioned by Kristeva is structured around the dichotomy between masculine and feminine. Kristeva's line of thought points out the importance of the "diversity of our identifications and the relativity of our symbolic and biological existence" (369). What is being emphasized here is a necessity to go beyond the Manichean attitude of gender identities and recognize that "the time has come when we must no longer speak of all women (373). Although Kristeva recognizes the role of a community of women, she also clarifies that a community should be constituted of particularities and not a uniform mass. The implications of Kristeva's argument, from a political standpoint, are the constitution of a new *ethos,* conscious of its relative position in the order of words and things.

The constitution of male and female subjects in contemporary society, aware of its psychic conditioning in language, paves the way to a utopian ethos that Kristeva describes in these terms: "I for my part say that love relation is the only chance to go through narcissism toward the recognition of the symbolic moment" (381). It is important to emphasize that Kristeva does not undermine the fact that reconciliation of differences can sometimes be impossible, or that dissociation is a complex mechanism necessary to constitute the speaking subject. What is important to understand in this concept of love that Kristeva refers to is its openness to the possibility of difference. In socio-political terms, such openness reveals itself in the creation of a society that is diverse enough to allow for existence of different modes of being and thinking. Moreover, it is important that this society be willing to fight against intolerance and bigotry. In the case of Madalena and Macabéa, the tragedy of their lives is directly related to an environment that is oppressive and discriminatory. These characters enable us to have extremely valuable insights regarding the condition of women in Brazilian society, and, most importantly, of the models of femininity they represent. Even though both protagonists have a tragic end, the very fact that such novels exist and have made an impact in Brazilian culture, means that the plight of the non-white, of the ex-centric female subject has become more visible. To judge from the enormous amount of scholarship on both novels, as well as from their enduring presence in book sales, one can conclude that they are widely read and studied, and that the complexity of these women characters are becoming more understood and appreciated. One may hope that perhaps in the near future all Brazilian women — as well as men who do not conform to the patriarchal views of masculinity — will be able speak in their own voices and represent themselves in the Brazilian political and cultural arena as equals. Just as President Dilma Houssef now can. Much remains to be done, but it is reassuring to see that some progress has already been achieved.

Notes

1. Translated into English as *The Hour of the Star* in 1992 by Giovanni Pontiero (New York: New Directions, 1992).

2. Qtd. in Nelson H. Vieira. "The Stations of the Body, Clarice Lispector's Abertura and Renewal." *Studies in Short Fiction*. January 1, 1988. (55–69): 56.

3. Unless otherwise noted, all translations of this and other texts are mine.

4. In "'Languages' and 'voices' in Brazilian Literature." *Revista de Letras*. 36 (1996): 189–210, Eva Paulino Bueno argues that these markers are historical *through* literature. She is referring Lispector's use both of a phrase in Euclides da Cunha's 1902 *Os sertões* (a literary account of a historical fact), of another phrase in Manuel Antonio de Almeida's 1852 novel *Memórias de um sargento de milícias*.

5. Getúlio Vargas (1882–1954) is the quintessential authoritarian figure in Brazil from the 1930's until his suicide in 1954. He was a dictator from 1930 to 1945, and returned to power in 1951, this time as the elected president. During his rule of 18 years, while he accomplished many things in his attempt to develop Brazil into an industrialized country, he also cracked down against the opposition. Ramos was sent to prison from 1936 to 1937, charged with participating in the communist uprising of 1936. The charges were never proven. *Memórias do cárcere*, published posthumously (*Memórias do Cárcere*. Rio de Janeiro: Livraria José Olympio, 1953), tells the story of his time in prison as well as of the suffering he and his fellow political prisoners endured.

6. Like the Chilean and Argentine dictatorships during the same period, the Brazilian

totalitarian regime was responsible for the death and torture of civilians, as well as censorship and repression of intellectuals and of the cultural opposition.

7. Patricia S. Yeager has an excellent discussion of the matter of the "anguish" of writing in Coleridge and Derrida. She says that, whereas for Derrida "the writer's anguish comes from the undifferentiated play of signifiers, from having too much or too little to say, Samuel Coleridge ... believed ... [anguish] is the vehicle through which divinity passes into humanity" (89). Patricia S. Yeager. "Coleridge, Derrida, and the Anguish of Writing." *SubStance* 12.3 (1983): 89–102.

8. The term *écriture feminine* was first used by Hélène Cixous in her essay "The Laugh of the Medusa," which appeared in English in 1976. Cixous opens the essay calling on women for them to write: "Woman must put herself into the text — as into the world and into history — by her own movement" (875). Even though many of the tenets of Cixous' ideas have been debated and challenged because they essentialize the female body, the idea that women must use existing language to inscribe themselves fully into discourse and power has had an enduring effect in feminist writing and thinking.

9. According to Fernando Arenas, Macabéa is the "objectified surface onto which the selves of the author/narrator (and even the readers) are projected" (110). The material poverty of Macabéa, Arenas continues, reveals the richness of the author/narrator and reminds everyone involved in this relationship with Macabéa of another kind of poverty, an emotional and spiritual one: "We (author/narrator/readers) are bound to Macabéa in sympathy, as well as in solidarity. In Macabéa we see ourselves; we see life's contingency" (110). See from Arenas, *Utopias of Otherness: Nationhood and Subjectivity in Portugal and Brazil* (Minneapolis: University of Minnesota Press, 2003).

10. Joseana Paganini (2000) points out the inappropriateness of considering *A hora da estrela* as a mirror of certain social reality. According to her, in Lispector's novel the reader is able to perceive a "poetic engagement" with reality that is able to articulate a double dimension of criticism: a reflection on aspects of society and on the language itself. In "Engajamento poético e transfiguração," *Estudos de Literatura Brasileira Contemporâne* 10. Brasília: UNB (Nov — Dic 2000): 3.

11. In "Can the Subaltern Speak?" Spivak questions Western representations of the "Third World" subaltern, more specifically the female subject. Spivak is interested in the political struggles of disempowered social groups and particular individuals who have been historically subjugated by European colonialism. She makes a distinction between different forms of oppression. Subaltern groups, for Spivak, do not have access to the cultural capital and the social validation to represent themselves and legitimize their own discourse (308).

12. See the discussion of the aspect of sacrifice in the novel in Waldman, B., 1998. "O estrangeiro em Clarice Lispector: uma leitura de *A hora da estrela*." In: R. Zilberman, ed. *Clarice Lispector, a narração do indizível*. Porto Alegre: Artes e Ofícios, 93–104.

13. Already in her first book, *Perto do coração selvage—Near to the Wild Heart*, Lispector is aware of the difficulties of expressing the deep truth of the self through language, and how this expression can transform the truth into something else. The protagonist, Joana, says, "É curioso como não sei dizer quem sou. Quer dizer, sei-o bem, mas não posso dizer. Sobretudo tenho medo de dizer, porque no momento em que tento falar não só exprimo o que sinto como o que sinto se transforma lentamente no que eu digo" (17) — "It is strange that I don't know how to express who I am. That is, I know it well, but I cannot say it. Above all I am afraid of saying it, because in the moment I try to speak I not only express what I feel, but also what I feel slowly becomes what I say" (my translation). See *Perto do coração selvagem* (Rio de Janeiro: Editora Sabiá, 1969.) If it is difficult for a person to express her own self, how much more difficult it is for anyone to express the Other as Other? Of course, this matter does not stop with the fictional text. Indeed, we can see how it permeates the critical discourse as well: even though Hélène Cixous was the first French critic to take up Lispector's work and is one of the main reasons why her work became known in Europe

and in the United States, the same question of the appropriateness of representation is raised by Elena Carrera reading Cixous reading Lispector. Carrera says that, in her readings of Lispector, "Cixous seems to be so preoccupied with herself that she can only speak in the first person and project her own subjectivity on to her reading" (90). See Carrera, Elena, "The Reception of Clarice Lispector via Hélène Cixous: Reading from the Whale's Belly." *Brazilian Feminisms*, ed. Solange Ribeiro and Judith Still (University of Nottingham Press, 1999): 85–100.

Works Cited

Bailey, Cristina Ferreira-Pinto. "Clarice Lispector e a crítica." in *Clarice Lispector: novos aportes críticos*. Eds. Cristina Ferreira Pinto and Regina Zilberman. Pittsburgh, PA: Instituto Internacional de Literatura Iberoamericana, Universidad de Pittsburgh, 2007. Print.

Bosi, Alfredo. *História concisa da literatura brasileira*. 3d.ed. São Paulo: Ed. Cultrix, 1995. Print.

Brunacci, Bel. "Graciliano Ramos e o autoquestionamento da literatura." *Revista Cultura Crítica* 08, Romance Regionalista, 2d semestre de 2008. Web.

Candido, Antonio. *Ficção e confissão: Ensaios sobre Graciliano Ramos*. Rio de Janeiro: Ed. 34, 1992. Print.

Cixous, Hélène. "The Laugh of the Medusa." Trans. Keith Cohen, Paula Cohen. *Signs* 1.4 (Summer, 1976): 875–893. Print.

Fávero, Alfonso, et al. "Resolving Doubts with Roberto Schwarz, an Interview." Trans. R. Kelly Washbourne. *Cultural Critique* 49 (Fall, 2001): 155–180. Print.

Foucault, Michel. *The Order of Things: An Archaeology of the Human Sciences*. New York: Pantheon, 1971. Print.

Helena, Lúcia. *Nem musa nem medusa*. 2d. ed. Niterói, RJ: Editora da Universidad Federal Fluminense, 2006. Print.

Kristeva, Julia. "Women's Time." In *The Kristeva Reader*. Ed. Toril Moi. New York: Columbia University Press, 1986. Print.

Lispector, Clarice. *A hora da estrela*. Rio de Janeiro: Editora Rocco, 1977. Print.

_____. *Near to the Wild Heart*. Trans. Giovanni Pontiero. New York: New Directions, 1990. Print.

Ramos, Graciliano. *São Bernardo* (1934). Rio de Janeiro: Editora Record, 2002. Print

Sá, Olga de. *A escritura de Clarice Lispector*. 3d.ed. Petrópolis: Vozes; Lorena: Faculdades Integradas Teresa D'Ávila, 1979. Print.

Spivak, Gayatri Chakravorty. "Can the Subaltern Speak?" In *Marxism and the Interpretation of Culture*. Eds. Cary Nelson and Lawrence Grossberg. Urbana: University of Illinois Press, 1988. Print.

Sussekind. Flora. *Tal Brasil, qual romance? Uma idologia estética e sua história: O naturalismo*. Rio de Janeiro: Achiamé, 1984. Print.

About the Contributors

María Claudia **André** is a professor of Hispanic American literature and Latin American studies at Hope College, Holland, Michigan. She has presented papers at national and international conferences and published articles in several literary journals. Recent publications include *Iconos femeninos latinos e hispanoamericanos* (Floricanto Press, 2006), *Encyclopedia of Latin American Women Writers* (with Eva P. Bueno, Routledge, 2008), and *Dramaturgas argentinas de los años 20* (Editorial Nueva Generación, 2010).

Marcus V.C. **Brasileiro** has a Ph.D. from the University of Minnesota, and is an assistant professor of Brazilian Literature at Utah State University. His work deals with issues of subjectivity, cultural identities and sexuality. He has published articles on the work of Mário de Sá-Carneiro, Torquato Neto and João Gilberto Noll.

Eva Paulino **Bueno** has a Ph.D. in Hispanic languages and literatures from the University of Pittsburgh. She has published books and essays on Latin American literature, Latin American popular culture, Brazilian literature, Brazilian film, comparative literature, visual art, and English language teaching in Japan. She also writes for the monthly *Revista Espaço Acadêmico* and teaches Spanish and Portuguese at St. Mary's University in San Antonio, Texas.

Alice **Edwards** is professor of Spanish at Mercyhurst College in Erie, Pennsylvania. A graduate of the University of Pittsburgh, Edwards writes on Latin American women's fiction, in particular women's life-writing and the Bildungsroman. She has published on the work of Norah Lange, Maria Luisa Bombal, and Gioconda Belli.

María **Fernández-Lamarque** is an associate professor of Spanish and the director of Spanish Graduate Studies at Texas A&M University, Commerce, Texas. She has a Ph.D. in Spanish and Latin American literature from Louisiana State University.

Her main areas of interest are Clarice Lispector, Patrícia Galvão, and children's literature. Her publications have appeared in *Hispania, Espéculo, Romance Notes, Neophilologus, Crisolengas and Destiempos.*

Héctor **Fernández-L'Hoeste** (Ph.D. in Hispanic languages and literature, Stony Brook University 1996) is an associate professor of Spanish at Georgia State University in Atlanta. His publications include *Narrativas de representación urbana* (Lang, 1998), and *Redrawing the Nation* (Palgrave Macmillan, 2009), a collection of essays on Latin/o American comics and graphic novels.

Jerry **Hoeg** received his Ph.D. in Spanish from Arizona State University. He is a professor of Spanish at the Pennsylvania State University and the author of *Science, Technology, and Latin American Narrative in the 20th Century and Beyond* (Lehigh University Press, 2000), *Reading and Writing the Latin American Landscape* (Palgrave, Macmillan, 2009), and several edited volumes. He is also the editor of the scholarly journal *Ometeca*.

Linda **Ledford-Miller** holds a Ph.D. in comparative literature from the University of Texas at Austin, where she specialized in the literature of the Americas. She is a professor at the University of Scranton, where she teaches Spanish and Brazilian Portuguese languages, Spanish American and Lusophone literature and culture, and literature of American minorities in English. She has published widely on women writers and travel writing.

Lisa **Merschel** (Ph.D., University of North Carolina–Chapel Hill) is a lecturer in the Department of Romance Studies at Duke University. Her work concentrates on task-based teaching, learning and assessment, foreign language technologies, and undergraduate study abroad. She wrote about María Flora Yáñez in *Latin American Writers: An Encyclopedia* (New York: Routledge, 2007). She is researching the use of machine translation in Spanish language classes.

RoseAnna **Mueller** (Ph.D., comparative literature), is an associate professor in the Humanities, History and Social Sciences Department at Columbia College Chicago and the coordinator of the women's/gender studies minor. She teaches courses on Latin American women in the arts, and women's/gender studies. Her articles and book reviews have appeared in *Hispanet, Hispania, Letras Femeninas, The Hispanic Connection, Latin America as Its Literature, The Latin American Feminist Encyclopedia,* and other publications. A Fulbright fellow to Venezuela in 2003, she is writing a book about Teresa de la Parra.

Jeanie **Murphy** is an associate professor of Spanish and Latin American studies at Goucher College in Baltimore, Maryland. She received her doctoral degree from the University of Arizona. Her book reviews and articles in the areas of contemporary Latin American literature and pedagogy have appeared in *Hispania, The Journal of the Midwest Modern Language Association*, and in edited volumes.

Jeffrey **Oxford**, a professor of Spanish at the University of Wisconsin-Milwaukee, received his Ph.D. from Texas Tech University. He is the author or (co-)editor of nine books and 36 academic essays, many of which research women's roles or issues in Spain and Latin America. He is writing a book on the Spanish female detective as portrayed by female Spanish authors.

Aldona **Pobutsky** teaches at Oakland University (Michigan), and is associate editor of *Studies in Latin American Popular Culture*. Her field is contemporary Latin American literature and popular culture. She has published in *Hispanófila, Revista Iberoamericana, Romance Notes, Hispanic Journal, Letras Femeninas*, and *Revista Canadiense de los Estudios Hispánicos*, among others, and is writing a book on drug trafficking in Colombian popular culture, entitled *Narcocultura Inc.*

Leonora **Simonovis** received her doctoral degree from Washington University in St. Louis. She currently teaches Spanish and Latin American and Caribbean literature and culture at the University of San Diego. Her research focus has included the relationship between music and literature of the Hispanic Caribbean and the role of popular culture in the construction of cultural identities. She is writing a book on the representation of women of African descent in Caribbean literature, art, and music.

Patricia L. **Swier** teaches Spanish at Wake Forest University. Her primary area of research is late 19th and 20th century Latin American literature with a concentration on gender and its relationship to national identity. She is the author of *Hybrid Nations* (Fairleigh Dickinson University Press, 2009) and several articles that focus on the connection between gender, power and nation. She is writing a book, *Dictatorships in the Hispanic World: Transatlantic and Transnational Perspectives*.

Index

227